AHEAD BETTER THAN ALL THE REST.

THE WABASH

Rivers of America books already published are:

THE
RIVERS OF AMERICA

Edited by

STEPHEN VINCENT BENÉT
CARL CARMER

As Planned and Started by

CONSTANCE LINDSAY SKINNER

Art Editor

RUTH E. ANDERSON

THE
WABASH

by

WILLIAM E. WILSON

Illustrated by

JOHN DE MARTELLY

FARRAR & RINEHART

INCORPORATED

New York   *Toronto*

For

My Father and Mother

Contents

PART FOUR. UTOPIAN INTERLUDE

PART FIVE. SHE COMES IN FREE

PART SIX. ABE LINCOLN: 1816-1830

PART ONE

Beginnings

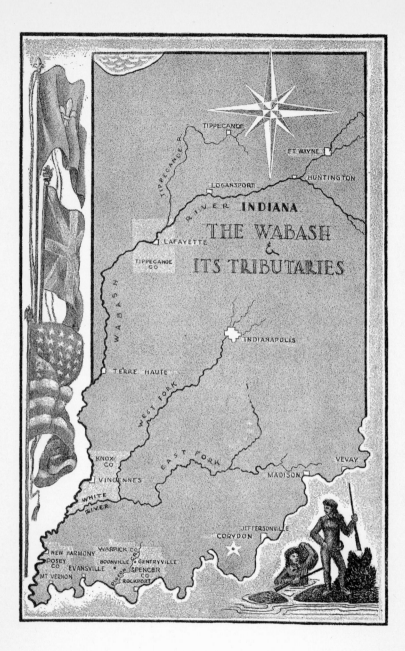

INDIANA

THE WABASH
&
ITS TRIBUTARIES

TIPPECANOE

FT. WAYNE

HUNTINGTON

LOGANSPORT

TIPPECANOE R.

RIVER

LAFAYETTE

TIPPECANOE
CO

WABASH

INDIANAPOLIS

TERRE HAUTE

WEST FORK

EAST FORK

KNOX
CO

VINCENNES

VEVAY

MADISON

WHITE
RIVER

JEFFERSONVILLE

CORYDON

NEW HARMONY

WARRICK CO

POSEY
CO

BOONVILLE   GENTRYVILLE

EVANSVILLE

PIGEON CREEK

SPENCER
CO

MT VERNON

ROCKPORT

I

Summer Evening

Iᴛ is evening in Indiana, a summer evening. The supper dishes have been washed, and Mother and the daughter whose turn it was to dry them have just come out on the front porch. Some of the children have gone off to the movies or to linger over a soda fountain on Main Street, but the rest of the folks are there. Father is in the swing, his after-supper cigar sending up tendrils of smoke that curl about the moonvine on the trellis. Grandma is in a rocker, resting her feet and rocking gently, to stir up a little air. On the steps a small boy is nuzzling his second slice of watermelon. From time to time he spits out the slippery seeds that collect in the pockets of his cheeks and wipes the back of his hand across his face from ear to ear.

"Be careful, son," his father admonishes. "Don't swaller any seeds, or you'll have a watermelon vine a-growin' out your ears!"

The boy only grins and digs his nose deeper into the fruit. He knows how to eat a watermelon. He knows a lot of things that his father has probably forgotten. He knows how to make pokeberry ink and where to find the best pawpaws, butternuts, and sassafras root. He can knock the bow and spin in the stern's place with his taw. He knows how to fish for camelworms and catch a bullfrog with a red flannel rag. He knows where to find dewberries and how to catch a coon and the best way to take walnut stains off his hands. He can take care of himself, that boy!

The boy's sister and older brother are on the porch too, and Aunt Mollie, who has come over with a dish of her apple slump; and when Mother and her helper come out, it is truly "quite a getherin' "—as Grandma might say. But it is a quiet, comfortable, Hoosier-fed gathering, and, no matter how small the porch may be, there is still room for a neighbor or two.

Everyone looks up when Mother appears, but no one stirs. It isn't time yet. Mother sighs softly, unties her apron, takes down a palm-leaf fan from the rack, and settles herself in a rocker. "Hot!" she says but that is all and nobody answers. They continue to sit in silence, listening to the drone of the locusts and smelling the deep, rich smells of an Indiana summer evening—honeysuckle and heaven trees and other people's suppers. It is as if they were waiting for something. And they are. The soft Hoosier air itself is breathless, and the gathered family are silent as they wait.

It is the boy who sees it first. He stands up on the steps and points through the ghostly, mottled branches of the sycamores.

"Look!" he cries. "There she comes!"

Mother stops fanning herself, and Grandma's rocking ceases. Father turns slowly in the swing, taking his cigar from his mouth. Aunt Mollie utters a little cry of wonder, and the other children run to the boy's side. Then, for a while, everyone is silent again; for a great, red moon is lifting slowly into the sky. Half the heavens it covers, almost, in the first few minutes, before it spills its blood upon the sultry evening air and sails more freely upward; and, no matter how many times they have seen it before, the folks on the porch are awed as they watch.

At last, Father turns to Mother and she nods in answer to his unspoken question. She is cool and rested now from her dishwashing.

"A harvest moon," she murmurs; and Father clears his throat, as if he were about to suggest a wholly new and unimagined thing, although everyone knows what he is going to say. It is what they have been waiting for.

"Well, folks," he says and clears his throat once more, "let's all go down and take a look at the river."

2

Let's Look at the River

A MAN who lives near a river cannot go for long without a visit to the riverbank. Anyone who has lived near flowing water—and most Americans have—knows that. The river draws him to it, like a magnet, and on its banks he will stand for hours, simply watching the water glide past. He cannot tell you what attracts him or what holds him there. Perhaps it is the river's beauty. Perhaps it is the current's symbolism of eternal change within eternal changelessness. Perhaps it is the reassurance that the river gives him of the permanence and stability of his world; for the river is his first and natural boundary, and he knows that a strange place, without a river from which he could take his bearings, would seem to him strange indeed—shapeless, confusing, and without reason for being. Perhaps going to look at the river is not a spiritual ceremony at all, but only the river dweller's excuse for idleness. But whatever the motive and whatever the nature of the river—whether it is the clear, blue water that runs from the mountains to the sea or the yellow stream that winds through thousands of miles of bottom land before it reaches the Gulf, whether it is dotted with rich men's sails or cluttered with poor men's houseboats, whether it is navigable only to canoes or bluntly plowed by barges and paddle-wheelers, whether it yields shad or trout or the sleepy mud cat, swift or slow, turbulent or quiet—it is all the same. A man must go and look at the river now and then.

To know America, you have to take a good, long look at the Wabash River. This is not provincial Hoosier pride. Other rivers in America are just as important. But, on the banks of the Wabash, the shape and size of the United States were determined during the Revolution, setting the southern border of Canada for all time at the Great Lakes, rather than the Ohio, and opening the Far West to American development. And on the banks of the Wabash has been nurtured the rare fusion of southern grace and Yankee industry which, for more than a century, has made the Hoosier one of the finest of American types.

They called the river the Ouabache originally—the French, who came to the country first, in the seventeenth century. That was their spelling of the Indian word, which meant "white." In those days, before the soil began to erode, the river was white, a glistening silver-white under the summer sun and a pale oyster-white when it reflected a winter sky; and where it flows over limestone or gravel and sand, yielding the famous Wabash pearls, there are stretches of the river that merit still the name the Indians gave it. Perhaps the pronounced coloring of the river, as much as tradition, was responsible for the failure of the French attempt to rechristen it "the St. Jerome."

The Indians called the lower Ohio "the Wabash" too, and considered the Ohio a mere tributary of their stream. For a long time the French accepted this nomenclature; but when the English got possession of all the

Ohio, they revised the map and rearranged the names as they now stand.

Whatever they called it and however they defined its course, they all agreed that it was a beautiful river and its valley a paradise. The Indians gave their lives to keep possession of it. The French sent back to their king glowing reports of its riches. The English fought stubbornly to win and to hold it. Finally, George Rogers Clark saw that, if the newly organized colonies were to survive and prosper, they must possess the Wabash; and he made a desperate conquest of it in the name of Virginia and the United States.

As soon as the conquests were over and the pioneers were able to rest from their pioneering, men and women turned to a less hazardous battle of words over the question of their river's source. The United States Topographical Survey settled the dispute at the turn of the present century; but, as late as 1931, three men set out on foot from Portland, Indiana, to find for themselves the river's origin. They ended up in a drainage ditch four miles south of Fort Recovery in Ohio. Had they been anyone but Hoosiers—or possibly Missourians, who also have to see for themselves—they would have been satisfied with the topographical report, which establishes the source a few miles south of St. Henry, Ohio, and indicates Beaver Creek as the first real contributor to Wabash waters.

On high, flat ground in western Ohio there is a lake called St. Mary's. The townspeople of St. Mary's and Celina, Ohio, are particularly proud of this lake; for, from it, the waters which flow eastward empty into the Great Lakes and eventually the Atlantic Ocean, and the waters which flow westward ultimately reach the Gulf of

Mexico, via Beaver Creek, the Wabash, the Ohio, and the Mississippi. In Celina and St. Mary's they reckon there is nothing else in the country like their lake—unless, perhaps, it might be the Continental Divide.

Celina has the more spectacular side of the lake, the westward side that feeds the Wabash. The village lies behind a great wall or dam some three miles in length. Summer cabins line the land side of the dam, and on the water side, at intervals of a hundred feet or so, are wooden piers. There, sitting on little platforms under large umbrellas, the summer colonists fish for bass, pickerel, and pike. But they are not robbing the Wabash. The wasteweir—or "wasteway," as some of the people there call it—that empties its parsimonious trickle into the sluggish and unromantic beginnings of Beaver Creek is fitted with heavy screens. The plentiful fish of the Wabash River come from no such slavish stock as that of the artificial lake. Like the soil of the Wabash valley, they are free—until the Hoosier boys tempt them too strongly with night crawlers!

The river itself is soon free after its waters leave the pool below the St. Mary's wasteweir, and it flows quietly, but in a beeline, among the willows, for the Indiana border. Through the black loam of Jay and Adams counties it meanders northward until it is joined by the Little Wabash, coming down from the once invaluable portage that linked the Wabash with the Maumee and, thereby, the Gulf of Mexico with the Great Lakes. After this pleasant excursion, the river glides westward across the state, giving a name to the town of Wabash, which was the first city in the world to be lighted by electricity ("first" and "biggest" are two words that loom large in the Hoosier's vocabulary), and fertility to the soil of

Miami County, which produces every crop that can be grown in Indiana (and that's a sight o' crops!).

At Peru, in Miami County, the Wabash is joined by the Mississinewa, a swift and beautiful stream from the south. On its banks, where once an Indian trading post flourished two miles east of the town, there is now a large, well-fenced community of yellow barns and sheds, where the lions and elephants of the John Robinson, Sells Floto, and Hagenbeck Wallace circuses spend the winter months. Logansport, the next large town on the Wabash, stands in the delta where the Eel comes in from the north, occupying the site of an old Kickapoo village that was destroyed by General Wilkinson in 1791. Below it is Delphi, high and airy on its hill at the edge of the "Grand Prairie."

From Delphi on, the Wabash seems to take more seriously its obligation to the Ohio, slanting off south-ward through the "Grand Prairie" and under the high, green hills round Lafayette, where William Henry Harrison put Tecumseh's redskins to rout and Purdue University still battles, though less spectacularly, with the modern enemies of agriculture. Along the plains named for Major Fountain of Kentucky and General Warren of Bunker Hill the river flows, through the "shoestring," with its vermilion soil and block coal, past Montezuma and Numa, until it reaches a city that was named Terre Haute by those who settled it and is called "Terry Hut" by those who live in it today.

Below Terre Haute, the Wabash, veering to the west, draws the line between southern Indiana and south-ern Illinois. After Prairieton and Tom, it is almost a straight drop southward between the two states, wash-ing the fertile land of Daniel Sullivan, who was killed

by Indians on the Vincennes Trace, nourishing the soil
so generously that melons grow large enough overnight
in that country to change surveyors' maps. Or so they'll
tell you. Through the county named for General Henry
Knox, first American secretary of war, the river flows
peacefully, and past Vincennes, which once was the capital of Michigan and Illinois as well as Indiana.

Down in Gibson County, the land grows even
richer, and the landowners of Princeton and Patoka are
indeed aristocrats of agriculture, while, finally, in Posey
County, the soil is the richest of all. There, in "the
Pocket," accumulate the deposits of the full stretch of
the river and of all its tributaries—the Tippecanoe, the
Eel, the Salamonie, the two forks of the White, the Vermilion, the Little Vermilion, the Mississinewa, the Embarrass (which is still called "Ombrah"), the Patoka, the
Black, and the two Little Wabash rivers, as well as Wild-
cat, Bonpas, Busseron, Coal, Sugar, Raccoon, and Turtle
creeks. From earliest times, Posey County has been blessed
with expert farmers, beginning with George Rapp, who
brought his German idealists to Harmony in 1815 and
consulted with the Angel Gabriel on the Wabash shore,
down to the present wise and merry-eyed men of "Hooppole" Township.

Although it is constantly coiling and uncoiling, like
a snake in the sun, and is never exactly the same two days
in succession, the Wabash is officially 475 miles long. It
begins at an altitude of 1,285 feet and ends at 313 feet
above sea level; but the speed of its current depends
mostly on the stage of the Ohio. If the Ohio is high, the
Wabash flows slowly; but when the Ohio is at a low
stage, it sucks the waters of the Wabash down to it
lickety-split. The drainage basin of the Wabash River is

33,100 square miles and is populated by almost three million people, of whom only one-fifth live in urban centers. In a recent census, the total value of farm lands, buildings, crops, and livestock in the basin was over two billion dollars, and the principal crops, besides corn, which composes twenty per cent of the produce of the region, were oats, wheat, timothy, clover, and other hays. The Wabash country has abundant deposits of coal, clay, gravel, and, of course, limestone—for which, along with corn, literature, politics, friendliness, and good cooking, the state of Indiana is famous. The river is no longer navigated, except by small boats and ferries. It is spanned by seventy-three bridges.

3

The Mound Builders

Iғ they could rise, reincarnated, from the ancient graves in which they lie buried, the first inhabitants of the Wabash valley would be mistaken for Indians. They were almost naked, and their skin was copper-colored. Like Indians, they wore feathers in their black hair and moccasinlike sandals on their feet. But their loincloths were of woven and beautifully designed fabric that no Indian could have made, and the ornaments of copper and bear teeth and fresh-water pearls strung about their necks and wrists were carved with a skill that the Shawnees and Piankeshaws and even the Miamis never possessed. The Mound Builders had much more in common with modern, civilized Hoosiers than with the savage followers of Tecumseh and Cornstalk.

Like the modern, white Hoosiers, the Mound Builders were mostly farmers. They raised corn in abundance in the river bottoms, because there the soil was loose and fertile and all they needed to cultivate it were their hoes and digging-sticks with mussel-shell blades, which were the best they could devise. In their well-plotted garden-beds, near their homes, grew the first of the famous Wabash squash, pumpkins, and beans, as well as the tobacco they smoked in their many pipes, carved to resemble the

13

intertwined necks of wild geese, perching owls and par-
rots, and squirrels that sat up on their haunches and
munched at nuts.

Like the Hoosier women of today, the Mound Builders' women were skilled at cooking. The variety of their
kitchen utensils bears witness to a well-practiced and
highly developed culinary art. Certainly they knew better than simply to boil animals whole, without removing
their skins, as the later Indians often did; and when the
meals were finished and the pots and pans scraped and
washed, they buried the garbage in specially dug refuse
pits, as any modern, civilized woman would.

Some of the Mound Builders operated quarries and
mines, gathering flint and limestone and granite and copper and iron from the earth wherever they could find
them. Others carried these raw materials up and down
the river in canoes and traded them for finished products,
such as pottery and textiles and ornaments and instruments of war. Still others dug for fresh-water clams in
the Wabash and extracted the pearls that formed about
grains of sand in their shells.

Not all the Mound Builders engaged in utilitarian
pursuits. The quantity of purely artistic objects which
the prehistoric race interred in their mounds would indicate that art may have been a profession among them.
Carved pendants made from bear teeth, strands of pearls,
earrings of chlorite and copper in the shapes of spools
and perfect circles, finger rings, and ornamental breast-
plates and headdresses have been found in abundance by
excavators and are proof that the Mound Builder
adorned himself with jewelry worthy of men and women
of some taste and refinement. The Mound Builder also
made terra-cotta figures and figurines in his own image

THE ONLY POSSIBLE SITE FOR THE BUILDING OF
BARNS AND HOMES IN THE LOW BOTTOM LAND.

and designed medallions in sheet copper. He sketched the human form on copper plate, engraved patterns on stone and human bone, carved ornaments of shell, and molded his pottery into fanciful shapes. He was not content with his world as he found it, and, not being content, he must have been superior to most of the Indians who succeeded him.

Of the Mound Builder's form of government and social organization almost nothing is known; but it is obvious that the warrior was not so important in Mound Builder society as he was among the later Indians. The Mound Builder was apparently a peace-loving man. Otherwise, he could not have developed the complex and widespread civilization that once ranged over all the river valleys of the Middle West and the South. Had his first interest been warfare, he would have built his mounds only as earthworks and burial places. He would have found no time to work out elaborate designs for them, shaping them into the forms of snakes and turtles and birds and the images of his own kind. Perhaps he would have had no time to build mounds at all; for their construction was a stupendous task that still baffles modern engineers.

In his woven basket, the Mound Builder was able to carry only twenty or twenty-five pounds of earth. Yet some of the mounds he accumulated range thirty feet high, over two hundred feet long, and a hundred wide. They are composed of tens of thousands of wagonloads of dirt that the primitive man dug up, transported, and piled into picturesque shapes. How he did it no one knows.

No one knows, either, exactly where he came from or where he went—or why. He was there for a while:

then he was gone—centuries, perhaps, before the Indians came. All that anyone knows certainly concerning him is what has been proved by the remains he left in his mounds.

They are still there—those mounds—from the river's source to its mouth, containing the ancient man's tools, his ornaments, and his bones. They cluster, especially thick, along the southern course of the Wabash, for there the soil was richer and easier to cultivate. At the juncture of the White and Wabash rivers, they are the dominant characteristics of the scenery, their round green hummocks rising on all sides, like chains of giant molehills. In those first-bottoms, the Hoosier farmer owes a special debt to the Mound Builders. They constructed the only possible sites for the building of barns and homes in the low bottom land.

4

Down from the North

IT was midwinter in the year 1669, and the water of the Ohio was yellow and fast and choked with floating ice. A thousand unpredictable eddies darted back and forth, weaving a treacherous tangle; and where the eddies met and were repelled, they left great dimples in the water that sucked branches and twigs and dead leaves into their syrupy pits. Trapped in one of those whirlpools, a canoe would have spun like a leaf and capsized.

The solitary white man, paddling in the middle of the river, roused himself suddenly to the danger. Bundled in a great beaver robe in the stern of his canoe, he tightened his grip on the smooth paddle, twisting the blade with all the strength left in his wasted wrists. He had shot the Falls of the Ohio. He knew the sauts of the Great Lakes. But he had never before found himself in such a maze of crosscurrents. Like invisible hands, they reached up unexpectedly from the bottom of the river and wrenched the canoe out of its course.

The canoe itself was a stranger to the brown and treacherous Ohio. Its ribs were the red roots of fir trees, heated over a fire and twisted into shape; and the hull was made of squares of birch bark, sewed together with dried moose sinews, the seams tarred with balsam gum. On the shores of this river, the birch, the fir, and the balsam did not grow; and the home of the moose was many miles away.

The beady, Gallic eyes of the young man in the canoe seemed never to lift from the swirling waters about him; and yet they saw everything. His life with the Iroquois in Canada had taught him that trick. He could take advantage of each ripple and wave; he could glide past rotting snags with only a hairbreadth between his fragile craft and destruction; he could steer a course through blocks of ice as tortuous as a rabbit's tracks among the trees of a forest; and, all the while, with some sixth sense, he was able to record in his mind every sound, every shift of the wind, and every bush and tree on both shores of the river. He had been doing it for days on end, alone and in a strange country; and now, although the river was suddenly demanding every ounce of his strength and his full attention, he was still able to do it.

He knew that he was between two large islands. He knew that the surrounding country was flat, except for the strange mounds that he had been seeing all along his course. And he knew, by the widening expanse of the water and the increasing complexity of currents, that he was approaching a large river that came down from the north.

He saw a bayou in one of the islands and steered for it. There was little danger from hostile Indians; but if there had been, he would have welcomed it. He had not seen an Indian of any kind for days and days; and the emptiness of the new country was growing oppressive, more oppressive even than the memory of his followers' desertion weeks before. The vast emptiness and stillness of

those snow-blanketed shores—that ever-changing pano-
rama of deep forests, wide prairies, and deep forests again
—had affected him even more than his own illness and
the cold and hunger that were gnawing at him, like a rat
in his stomach. He would have welcomed an Indian with
war paint and a scalping knife as heartily as if he had
been old Father d'Hocquelus in Rouen, who long ago had
awakened his first boyhood dreams of adventuring in far
lands.

Reaching above his head, he grasped the branch of a
willow and held his craft steady against the shore. His
arm ached. He was afraid he was going to be sick again.
But he held on.

The island was in the middle of a shoreless lake
whose waters were ripped by slanting trees and spotted
by nipples of brown earth, which the young man recognized as the crests of more of those strange and obviously
man-made mounds. Above him stretched the yellow,
treeless avenue of the river from the north. Gazing at it,
he wondered for a moment whether he had at last found
the great river he was seeking. In the swirl of currents,
it was difficult to tell whether the Ohio flowed into the
river above him or whether the river above flowed into
the Ohio.

His heart beat faster, and his shivering body was
suffused with warmth.

What if, in another week or so, he should reach the
warm ocean! What if, at last, he had found the river
route to China!

He remembered that giant of a man, Louis Joliet,
whom he had met for the first time only a few months
before, on the shores of Lake Ontario. Louis Joliet's name
had been a thorn in his own vanity ever since he had come

to Canada; and although, when they met, he had treated his great rival with respect, he had found it impossible to like him.

What a story it would be, up north in the narrow, crooked streets of Ville Marie and Trois Rivières and Quebec! What a legend he would become in the court of Louis XIV in France! He could hear the announcement of the news:

"Robert Cavelier, Sieur de La Salle of Rouen has found the northern reaches of the great river!"

And a murmur would go over the assembled court: "He got there before Joliet!"

But his calculations of longitude, clumsy and inaccurate as they were, told him that this was not the river he was seeking. Moreover, since Father Dollier and Father Gallinée had left him on the great lake, he had not traveled far enough west to reach the great river. There were still many miles to go.

The downflowing stream from the north yawned with the winter floods, spreading its yellow mouth wide, obliterating the face of the land. But La Salle, his first disappointment past, was beginning now to see it as it would be in summer. Beneath the racing, muddy waters, he could almost feel the outlines of its shores; and, as he watched, his feverish eyes began to see something more— something that no other man could have seen in that country.

For a minute or two, his vision of the future seemed to him like reality itself. Corn was growing in endless acres—the Indian corn that his own people called "turkey wheat." There were fertile gardens and white farmhouses and villages along the river. He saw men and women living there industriously and peacefully—

French men and women, sturdy Normans, like himself. Among them, there were robed priests, carrying the cross. He saw Franciscans and Sulpicians, like his brother, Jean, in Ville Marie; and, yes, he feared that he saw Jesuits, too, although he did not like the Jesuits. There were granaries and mills and sailing vessels that had come from the warm seas with cargoes from China. There was the laughter of many children. There was the lowing of cattle. There was the stamp of horses' hoofs. And, dominating the whole country, strong fortresses rose, garrisoned by French soldiers and flying the fleur-de-lys of France.

The canoe gave a lurch, the vision vanished, and La Salle knew that he could hold on to the willow no longer. He dipped his paddle into the water of the bayou and shot out into the shuttle of the two rivers' currents again. In a few minutes, he was past the northern river's mouth and entering a vast marsh. The combined waters of the two streams spread so wide that no channel could be distinguished among the submerged trees. He took one last look backward. Then he began to paddle slowly downstream.

Another day, perhaps, he said to himself. Two days, at the most. Then his waning strength would give out. If he was ever to get back to Canada, he would have to abandon his birchbark canoe somewhere in these marshes and strike out on foot, overland, northeast, across the upper reaches of the river he had seen, to the straits of Detroit and to his home near Ville Marie, where his brother Jean would be waiting. But he would not turn back until he had to. He would keep on as long as he had strength. He was thinking again of his giant rival—Joliet.

Ten years later, the young man wrote a memorial to his king. In it, he referred to himself modestly and always in the third person:

"In the year 1667, and those following, he made divers voyages with much expense, in which he for the first time explored many countries to the south of the great lakes, and among others the great river of Ohio; he followed it to a place where it empties, after a long course, into vast marshes, at the latitude of thirty-seven degrees, after having been increased by another river, very large, which comes down from the north. . . . Those lands surpass all others in everything. They are almost so beautiful and fertile, so sparsely covered with forest and so well adorned by prairies, streams, rivers, fish, game, and venison that one can find there, in abundance and with very little trouble, everything necessary for the maintenance of powerful colonies."

Robert Cavelier de La Salle was only twenty-six when he made that voyage of discovery down the Ohio in 1669. On that journey, his strength did not last and he failed to reach the Mississippi. Joliet was to see it first, after all. But La Salle, on that voyage, became the discoverer of the Ohio—and the Wabash, that "other river, very large, which comes down from the north."

5

The First Villain

AHALF century elapsed between La Salle's discovery of the Wabash and the establishment of the trading posts of Vincennes and Ouiatenon in what the French called "the Illinois Country." But by that time the fur trade of the Wabash valley was already thriving, as it was to continue to thrive until the passing of men's fancy for beaver hats put an end to it. The white men who, in that interval of fifty years or so, developed the routes along the Wabash and made the first bargains with the Indians were called "coureurs de bois." They were not very popular among members of their own race.

The coureur de bois was the white man in America gone native. By the end of the seventeenth century, he was to be found in every Indian village. Coming out of the oval council house of a Kickapoo town on the Wabash, near the mouth of the Vermilion, he looked, for all the world, like the warriors with whom he had been conferring. He was naked. His skin, from long exposure, had acquired a copperish glint. He wore moccasins and in his braided black hair were the three turkey feathers of the Kickapoos. He walked like an Indian, too, with long, gliding steps, toes turned in, and he was careful not to disturb any of the pack of dogs that prowled about the village, for the dog was sacred to the Kickapoos. At the end of the dusty street, he would turn in at one of the bark or flag-reed houses, and a Kickapoo squaw would greet him with a familiar grunt. In the Kickapoo tongue, he would ask her when his dinner would be ready; and if she was slow in answering, he would kick her, as he would not have dared to kick one of the dogs.

But he was not altogether like his Kickapoo companions. Unlike them, he might be found the next week among the Potawatomies to the north, or in the Wea town that was later to be Ouiatenon to the east, or down in Chippekawkay where the Piankeshaws lived on the site of what the French would one day call Vincennes. There he still looked and walked like an Indian, but his headdress was changed to conform to the mode of the tribe he was visiting and his language had become theirs also. And there, leaving the council house, he would enter another Indian dwelling, and another squaw—Potawatomi, Wea, or Piankeshaw—would greet him with the same familiarity and receive the same familiar kick.

The coureur de bois was interested only in himself and in what he could get for himself in the fur trade. He had no allegiances. For that reason the Indians accepted and trusted him. He lived and spoke and dressed like themselves. He was brave. He was strong. He traveled alone—never in murderous packs, like the invading French and English armies. And even when he was drunk and on a carouse, he never betrayed a secret. A word spoken to him was not spoken to the winds to be carried into every white settlement and to every other tribe in the country. It was a word spoken as if to oneself. The coureur de bois wanted only furs and goodwill. He knew a good thing when he saw it.

Naturally the coureur de bois was damned by his more conventional countrymen. He was getting rich, and he was having fun doing it. Yet they were responsible for his being what he was. The Puritanism of the Canada from which he came was oppressive. Attendance at balls, the wearing of lace and ornaments, cardplaying, and masquerading were frowned upon in Ville Marie and Quebec; and yet the education of young Frenchmen prepared them for little besides gaiety and fighting. What was a young man of high spirits to do? Finding the company of Indians more attractive than that of his gloomy and pious elders, he had no choice. As soon as he was old enough to escape from his somber home, he took to the woods.

In 1685, Bishop Saint-Vallière of Quebec wrote back to France:

"The youth of Canada are for the most part wholly demoralized; there are married men who, in addition to their own wives, keep squaws whom they publicly deceive; and the most frightful crimes are perpetrated by the young Frenchmen who resort to the woods."

Thus were the coureurs de bois denounced from Quebec and Ville Marie, and no doubt they deserved all that was said about them. Finally, laws were made that ostracized them from white society. They might come back to staid and stolid Ville Marie and Quebec only on pain of death.

Such remained the official attitude of proper French folk for more than a decade. Then the authorities discovered that the coureurs de bois were of some value, after all. The encroachments of the English were growing troublesome. The coureurs de bois were the one strong link that bound the Indians to the French. Why not use the coureurs de bois to stir up the Indians against the English? Overnight, the renegade youth of Canada were transformed, then, from criminals to heroes; and, in 1701, the King of France granted them a general amnesty.

But the King of France succeeded only in robbing the life of the coureur de bois of one of its attractions. The rebellious young men of Canada had no desire to become respectable. By the year 1765, when the English took over the country southwest of the Great Lakes, the coureur de bois was no more.

HE HAD AT LAST FOUND T[

EAT RIVER HE WAS SEEKING.

PART TWO

The Drowned Country

6

Red and Green Serge

CAPTAIN FRANÇOIS BUSSERON was a phlegmatic man. Other Frenchmen in Vincennes, on a certain July morning in 1778, may have been keyed up to high pitch of excitement; but Captain Busseron, upon whom so much depended, was calm.

With customary concern for his wife's slumber, he eased himself cautiously out of bed, planted his feet wide apart and firmly on the Indian mat at the bedside, and stood up slowly, so that the network of ropes beneath the feather mattress would not creak. Then he padded in his bare feet across the puncheon floor to the wardrobe and began to dress.

From the leather and homespun shirts and pantaloons and the silk petticoats and Paris dresses in the wardrobe, he selected the beautiful white uniform of a French officer. In it he had once served the King of France. But that was years ago. Now, with the British in command of Fort Sackville, he wore it in the service of the King of England, as an officer of militia. The brocade was slightly tarnished and the sleeves were frayed, but the cloth had been beaten snow white with a mallet only yesterday, and Aspasie, the Negro slave, had done a good job of starching and ironing.

Downstairs, Aspasie was already stirring about; and, as he finished his toilet, the yeasty fragrance of new bread began to float up from the bakehouse to tease the captain's nostrils. But he did not hurry. Only when he was satisfied with each buckle and lacing on his stocky, well-fed person did he descend the stairs and, settling himself in a rush-bottomed chair at the dining-room table, call for his breakfast.

The meal finished, he lighted his pipe and went into the parlor, where he paused for a moment and ran his stubby fingers affectionately over the green cloth of the billiard table. This was a morning ritual that he could not omit even today. It had cost him a pretty penny to get that table up the Mississippi, the Ohio, and the Wabash from New Orleans, and his pride in it was the greatest of his many little vanities. He hefted one of the crooked cues in his hand and let the butt of it drop with a light thump on the floor. Then he bent over and, sighting down the cue at an uneven ball, winked with satisfaction at his skill and made a clucking sound with his tongue. Tomorrow, when everything was settled, he would have a game with Father Gibault.

That was the only time during the day that Captain Busseron deviated from the line of duty. Immediately after taking aim at the ball, he laid the cue in its rack, straightened his shoulders, glanced about guiltily, as if he feared someone might have been watching him, and went out into the bright morning sunlight. Once more, as he marched down through his orchard under boughs heavy with apples and pears and out through the gate of his high picket fence, he was the perfect soldier.

Captain Busseron was born first to obey and then to command. He had no conception of loyalties higher than those he owed to his immediate superior, to whom he gave the same blind obedience that he expected of his men. Under French rule, he had been a devoted subject of Louis. Since 1765, he had served George of England equally well. Neither sovereign meant more to him than a name. What counted with him was his allegiance to the officers sent out from the remote lands of England or France to command him. Without them, he was lost.

For more than a month, now, he had been thus lost, and it had been a trying experience. In the spring, Lieutenant Governor Abbott had gone back to Canada and left him in charge of the garrison at Vincennes. The captain had done his best, but he knew that it was a very poor best. The discipline of the fort was lax. The citizens had become careless. Things most certainly were not as they should be. And yet, with no one to give him orders, Captain Busseron failed to see how things could be otherwise. Fort Sackville needed a real commandant, not just a captain of militia, to govern it. The captain had been quite despondent over his many problems until two days ago when Father Gibault arrived in Vincennes and made him, once more, a useful and efficient soldier. Father Gibault, while he was not an army officer, was born to command.

Captain Busseron worshiped Father Pierre Gibault. In his opinion, and in the opinion of most of his friends, the priest was the greatest man in the Wabash country. For ten years he had been there among them—now at Vincennes, now at Kaskaskia, now at Ouiatenon, going and coming tirelessly through the forest, placating the Indians, advising the English, shepherding the French, even converting an occasional American, and performing his duties as vicar-general as no other man could have performed them. A saintly man, Father Gibault was, nevertheless, a soldier's priest. He feared nothing; his frail, ascetic body could endure the severest hardships; and, without diminishing in the slightest degree the dignity and sanctity of his calling, he entered into the pastimes of rough and vigorous men with a heartiness that excelled their own.

"Un vrai bon soldat de Jésus!" they said, as they raised their glasses in respectful toasts to him in the wine-shops of Vincennes.

"Yes," Captain Busseron thought, "and a good billiard player, too!"

The captain was alone in the street, and he walked briskly. It was a beautiful morning. A fresh breeze was blowing up from the Wabash, and the silent, white-washed houses glistened in the early morning sun. They stood close to the street, behind high picket fences. Most of them were of logs, set upright in the ground, but some were more ambitious, with puncheon walls and shingle roofs and piazzas running round all four sides, like the captain's own home. Some were even built of stone, but not many. All of them were clean and white and surrounded by hollyhocks and fruit trees, with long gardens stretching behind them.

"Old Laderout's squash look good this year," the captain muttered to himself, forgetting tomorrow's billiards momentarily as he caught glimpses of the gardens through the endless rows of fence. "There's a blight on Gamelin's potatoes, I see. . . . The widow Racine will have good wine again this season. . . ."

At the end of the street, he paused to look down at four Indians paddling swiftly and silently past in a long pirogue. He recognized them as Kickapoos, come down the Wabash from the Vermilion, and made a mental note of their passing, hoping it did not forebode trouble.

As he started on again, he found himself suddenly face to face with another Indian. The captain was startled. It was as if the savage had sprung up from the dusty earth. But he quickly recovered himself when he recognized the Indian as Tobacco's Son, the chief of the friendly Piankeshaws who lived in Vincennes.

"Bonjour," he said, offering his hand.

Tobacco's Son took the extended hand in solemn friendliness. In spite of his age, he was a tall, lithe, and muscular animal. His other name was Grand Door of the Wabash. It had never occurred to Captain Busseron to smile at such a name—even the first time he heard it. The captain was not that kind of man.

"You woke up with the birds this morning, captain," the Indian said.

"I have to get ready for the meeting in the fort. You are coming with your warriors, I hope, Tobacco's Son."

The Grand Door of the Wabash shook his head.

"The shifting wind shakes the fruit from the tree before it is ripe," he said cryptically, and bowed.

Captain Busseron gave a little shrug. He had never been able to understand the nonsense the Indians talked. They were always prattling away about the winds and the good little birds and the bad little birds.

"Tiens!" he said; and the Indian smiled.

"But the Piankeshaws and the French will remain one people, no matter what happens."

"C'est entendu."

They bowed to each other again, and Captain Busseron marched on.

At the door of a cottage on the next corner, he knocked loudly, and a woman appeared. She wore a pale-gray skirt that reached only to her knees, and below it was a flame-colored petticoat that continued to her ankles. The captain found time for an admiring glance before he spoke.

"Good morning, Madame Godare. You have finished the little job I gave you, I hope."

The woman smiled and nodded and then disappeared, returning in a moment with a roll of red and green cloth.

"Good luck with it, monsieur le capitaine," she said.

"The lovely hands that made it, madame, could bring us nothing else."

As he paid her for the cloth, Madame Godare gave him a coquettish smile.

"If the captain fights as well as he speaks, we need have no fear," she said; and, with a curtsy, she closed the door.

In the street again, Captain Busseron stopped and drew a slip of paper from his pocket.

"St. Marie," it read, "5 ells of red serge. . . . M. Defonet, 3¾ ells of green serge. . . . Mme. Godare, sewing . . ."

The figures in the right-hand column represented a fair sum. The captain pursed his lips and shook his head. He hoped that someday he could collect the money he had spent. But, of course, he would! He trusted Father Gibault.

He saw the priest coming out of the log church and crossing the street to the fort. Calling to him, the captain quickened his pace and came up puffing, the roll of red and green serge under his arm.

Father Gibault's eyes twinkled under the bushy eyebrows that jutted above his long, pointed nose and cadaverous, deeply lined cheeks.

"I see you have it," he said, touching the cloth with a brown hand.

"Yes, father, and everything else is ready."

"Good! They should be gathered in another hour. Let us go to the fort at once."

The captain nodded and the two men, their heads bent close in consultation, entered the gate of the log stockade.

7

Soldat de Jésus

On that July morning in 1778, Pierre Gibault was just entering his forty-second year. Born in Montreal, he had been especially trained for work among the Indians; and when he was ordained a priest in 1768, he was sent immediately to the Illinois country. He had been there for ten years now, and François Busseron's opinion of him was fully justified. There was perhaps no other man in all that country with the influence that Father Gibault exercised. He was a Jesuit—one of that order which La Salle had feared to see enter the new land— but he wore his authority and his power with a wisdom and tolerance that the discoverer of the Wabash would have admired.

As he stood before the French people of the village of Vincennes, in the stockade of Fort Sackville high above the Wabash River, his manner inspired confidence. While they knew that his brain was quicker than theirs and his eloquence might readily deceive them if he wished it to, there was not one among them who envied him or mistrusted him. They stood in respectful silence and listened, as the line of militia behind Captain Busseron came to attention and the priest's words rang out in the morning stillness and echoed across the river.

He spoke briefly, and not as a priest but as one of their own number. His manner was quiet and persuasive. His fine, gaunt, ascetic face was earnest.

"I have just come from Kaskaskia, as you know, and there, within the past few days, I have witnessed a miracle. It was not a miracle of the church, but a miracle of the sword—a kind of miracle to which we are not accustomed in this wild country of ours.

"On the fourth of July, the people of Kaskaskia, like the people of Vincennes, lived under English rule, and their garrison was commanded by the Chevalier de Rocheblave, in the absence of the English commandant, just as your fort is governed by Captain Busseron while Lieutenant Governor Abbott is away. On the fourth of July the Kaskaskians believed that the nearest Americans were miles away above the Falls of the Ohio, and no one dreamed that the war between them and the English would be brought into the Illinois country. On the night of the fourth, everyone in Kaskaskia went to bed as usual, feeling they would rest secure and undisturbed.

"But when the people woke on the morning of the fifth, they found the garrison occupied, not by the Chevalier de Rocheblave and the militia under the English flag, but by a small army of Americans, commanded by a young man named George Rogers Clark, of Virginia. This army had traveled down the Ohio and then overland one hundred and twenty miles to Kaskaskia without being discovered, and they had captured the fort during the night.

"The miracle was not the long journey undetected, nor the victory—although they in themselves were remarkable. The miracle was the completion of that march and that victory without a single loss of life. Stranger

still, no one was imprisoned and no attempt was made
to employ the Indians in a civil dissension that might
have ended in a massacre.

"But we were not aware of these startling facts at
first. We only knew that the Americans were there
among us and we were afraid. Many of our people cow-
ered in their homes, fearful of what the ragged and un-
kempt invading army would do. It was with such fears
in my own heart that I went to Colonel Clark and asked
whether the usual services might be conducted in the
Church of the Immaculate Conception.

"His answer astounded me.

" 'But of course, Father Gibault!' he replied. 'My
army has nothing to do with the affairs of churches, except, under the laws of Virginia, to protect them from
insult.'

"This man, who is not of our church, allowed us
then to proceed to worship in our own way, promising to
defend our right to do so; and when the people learned
that they were not to be molested, their mourning turned
to excess of joy. They decorated the streets with flowers
and pavilions of many colors and cheered the conquering
army. Only the Chevalier de Rocheblave suffered from
the change of government, and his sufferings were largely
his own fault, for he had refused to surrender gracefully.
His slaves were sold at auction and the proceeds were
given to Colonel Clark's men. But, in the end, even the
Chevalier de Rocheblave was paroled.

"Within a week after the appearance of this miraculous army, the towns of Prairie du Rocher, St. Philippe,
and Cahokia were captured in the same bloodless manner,
and Colonel Clark succeeded in pacifying Indian chiefs
whom even I, protected by the cross, have feared at times

to approach. There was peace and order in the Illinois country when I left it, and a new kind of liberty was being enjoyed by everybody.

"Now, I am here today, because Colonel Clark has asked me to come and tell you of his conquest and explain to you that the war the Americans are waging against their English rulers is being fought in the cause of liberty. Colonel Clark is determined to take possession of Vincennes, but he is eager that the victory shall be gained in a peaceful manner. He has asked me to propose to you that you take the American oath of allegiance now, so that bloodshed may be avoided and it will be necessary for him merely to send an American officer to take charge of the fort in the same manner that he took over control of Kaskaskia."

The priest paused and allowed the villagers to discuss the question among themselves, while he turned to Dr. Laffont, who had accompanied him from Kaskaskia, and talked quietly of the beauty of the summer day.

Finally, one of the leading merchants of Vincennes stepped forward.

"Father Gibault, we are at a loss to know what to decide. We should like your advice in the matter."

For a moment, the priest appeared to hesitate. Then he spoke again, calmly, and with no attempt to exhort his followers.

"Because of my calling, I have no part in temporal affairs; and yet the welfare of my people must always stand foremost in my heart. For that reason, I feel justified in giving you an opinion.

"If you become citizens of Virginia, I believe you will not only avoid needless bloodshed, but will also strengthen the security of your persons and your property and extend your commercial privileges far beyond those that your present English governors allow you.

"But that is merely my opinion. I do not wish to persuade you against your will. You must make the decision for yourselves."

Again the citizens of Vincennes debated among themselves. Then the merchant stepped forward once more.

"Father, it is our wish to become citizens of Virginia and to take the oath of allegiance immediately."

Father Gibault, prepared for the decision, administered the oath himself. While he was doing so, Captain Busseron, also prepared, stepped up to the flagpole and ran down the British flag. Taking the bundle of red and green serge that he had got from Madame Godare that morning, he tied it to the cords and raised it to the top of the mast, where it unfurled in the morning breeze and floated, as a symbol of the sovereignty of Virginia, above the heads of the cheering citizens.

A few days later, Captain Leonard Helm and one soldier arrived from Kaskaskia and took command of Vincennes in the quiet and unoppressive manner that George Rogers Clark had promised. Like Colonel Clark, Captain Helm knew how to win the confidence of the Indians. Within a few days, Tobacco's Son, the Grand Door of the Wabash, who had spoken so cryptically to Captain Busseron on the morning of Father Gibault's address, announced that henceforth he was not a British subject but an American. And a loyal American he remained throughout all that happened thereafter.

8

The Beavers Help the British

FOR three years Lieutenant Colonel Henry Hamilton, the British governor of Detroit, had been allowing the Indians to do his work for him. Through his Indian agent, Major Jehu Hay, a Pennsylvanian, he had been buying the scalps of American settlers and allowing that commercial enterprise to substitute for more direct warfare. On September 16, 1778, he was writing:

"Since last May the Indians in this district have taken 34 prisoners, 17 of which they have delivered up, and 81 scalps, several prisoners (children) taken and adopted not reckoned in this number."

The Indians were good instruments of terror, but their scalping activities did not establish British troops in American forts or add territory to the British command. Furthermore, Colonel Hamilton was bored with the smoking of Indian pipes and dickering over the price of scalps, and he was growing restless. A long-nosed, horse-faced man, with a thick, protruding lower lip, a contemptuous smile, and sharp, cynical eyes, he looked upon his adversaries in the rebellion of the colonies as a gang of tatterdemalion ruffians. Exasperated by their persistence in fighting for their silly cause, he determined, in the summer of 1778, to dally with them no longer, but to strike at Pittsburgh, crush it, and thereby establish British sovereignty throughout the west. Then, on the sixth of August, he learned of Clark's victories at Kaskaskia and Vincennes; and he knew that, before he could be successful at Pittsburgh, he must clean up the unexpected situation that had arisen to the southwest of his headquarters.

It was with considerable disgust for the task that he began his preparations. A campaign in the wilderness of the Wabash and Illinois country had few charms for a man who loved his comforts. Moreover, he was being forced to postpone a more brilliant campaign against Pittsburgh that would have won him considerable renown in the mother country. Who, in England, knew the whereabouts of Kaskaskia or Vincennes? Who, indeed, even knew they existed? But he was a good soldier and he knew where his duty lay. While he was at it, he would make a thorough job of it, clean out the American rascals completely and not only vanquish Kaskaskia and Vincennes, but also establish a fort at the mouth of the Ohio which would give him control of the Mississippi.

By October 7th, Hamilton was ready and he set out, his two hundred white troops and four hundred Indians, completely armed, even with cannon, poling and paddling up the Maumee River until they reached its headwaters, where they disembarked and began the nine-mile portage to the Wabash.

They did not travel light, and the portage was a great trial to the men, who had been living an inactive life in barracks for three years. The British soldiers were members of the King's Eighth—most of them Irishmen who had little interest in the war—and they soon began to grumble. The Indians downrightly refused to touch the black cannon, fearing they might bark. When the army finally reached the Wabash, their troubles came to a climax. It had not rained for days, and the Wabash waters were too shallow to float the boats after the heavy cargoes were taken on.

"We'll not be carrying these damned cannon all the way down to Vincennes on our backs!" the Irish growled.

But even as they rebelled, a scout returned with the news that four miles down the river beavers were building a dam and in no time the stage of the river would be high enough for their keels to clear the sandy bottom.

In less than no time, this did happen, and Colonel Hamilton's army found itself once more afloat. When they reached the beaver dam, they cut through it a passage that not only allowed them to sail on, but also flooded the stream farther down with the pent-up waters of the beaver lake.

Once again, on that journey, the beavers of the Wabash took sides in the American Revolution and helped the British to advance by building a second dam. But, even so, it was not an easy voyage. The weather had turned bitter cold and the river was often flooded with ice. The army did not reach Vincennes until December 17th, seventy-one days after its departure from Detroit.

9

Captain Leonard Helm

ON THE morning of December 17th, only four months after he had hauled down the cross of St. George above Fort Sackville and run up Madame Godare's red and green flag, François Busseron, a major now, lay in bed listening to the boom of Captain Leonard Helm's cannon summoning him and his militia to the fort's defense. He did not ease himself calmly and cautiously out of the feather mattress, as he had done on that bright morning in July. Instead, he closed his eyes against the snowstorm blowing past his bedroom window and tried to go back to sleep. Yesterday and the day before he had answered the boom of Captain Helm's cannon, but only a few of his men had appeared with him. This morning he would remain abed.

Major Busseron had heard the report of Colonel Hamilton's approach. Two hundred British regulars and French-Canadian militiamen, several cannon, and six or seven hundred scalp-hunting Indians collected on the route from Detroit! Major Busseron was a good soldier, but he did not believe in suicide.

In the fort, however, Captain Helm was showing another spirit. With his garrison of one lone American soldier standing beside him, he continued to add sen-

tences to the report he had begun to write to Colonel
Clark several days before, jotting the words down from
time to time in the midst of preparations. As he scribbled
the closing lines, he could glance through a porthole and
see Major Hay and his detachment of regulars and Indians dragging a six-pounder into position and Colonel
Hamilton's flotilla gliding down the river toward the
town through the blinding snow.

"Dr Sir," the letter ran:

"At this time theer is an army within three miles of this
place. I heard of their comin several days before hand. I sent
spies to find the certainty. The spies being taken prisoners, I
never got intelligence till they got within three miles of the
town. As I had called the militia, and had all the assurance of
their integrity, I ordered, at the firing of a cannon, every man
to appear; but I saw but few. Capt. Burron behaved much to
his honor and credit; but I doubt the certain[ty] of a certain
gent. . . .

"Excuse hast as the army is in sight. . . .

"My determination is to defend the Garrison, though I
have but 21 men but what has left me. I refer you to the
bearer, Mr. Wms, for the rest. . . .

"The army is in three hundred yd of the village. You
must think how I feel; not four men that I can really depend
on, but am determined to act brave. . . .

"Think of my condition. I know it is out of my power
to defend the town, as not one of the militia will take arms,
thoug, before sight of the army, no braver men. . . .

"Their flag is at a small distance. I must conclude.

"Yr Humble servt
"Leod Helms"

By the time he had finished, Captain Helm saw that
his case was hopeless; but, undaunted, he gave the letter

to Mr. Williams, his one soldier, with orders to carry it to
Kaskaskia, and then he set about by himself to meet the
invading army of at least eight hundred men.

The attack began with Colonel Hamilton advancing
toward the gate of the fort under a flag of truce. Immediate surrender was his demand.

Captain Helm had a sense of irony even in desperate
circumstances. "Before sight of the army," he had written, "no braver men. . . !" To the splendid figure in
scarlet outside Fort Sackville's gates, he said drily:

"I reckon I'd better know first who sent you here,
mister."

Colonel Hamilton drew himself to his full height,
and his lower lip protruded contemptuously. Had he not
come himself to treat with this ragged rebel upstart! And
now he was being asked for his credentials! He, with two
hundred British soldiers behind him and a mob of savages waiting breathlessly for the war cry! And this one
man in the fort insisted upon credentials! It was prepos-
terous.

"I am the king's lieutenant governor from Detroit,"
he replied.

Captain Helm studied him calmly for a moment;
and then, as if he were not only ready but able to blow
the lieutenant governor's army to bits, he asked what
terms he should have if he yielded.

Hamilton was speechless. Terms! But slowly he
found himself admiring the courage of the lone man before him.

"Humane treatment," he replied quietly, and with
a note of respect in his voice.

Leonard Helm was silent for several minutes, as if
he were calculating the number of redcoats and savages

he could handle before he was himself killed. At last, he said slowly:

"It looks like you might as well come on in, colonel."

British sentries were posted in the fort at once, but they were not strong enough to restrain Hamilton's Indians.

"They bore down the sentries," the colonel wrote later to his king, "and, seeing that I had posted another at the door of the commandant's headquarters, they went to the window which they broke and fell to plundering."

Captain Helm refused to take down the red and green flag; and the colonel had to give orders to one of his men to run it down and replace it with the cross of St. George. Thereupon the entire army marched into the garrison and Vincennes was once more a British town.

The next day, in the church, from which Father Gibault had been taken as a prisoner of war, six hundred and twenty-one French inhabitants of Vincennes filed past a British officer and signed a document specially drawn up for them.

"We, the undersigned, declare and acknowledge to have taken the oath of allegiance to Congress, in doing which we have forgotten our duty to God and have failed in our duty to man. We ask pardon of God and we hope from the goodness of our legitimate sovereign, the King of England, that he will accept our submission and take us under his protection as good and faithful subjects, which we promise and swear to become before God and before man. In faith of which we sign with our hand or certify with our ordinary mark."

Thus once more, after a period of uncertainty, François Busseron, who was born first to obey and then to command, became a useful and efficient soldier, although by this time a seed of skepticism regarding his superiors had begun to take root in him. When he learned that the British intended to buy the whole of the town's goods for their own use, he buried the greatest part of his powder and ball.

Tobacco's Son, on the other hand, the Grand Door of the Wabash, who in July had at first been wary of the shifting winds, was no such opportunist. He remembered the oath Captain Helm had persuaded him to give. He acknowledged nothing superior to his own honor. When Colonel Hamilton invited him to transfer the allegiance of his tribe once more to the British cause, he listened in stony silence; and his only reply was to withdraw his warriors to the outskirts of the village, where he maintained an orderly, but disdainful neutrality.

10

A Desperate Case

"ON THE 4th of [February] I got everything complete, and on the 5th I marched."

That was how he afterwards stated it, and that was indeed how be began it.

Like so many of the men who wrote the first chapters of the story of the Wabash, George Rogers Clark was a Virginian. Born on his father's 400-acre farm on the Rivanna River, just two and a half miles from the birthplace of Thomas Jefferson, he might easily have contented himself with a place in that Old Dominion society as a country gentleman. James Madison and John Tyler were his schoolmates; and, although George Rogers did not take kindly to his Scottish schoolmaster's brand of Greek, Latin, and French, scholarship was not one of the requisite qualities of a gentleman in those days. George Washington himself never learned to spell correctly. It was not an inability to master grammar, then, that sent George Rogers Clark out of that well-ordered and aristocratic world into the wilderness and on to immortality on the banks of the Wabash: it was, instead, the nature of George Rogers Clark himself. He was destined for adventure.

Physically, he was a giant. Well over six feet tall, his

body was as supple and strong as a hickory rod. His eyes were black, startlingly black and penetrating and full of fire, as if they had caught some of the flame from the shock of red hair that crowned his large and handsomely shaped head. He moved with the Southerner's easy grace among a world of smaller men; and perhaps from the physical necessity of seeing above the heads of those about him, he acquired the habit of gazing at horizons— a dangerous habit for young men whose parents would keep them at home.

At nineteen, he took up the study of surveying under the guidance of his grandfather, and thereafter his one obsession was land—new land—for Virginia first, and only afterward for himself. He was not yet twenty when he went on his first journey of exploration westward, down the Ohio to the mouth of the Kanawha; and that first voyage sealed his fate. Within a few years, he was the acknowledged leader of all the pioneers in the new land of Kentucky. When his little army captured the fort at Kaskaskia in the Illinois country, he was still only twenty-five.

"On the 4th of [February] I got everything complete, and on the 5th I marched."

Reading that bald statement of the beginning of the campaign to recapture Vincennes, you might conclude that George Rogers Clark was either a very brash and overconfident young man or else a man whose previous successes had robbed him of imagination.

He was neither. He knew that his little army of Kentucky frontiersmen was inadequate. He knew that, with no base of supplies to draw upon, no avenue of retreat behind him, and no reinforcements to be hoped for, his chance of overpowering the new British garrison at

Vincennes or even of outwaiting them in a siege was worth about as much as a drunken Indian's promise. He knew that the Miamis in Colonel Hamilton's service would be everywhere in the forests about Vincennes; that the French, with their readiness to change allegiance with every turn of fortune, could not be counted upon; that even the Grand Door of the Wabash, although he professed to be listening to the good little birds and so far had refused to join the British, might at any moment change his unpredictable Indian mind.

It was with a complete knowledge of the situation at Vincennes that George Rogers Clark undertook his campaign. Father Gibault, released by Colonel Hamilton, had come to Kaskaskia and told him all that had happened. Francis Vigo, a Sardinian, who gave both his advice and his money to the American cause in the west and who, sixty years later, was to die a pauper, had also come from Vincennes and told him.

George Rogers Clark knew, too, as your modern Wabash valley dweller still knows—even in this day of dams and steel bridges and concrete highways—that February is no time of year for men to go tramping among the bayous of the Embarrass, the Little Wabash, and the Big Wabash rivers. To Patrick Henry, on the third of February, two days before he started, he wrote:

"I know the case is desperate, but Sr, we must either quit the country or attack Mr. Hamilton."

That bald statement of Clark's does not tell us that it was by strategy that he "got everything complete." The French inhabitants of Kaskaskia were none too eager to join a march across two hundred miles of "drowned" country. They had changed their allegiance to the Americans too recently, and they preferred the comfort of their homes and the pleasures of conversation and billiards and light wines to the hardships of the wilderness. But Clark was determined to have volunteers, for his own men were not enough. So he brought down from Cahokia a group of more daring Frenchmen who were willing to go to Vincennes, and, in the presence of the Kaskaskians, he entertained them expensively. At once, the young ladies of Kaskaskia took notice. They liked the Cahokians' uniforms. They liked the distinction of being seen in their company. They began to find the home-town boys dull and unromantic. And, at that point, the home-town boys themselves began to take notice. Sixty of them enlisted to join Clark's seventy Americans in the desperate campaign.

On the fourth of February, the Cahokians were put aboard a batteau, called the *Willing,* which was to make its way down the Kaskaskia River and the Mississippi to the Ohio, and up the Ohio and the Wabash to Vincennes. Two four-pounders, four large swivels, one nine-pounder, and forty-six men were aboard the vessel when she sailed. They were to assist Clark at Vincennes in his siege—if they arrived in time.

And on the fifth, George Rogers Clark, with his seventy Kentuckians and sixty Kaskaskians, marched.

11

Shoulder-Deep and Singing

"WE NOW had a route before us of two hundred and forty miles in length, through I suppose one of the most beautiful countries in the world, but at that time in many parts flowing with water, and exceeding bad marching. My greatest care was to divert the men as much as possible, in order to keep up their spirits."

He did it by beginning the march as if it were nothing more than a hunting expedition. He himself had "an inward assurance of success," and that assurance was shared by Father Gibault, who, before the troops left, blessed them in the same quiet and matter-of-fact manner in which he had addressed the Vincennes populace seven months before.

But, once on the march, Clark had to change his policy. There the matter-of-fact pose would not do. Out of sight of Kaskaskia, there were no longer admiring young ladies, weeping mothers, and proud, but troubled fathers to make them keep their chins up and their eyes straight ahead. Once on the march, the shrewd young Virginia colonel decided that the expedition must be made to seem like a lark.

He was riding a fine stallion and the other officers were also mounted; but daily they lent their horses to the men to go out and shoot game. While they were gone, the young commander and his aides frolicked like schoolboys, shouting and singing and running ahead of the men, through the mud and water, to urge them always onward. At night, when camp was made, the company that had been allowed to hunt during the day invited the rest of the army to a feast, where they all reveled like Indian war-dancers.

"Thus, insensibly, without a murmur," George Rogers Clark wrote afterward, "were those men led on to the banks of the Little Wabash."

And thus, by the time they reached the Little Wabash, they were convinced that nothing could stop them.

The Little Wabash tried. Choked with planters and sawyers—logs that stood upright and logs that floated—it was mad with the torrents of early spring. But it failed to hold the men back. They built a platform on the opposite shore and ferried their goods across to it; and when they discovered that the land on the eastern shore lay three feet underwater as far as they could see, they only laughed.

"We've crossed only one fork of the Little Wabash," a Frenchman explained to them. He knew the lay of the land, even though he could not see it. "The other fork is three miles away. There must be five miles of floodwater still ahead of us."

Beside him, a tall, gaunt Kentuckian pushed back his black felt hat on his forehead and, with the back of his hand, wiped the tobacco juice from the corners of his mouth.

"Is that all? Why, that won't even be worth me a-tuckin' my shirttail inside of my britches fur!"

And, without another word, he plunged into the

flooded bottom land, waist-deep, beckoning to the others with his rifle, held high above his head.

They were supermen, and they knew it. They danced and splashed and sang and boasted what they would do to Mr. Hamilton—"the hair-buyer general"—when they got their hands on him. When a little drummer climbed aboard his drum and paddled on ahead of everybody else, they laughed, until someone shouted:

"Lookie thar! That-air young'un's a-tryin' to beat us to it!"

With a war whoop they were after the drummer, scrambling and stumbling.

By the evening of the fifteenth, when they encamped on an isolated mound of dry earth, they had already, in their imaginations, taken Post Vincennes, divided the spoil, and marched halfway to Detroit.

But beyond that point, there was no more merrymaking. They were now within only a few miles of the enemy, who, if they discovered the army's approach, could dispatch a party in boats that would have all the advantages in a fight. Not only tactics demanded a less exuberant march, but nature also. Provisions were running short. They were hungry. Many were weakening. A few began to stumble and fall in the icy waters. The others helped them, even carried them on their shoulders, although it was burden enough for any man to carry only his goods and, in from three to five feet of water, to keep his arms and powder dry. There was no laughter after they crossed the second fork of the Little Wabash. But there was no grumbling, either.

" 'Tain't much farther, pard! Keep yer head up!"

"Jist wait till we git to Vincennes, an' 'en see what we'll do!"

"Non, m'sieu! Just my rifle. That's all. I can take care of myself."

"Courage, mes vieux!"

No one—neither Frenchman nor American—spoke once of turning back.

George Rogers Clark knew what was ahead better than all the rest. He had dispatched four scouts across the Embarrass to bring back vessels and intelligence. They returned with nothing more than the canoe in which they had set out, and the intelligence they brought was enough to shatter the young colonel's fondest hopes. For nine miles, between the army's camp and Vincennes, there was nothing but water. The whole country was flooded.

Yet, when he received the news, he plunged into water shoulder-high and beckoned his men to follow. They did not know it, but he was taking a roundabout route, setting out along the flooded shore of the Embarrass River to follow it down to the Wabash. He was setting out—afoot now, for the horses had been left behind—to follow the course of one hopelessly "drowned" river in order to find another that was even more hopelessly "drowned."

But he found it!

At daybreak on the eighteenth of February, the army heard the British morning gun; and by two in the afternoon, they felt, with their submerged and aching feet, the sudden slant of the Wabash shore and saw, with their dull and hunger-stricken eyes, an avenue of treeless water winding southward through the flooded woods.

"Thar she is!" they whispered hoarsely.

"The Wabash!"

"Ave Maria!"

Their rejoicing was not long nor loud. It could hardly have been called rejoicing at all. For the past three days, they had been silenced by their new and fearful enemy—hunger. Grimly they built a canoe and sent two men up the river to steal or borrow boats from the Vincennes French, and grimly they waited for their return. For those empty hours, as he recalled them in a report a year later, George Rogers Clark could find but a single word:

"Starving."

For the empty moment when the scouts returned unsuccessful, there were no words at all.

Two days longer they waited on the west shore of the submerged river, gazing southward for the appearance of their Cahokian friends in the batteau called the *Willing*. But they were waiting in vain. The *Willing* was not to reach them until long after their march was finished. In those two days, they had but one small deer for food. On the third day, they agreed with their commander that to delay any longer would be suicide. They must either advance or perish. In two canoes, they ferried themselves slowly across the Wabash to a little mound called the Lower Mammel, or Bubbie, and faced northward across the seven or eight remaining miles of flooded bottoms that lay between them and Vincennes.

Once more Clark sent out scouts; once more they returned without the boats they were sent for; and once more the redheaded young colonel from Virginia saved his men with his ready courage and his ready wits.

Scooping up the river water in his hand, he sprinkled a little of his precious gunpowder on it. Then he rubbed his hand over his face and, with a war whoop, emerged from the operation a painted Indian.

"Forward!" he cried, and plunged into the water.

For a moment, the men only stared at him dully. Then one of the gaunt skulls began to grin.

That redheaded son of a saw-toothed alligator! Nothing could stop him!

With a feeble yell, the skeleton in buckskin plunged in after his commander; and, in another minute, the rest were following, like a flock of dumb, half-frozen sheep.

"Sing!" Clark shouted.

The British might hear, but, without a song, they were lost.

"Sing!"

A Frenchman struck up an old favorite of the coureurs de bois, and the rest joined in, whether they knew the words or not.

> "Je suis jeune et belle,
>   Je veux m'engage
> Un amant fidèle . . ."

"Louder!"

The melody carried down the line of stumbling, splashing men, faint and off key, but undaunted.

At times the water was up to George Rogers Clark's neck—and he was a tall man. Then it was necessary for the other tall men to carry their shorter comrades or ship them ahead on floating logs and in the two canoes. At other times, when the water was shallower, Clark would run ahead to a clump of trees and shout, "Land!" At once, the line would straighten out and the march would quicken slightly. Time and again, they reached the clumps of trees only to find themselves still wading in icy, brown water. But the ruse saved them.

That lasted three days. The water was never once

shallower than the men's knees, and often it was over the heads of the shorter soldiers. Three days, covering only three miles a day—and with no food.

Slow, cruel, incredible it was—that march. And incredible the courage and strength of the men that made it. For they were not in retreat. They were not making a desperate, last effort to save their skins. They were advancing. They were marching into the face of danger. Starved and exhausted, with insufficient ammunition, they were advancing upon a fortified and well-drilled army that was fresh and better equipped than they. And, what is more, they knew what they were marching toward.

But they marched!

On the third day—the nineteenth day of the expedition—they reached a wood where the short and the weak were able to cling to trees while the tall and the strong plunged on to a ten-acre scrap of land that was actually land. There the stronger ones built fires and came back and carried their comrades to safety. But the wet fuel gave off little heat, and the weak did not revive. So the strong, standing on either side of them and holding them upright, marched them back and forth on the little patch of ground for hours, until the warm blood began to flow once more through their frozen bodies. Then the strong fed them with a quarter of buffalo, some corn, and some tallow, which they had taken from several squaws and Indian children who had paddled past the camp in a canoe. With their mouths watering for the food, but refusing to touch any of it, the strong stood by and watched the weak regain their strength. Then all of them, strong and weak alike, tightened their belts about their lean bellies and faced their commander.

They had marched two hundred and forty flooded miles in nineteen days. They might, without dishonor, have asked for a breathing spell. But Vincennes lay just on the other side of yonder hill.

"The men are ready, Colonel Clark."

"We're sp'ilin' fur a fight!"

"Forward!"

"En avant!"

12

Wait for the Flare of Their Torches

THE REST was a matter of wits.

South and east of the old town of Vincennes, the low plain is marked by a chain of little knolls that rise seven or eight feet above the common level of the earth. After he had sent a messenger to the French inhabitants of the town, Colonel Clark deployed his men among these knolls, marching them in and out and about through the plain so that most of the time only their banners were visible to the townspeople and the numbers of the little army appeared far in excess of what they actually were.

It is an old device. The people of the Wabash country still use it—or are accused of using it—before each election.

"Why, they ain't that many Demmycrats in the whole state of Indianny! They marched 'em down Main Street at least three times in that-air peerade!"

"Looks like the Republicans'll win? Not on yer life! Why, I counted every wardheeler at least five times marchin' past me!"

It was an old device even in 1779. But it worked. The town came over to the Americans immediately and opened their homes and their supplies to the army. Major Busseron, once more foreseeing a change of masters, got out the powder and ball he had hidden from the King of England. Tobacco's Son, the Grand Door of the Wabash, who had never wavered, was ready too.

"I took the oath of the Americans under Captain Helm," he said. "I have not forgotten it. I have a hundred warriors ready to join you."

But George Rogers Clark did not accept his offer. He was afraid that, in the night, the Grand Door's Piankeshaws might be mistaken for Hamilton's Miamis and start confusion in the ranks. His own one hundred and thirty ill-equipped and half-starved men would have to do the job by themselves.

The attack began on the night of the twenty-third. The cannon of Fort Sackville were mounted on the upper floors of strong blockhouses at each angle of the stockade, standing eleven feet above the ground and with ports so crudely cut that their range was limited. In the darkness, Clark's men crept under the cannon and opened fire.

Lying on his belly in the dark, the American took his time, holding his fire until a cannoneer's torch flared in a porthole. Then the opening was filled with a volley of lead. As soon as he had touched the hairtrigger of his rifle, the American rolled over and over on the ground to another position, so that the flash of his powder became a false target for the enemy. When, occasionally, the British did manage to touch off one of their big guns, the cannonball flew harmlessly over the Americans' heads.

Thus all night long the musketry rattled, and the useless cannon boomed. From time to time, between volleys, a howl of laughter would arise from one part of the town, where the young Virginian had ordered a small group of his men to gather and make merry, so that the British would think that the main body of the army had not yet gone into action. Then the Americans, on their bellies under the walls of the fort, would snipe off another cannoneer and the battle would recommence.

At dawn, George Rogers Clark demanded unconditional surrender and was refused. But by noon Hamilton changed his mind. With Captain Helm, whom he was still holding prisoner, and his Indian agent, Major Hay, he came out to the church for a parley with Colonel Clark and Captain Bowman.

"Unconditional surrender," George Rogers Clark repeated firmly; and his black eyes fell on the cringing figure of Major Hay. He was wondering how he could save the scalp-buying American renegade from the anger of his men—or whether, after all, he ought to save him.

Lieutenant Colonel Hamilton pondered, his lower lip thrust out. He had taken the measure of his opponent, casting a sidelong glance at the lean, hard figure. Those black eyes and that red hair foreboded no good. But his pride would not let him yield.

"No," he said finally; and, with his prisoner and his aide, he left the church.

But, once out of doors, he hesitated and came back.

"Why," he asked, "are you willing to accept only unconditional surrender?"

George Rogers Clark's handsome young face was stern.

"Because I know the greatest part of the Indian partisans are with you, and I want to put them to death as I see fit. Those men do not deserve the fate of soldiers, and the cries of the widows and fatherless on the frontiers demand their blood from my hands."

Major Hay, standing a little behind his superior

officer, was suddenly apprehensive; but Colonel Hamilton pretended not to understand.

"Pray, sir, who is it that you call 'Indian partisans'?"

Clark's answer was ready; and his black eyes fixed the trembling major as he spoke.

"Sir, I take Major Hay to be one of the principal."

Of the effect of his words on Major Hay, he later wrote:

"I never saw a man in the moment of execution so struck as he appeared to be,—so pale and trembling, scarcely able to stand. Governor Hamilton blushed, and I observed was much affected at his behavior in the presence [of danger]. Captain Bowman's countenance sufficiently explained his disdain for the one and sorrow for the other."

"No," Colonel Hamilton said at last. "No, I cannot do it."

The fighting was resumed, but not for long. Hamilton had had enough of the siege and, after Clark's speech, perhaps he had had enough of the company of Major Hay, too. By the end of the day, he was ready to accept Clark's terms, and he sent out an officer under the white flag.

George Rogers Clark was a generous man. Not one of the British was harmed—not even the scoundrel Hay, who, after all, was not British but an American renegade from Pennsylvania. When the garrison was occupied, Colonel Hamilton was paroled and sent to Kentucky and the soldiers were treated as prisoners of war. As for the Miami Indians who had accompanied the British—with humble admiration for their American conqueror, they gave him their oath of neutrality and returned, on parole, to their homes in the north.

Once more Madame Godare's red and green flag floated from the mast over the fort, which Clark renamed Fort Patrick Henry, annexing it and all the surrounding country in the name of the state of Virginia. By this act, he made Vincennes the first American seat of government northwest of the Ohio and himself the conqueror of a territory more than half the size of the thirteen original colonies.

Originally called the County of Illinois, under the government of Virginia, and, after 1787, known as the Northwest Territory for thirteen years, this region included all of what is now Ohio, Indiana, Illinois, Michigan, and Wisconsin, land that otherwise would have remained in English hands at the close of the Revolution.

PART THREE

Lo, The Poor White Man!

13

The Warm and Smoky Days

Y OU ARE, at last, reconciled to the passing of summer. The leaves are mostly gone from the trees. They lie in dry, brown heaps in the fence corners, rot in the furrows between the corn rows, and are caught, like fluttering birds, in the bushes. There has been frost in the ground for a month, and one or two light powders of snow have fallen. The corn is gathered and the potatoes are all dug. In the fields, cold winds rattle the corn shocks. The idle mules and horses huddle close together in the barn lot, and the hogs, which all summer were allowed to root for themselves or die, are fattening in their pens. It is the season when houseflies die on the kitchen ceiling and there is a crust of ice on the water trough in the early mornings, when hot fried mush and sorghum molasses appear on the breakfast table again and the house is filled with the heavy sweetness of cooking pumpkin; it is the season of shoes and stockings and schoolbooks, of long underwear and running noses. You are sure that winter has begun.

Then, without warning, comes a morning when you wake in a sweat under the blankets that still smell of mothballs and, getting up, you dash to the window to find that the sky is a bright summer blue again. The cows are frisking in the pasture, just as they do in spring. A mule rolls over on its back, kicking up its heels. A brown hen ruffles her feathers in a long-neglected dust pit. You stand at the window, incredulous. The very sounds of the morning are different—the creak of the chain in the cistern, the neigh of the mare, the far-off barking of a dog; once more they are the soft, lazy sounds of summer.

Time will be breathless now, for a while, and standing still. Forgetting to be winter, the season will slip backward into a brief, nostalgic dream of the summer that is gone. Women will linger in kitchen doorways and men will stand idle in the fields, as if they could never get enough of breathing the autumn smells borne so strangely upon summer air. During the warm and smoky days that are coming, nothing will seem quite real. Then, as suddenly as it has come, the dream of departed summer will end; the smoky haze will lift from the fields and the river; snow will fly once more; the winter will come back to stay; and you will doubt that it ever happened and, doubting, soon cease to remember.

The old man who leans against the roadside fence can best explain the warm and smoky season to you.

"Indian summer . . ." he will say dreamily. "Now, that's the best season of the year. It's like youth come back to an old man, like love come to a homely woman."

You must wait until his pipe is going before he will continue, for the fragrance of tobacco sharpens his wits and loosens his tongue. He shaves the edge of his plug with a barlow knife, crams the shavings into his corncob, and lights up.

"But it wasn't always so!" he says, at last. "No, sir!

In the olden times, folks hated the Indian summer worse'n they hated summer itself!

"You see, in more'n one respect a Indian's like a snake. When it's hot, he's quick as lightnin' an' shore p'ison. But when it's cold, all he wants to do is jist curl up an' sleep. That's why, in the olden times, folks lived in blockhouses in the summers, when the Indians was on the warpath; an' they didn't dast go out an' live in their cabins till the first cold snap come along. Then, jist about the time they got their corn an' taters in an' the hawgs all nice an' fat, along would come a unexpected warm spell an' the Indians'd be upon 'em afore they could run fur shelter.

"That's why they come to call the late-autumn warm spell 'Indian summer,' an', believe me, it wasn't no complimentary title in them days!"

Smiling, he pauses to let the blue smoke curl upward about his head—and to see whether you will listen to a story. If you have the time and patience to wait, he will begin again.

"I mind the things my gran'ma used to tell.

"They was two other old ladies used to come an' set with gran'ma an' bring their knittin', an' they never got together 'thout the three of 'em a-tellin' 'bout the first nights they was ever left alone in their cabins in the olden days.

" 'Law,' the one of 'em would say, 'the thought of Injuns had me skeered half to death! I built me a big fire of solid logs of wood so it would last all night. Then I lighted a candle an' sot it on the table, an' 'en I piled up everything I could find agin the door an' darkened the winder. After that, I clumb into bed an' pulled the kivers up over my head an' jist lay thar all night long, wide awake an' froze stiff with terror. They was a wind a-blowin', I remember, an' every time the branches of the trees cracked I thought it was the crack of a rifle, an' the ol' pussy cat a-paddin' around on the puncheon floor was the slip an' slide of moccasins. Skeered?—Well, I got used to bein' alone in the woods after a while, but the first night I was skeered aplenty!'

" 'Now, me,' the other ol' lady'd say, 'I did different. I sat up all night a-workin' an' keepin' myself busy. I recollect I made a whole quilt in that one night, a-sewin' as fast as I could, to keep my mind off the Injuns. An' when I got sleepy, I'd git up an' go to the door an' remind myself of the danger all over agin. I didn't need much remindin', though. I never seen the great trees look so bleak an' bare as they did that night, nor the shadders on the white snow look so lonesome.'

"Then my gran'ma she'd put down her knittin', I remember, an' say:

" 'Well, the first time I was left alone in my cabin it was summer an' I didn't have so much as a kitten fur company. As soon as it got dark an' I had the supper dishes cleared an' I set down alone in that deep silence, I thought I'd go clean out of my head. In five minutes I was so fidgety I couldn't stand it, an' you know what I did? Well, I got down pa's gun an' went out an' routed up the pigs from their pen, an' all night long I druv 'em round an' round that-air cabin till both me and the pigs was wore clean to a frazzle by sunup. To this day, the gruntin' of a pig stirred out of his waller is about the sweetest music I know!' "

The old man knocks out his corncob on the top rail of the fence and prepares to take his leave, until you stop him with a question.

"Me?—No, I've never seen a Indian in Indianny. But my gran'pa was kilt an' scalped by the Indians just north of here. But that was a long time ago—in the days of Tecumseh an' the Prophet."

14

"Brothers: The Whites Are Not Friends"

Y EARS after his death, when they were asked to describe Tecumseh, men often referred to pictures of Napoleon.

Tecumseh did not look like Napoleon. He was tall, slender, supple. His face was long and, in later life, rather sharply drawn. His eyes were a clear, translucent hazel that could be gentle and understanding or could burn like balls of fire. In his long hunting shirt, leggings, and moccasins, he was like most of the Shawnees—strong and finely formed, but not muscular; tan instead of red; and exceedingly graceful.

Yet, under the blue-and-white turban that he wore, there was something in his face that made men think of pictures of Napoleon. It may have been his mouth, proud and passionately curved. It may have been the intensity of his eyes, or the haughty, brooding tilt of his chin. But, more than likely, it was the spirit of the man behind all these physical expressions—the spirit of a man whom men recognize immediately as a ruler, born to command.

Like Napoleon, Tecumseh did not inherit his leadership but rose from the ranks by his natural and indisputable talents. His father was only one of many Shawnee braves who sniped at white settlers floating down the rivers on their flatboats and occasionally met their men in open and declared warfare. His mother was a strong and intelligent woman of the Carolina Shawnee blood.

When he was a boy of thirteen, Tecumseh got his initiation as a warrior; and his action under fire was by no means distinguished.

"I felt afraid. When I heard the war whoops and saw the blood, I ran and hid beside a log."

At seventeen, he was sickened by the sight of a white prisoner being tortured and burned to death.

But the qualities in Tecumseh that made him flinch in his early experience of warfare were the qualities that later made him the great man that he was. He was sensitive, thoughtful, and farseeing. He was able to translate immediate happenings into the terms of the greater cause that lay behind them. For that reason, when the killing of his father and the destruction of his native village by the whites seared his proud soul with hatred, he did not wreak his vengeance in the blind frenzy of a single skirmish or a bloody raid. He was a statesman. He saw his people not as loosely allied bands and tribes, but as a whole race. He understood the significance of the westward push of the pioneers and he knew they could not be stopped by the terror of sporadic attacks any more than their voracious hunger for land could be appeased by concessions and treaties. Between the white men and the Indians, it must be all or nothing. Either the red men must yield and accept annihilation or the white men must be driven back. And Tecumseh knew that the time for driving them back was rapidly slipping away. The red men must unite while there were still enough left, virile and uncorrupted, to hold the land that was theirs.

So, while other Indians were avenging the murder of their families, fighting scattered battles, making treaties, destroying the armies of Harmar and St. Clair, and in turn being destroyed at Fallen Timbers by Mad Anthony Wayne, Tecumseh was traveling throughout the land carrying his message.

"Brothers: The whites are not friends to the Indians. At first, they only asked for land sufficient for a wigwam; now nothing will satisfy them but the whole of our hunting grounds, from the rising to the setting sun. . . .

"Brothers: The red men have borne many and great injuries; they ought to suffer them no longer. My people will not; they are determined on vengeance. . . .

"Brothers: My people are brave and numerous, but the white people are too strong for them alone. I wish you to take up the hatchet with them. We all belong to one family. If we all unite, we will cause the rivers to stain the great waters with their blood. . . ."

He went among the Miamis, the Kickapoos, the Potawatomis, and the Weas along the Wabash. He went south among the Creeks, the Cherokees, and the Choctaws. He even crossed the Mississippi and pleaded with the Osages.

"Brothers: If you do not unite with us, they will first destroy us, and then you will fall an easy prey to them. . . ."

But Tecumseh was wise enough to know that people can never be united by reason alone. To unite effectively in self-interest they must be bound together by devotion to an ideal outside themselves, a common mystic hatred or a common mystic love. In the year 1805, Tecumseh found the instrument for that mystical union in his brother, Laulewausikau, who had just inherited the title of medicine man and was calling himself the Prophet.

Blind in one eye, tall and massive, the Prophet was a commanding figure. Great golden hoops dangled from his big ears and he wore a fantastic turban on his head. Another golden ring hung from the end of his long, drooping nose, flashing in the sun when his sensual lips moved in impassioned speech. The Prophet's teachings were half hokum and half divine inspiration, and Tecumseh knew it; but he needed the Prophet's mighty voice, and he gave it full license to preach.

"Brothers: The Master of Life has spoken to me and I must tell you what he has said. You are to give up the white man's ways and live to yourselves as your ancestors lived. You must wear the clothes of your ancestors, eat the food of your ancestors, fight with the weapons your ancestors used. You are not to touch the white man's firewater or take the white man's money. You are to shun the white man as you would shun poisonous snakes. And, in return, the Master of Life has told me that he will come again to the earth and put strength into your arms to drive the white man from your lands and to fatten your tomahawks with blood."

Thus spoke the Prophet; and, while his brother traveled over the land persuading red men to unite, he gathered the recruits into the fold in a village on the Wabash below the mouth of the Tippecanoe. The day of the Master's coming, he said, was not far off and the white men's hearts were filled with terror.

15

On His Mother's Bosom

In August, the trees hang still and heavy with thick foliage over the Wabash and the air is filled with the song of insects. As Tecumseh, in the first of a flotilla of eighty canoes, came down the river, he was stirred by the quiet beauty of the green tunnel through which the water flowed. He loved the land through which he passed as no white man could ever love it. For generations, his race had been nourished by it, and they had taken what it offered with their own hands. They built their homes of its logs and bark. They killed its game. They ate its pumpkins, squash, and corn, and gathered its nuts and berries. They made their clothing from the hides they tanned themselves. They built their fires with the buffalo chips and branches that they found. It was the land of Tecumseh's people, and he was dreaming of the day when the alien white man would be forced to retire from it, leaving it once more to the Indians who owned it.

At Fort Knox, above Vincennes, Captain Floyd came out to meet him.

"My intentions are peaceful," Tecumseh assured him. "Someday I shall drive the white man back to the great waters, but today Governor Harrison has asked me

TECUMSEH DREW HIMSELF TO HIS FULL
HEIGHT, CONTINUING TO GAZE AT THE WHITE
MAN SEATED BEFORE HIM.

to come in peace and talk with him and I have given him my word."

In a few more minutes, he was looking up at the high, red-brick mansion on the hill where the governor lived. Many men and women were gathered on the porch and on the lawn, under the elm and locust trees, and Tecumseh saw the gleam of muskets in the summer sun. He turned to his warriors and commanded them to beach their canoes on the bank of the Wabash in silence, to disembark, but to stay at the water's edge. Then he stepped ashore himself and, folding his arms across his chest, walked alone and unarmed up the hill toward the house.

As he approached, he recognized the governor sitting in an armchair under one of the elms. About him, at the end of a corridor of territorial soldiers, doubly armed, were gathered the judges of the supreme court of the territory. Behind them, the fashionable ladies and gentlemen of Vincennes sat on the porch of the mansion, chatting gaily.

When he came nearer, Tecumseh heard the suppressed laughter of the ladies, but it ceased when he raised his proud head and fixed them with his hazel eyes. Without seeming to move, he glided nearer to the tree where the governor sat, running the gantlet of the armed soldiers' suspicious eyes without glancing either to the right or to the left. When he was within a few feet of his host, he stopped and stood perfectly still.

"Your great father offers you a chair," the interpreter said, pointing to the empty armchair beside the governor.

Tecumseh drew himself to his full height, continuing to gaze, without expression, at the white man seated before him.

"This man is not my father. The sun is my father. My mother is the earth. I shall recline on her bosom!"

Thereupon, he sat down upon the earth at the governor's feet.

Embarrassed by his own superior position, the governor was forced to open the conversation in a conciliatory tone.

For hours they talked.

"Since the last peace was made," Tecumseh said, "you have killed some of the Shawnees, Delawares, and Winnebagos. Yet, no white man has been punished!"

"I have been liberal with the Indians," replied the governor. "The Miamis are the only tribe who have any real claim to the land, and yet I have made treaties with the other tribes too."

Tecumseh shook his head.

"The land belongs to all the Indians alike. No single chief has a right to sign it away to the white men."

"The Indians have stolen white men's horses and they have raided white men's settlements, taking scalps."

"The white men have moved in upon land that belongs to the Indians—all the Indians!"

"At the Prophet's Town, you have refused the annual payment of the white men's salt, which they are willing to give for the land."

"The Indians do not want the white men's salt. They have not sold their land. Only the traitors among their people pretend to sell land to the white men. They have no right to do so."

"Tecumseh has listened to the bad birds. His brother

is stirring up trouble on the Wabash. He is preaching bloodshed among the red men."

"The red men want only to be left in peace. They want the white men to leave the country and stop giving firewater to their weaker brothers. It is the white men who are making trouble."

"The white men act at all times in good faith. The Great White Father of the Seventeen Fires bears only love for his red brothers in the forests—"

Tecumseh sprang to his feet. His eyes flashed. His mobile mouth drew tight across his long, sharp face. He had had enough!

"What this man says is a lie!" he hissed; and, turning, walked slowly and with great dignity back to the river's edge, while the young governor stood in apoplectic wrath, glowering after him, his sword drawn.

The next day Tecumseh returned and apologized.

"I spoke the truth," he said. "But I should not have spoken it in anger."

The parley was continued for another day in a quieter vein; but nothing was accomplished other than a temporary truce. A year later, Tecumseh and the governor met again on the shore of the Wabash under the big elm; but again nothing but a temporary truce was achieved. Trusting the white governor to keep his promise of peace, Tecumseh announced, when he departed on that second occasion, that he was leaving the Wabash country for a time to go south and talk with his friends, the Creeks.

16

"I Am Much Pleased
With This Country"

Tecumseh should have known better than to place confidence in the pacific promise of William Henry Harrison. Had he studied the young governor carefully enough, he would have realized that the governor distrusted him, thus invalidating any agreement they made.

There was nothing in William Henry Harrison's experience to inspire him with faith in Indians. While he pitied them, he held them in contempt; for the only Indians William Henry Harrison knew were those he had seen fleeing before the army of Anthony Wayne at Fallen Timbers in 1794 and the drunken and degenerate dregs of the Piankeshaws at Vincennes, descendants of old Tobacco's Son and his followers, who had been corrupted finally by too much living with the whites.

Like Tecumseh, William Henry Harrison was himself an aristocrat of nature and a man of much experience in statesmanship. For several generations, his ancestors had been active in the government of Virginia. His father, Benjamin Harrison, was one of the signers of the Declaration of Independence. Although William Henry was only twenty-seven at the turn of the century when he came to Vincennes to govern the new Indiana Territory, which had been carved out of the lands ceded to

the nation by Virginia after the Revolution, he already
had served as an officer in the army, taking part in Anthony Wayne's campaign, had filled the post of secretary
to the governor of the Northwest Territory, and held a
seat in the national Congress. But, more than his experience, his background had molded him. He was of the
Virginia aristocracy. Born and brought up in the fine,
old mansion called "Berkeley" on the James, he came
naturally by the easy grace of a man of authority, who
governs because it is his God-given gift to govern, and
who regards all races other than his own as inferiors.

He was a charming, if not a robust man. Slender,
graceful, with fine, patrician features, a thick shock of
dark hair, and the soft, cultured drawl of a southern gentleman, he soon attracted to himself in Vincennes a
group of aristocratic ladies and gentlemen of his own
kind. He loved literature, and his speeches and the mes-
sages he wrote to his beloved hero, Thomas Jefferson,
were filled with classic allusions and Latin quotations.
As soon as he arrived at the shabby, little frontier outpost
that Vincennes had become—a half-forgotten village,
where the once prosperous French had lost their moral
fiber from too frequent acquiescence to change of government and the once proud Piankeshaws had sunk to a
tragic level of degeneracy from too much contact with
the French—William Henry Harrison began to create an
appropriate setting for himself, his books and his elegant
companions.

His efforts required three years, and the result was
"Grouseland," which still stands in the city on the Wabash as a monument to the young governor's good taste
and high aspirations for the land to which he had come.
Surrounded today by shabby houses and reeking oil tanks,

Grouseland nevertheless retains its charm; and, once inside its door and facing the white, curved soffit of the stairway that rises like the wing of a dove in the high-ceilinged hall, the visitor understands why there remains in the life of Indiana something of the leisurely gentility of the old South. William Henry Harrison and his friends brought with them to the wilderness not only the spirit and traditions of the plantations they had left, but they also tried to re-create the physical and material world to which they were endeared.

"I am much pleased with this country . . ." he wrote to a friend soon after he arrived, "nothing can exceed its beauty and fertility. I have purchased a farm of about 300 acres joining the town which is all cleared. I am now engaged in fencing it and shall begin to build next spring if I can find the means."

Like all Virginians of his day, he was a sportsman, and he enjoyed many long days in the forests and on the Wabash River, hunting and fishing. The evenings he spent among his books or with his friends and his rapidly growing family.

But his life in Vincennes was not all pleasure and gaiety. He did not neglect his duties, the chief of which was the solution of the Indian problem.

When he first arrived, he was deeply shocked by the condition of the Indians. They lived in abject squalor and poverty. They dozed in the sun all day in the doorways of their tumble-down huts and ragged tepees and caroused all night with their red skins full of the liquor the white men sold them. Drunkenness among them was worse than drunkenness; it was madness. They screeched and howled like wild beasts. They killed their own friends in blind, bloodthirsty frenzy. They burned down their

own houses. They beat their wives. They sluiced the fiery
liquor down their yawning, drooling throats till they
were reduced to sheer idiocy and fell, unconscious, in the
streets. And, all the while, their women and children
grew filthier and more shiftless each day.

Chiefs waited constantly upon the young governor
to plead with him for help. It was not only the Piankeshaws in Vincennes for whom they were concerned.
After all, the Piankeshaws were beyond redemption. But
the Indians of the forest, too, were being corrupted.
White traders followed the Indian hunting parties and,
as soon as the kill was made and while the blood was still
warm on the animal's wounds, they began to ply the
hunters with whisky and to dicker for the "green" skins.
They moved in and squatted on land still reserved for the
Indians. They fenced off the common hunting ground.
They killed game with abandon. They killed Indians too,
whenever they "trespassed" on their own lands, knowing
that no white jury of the territory would convict them
of murder.

"The only good Injun is a dead Injun," they said,
and continued to slaughter and trespass and transgress
with impunity.

With the true patrician's care for his subjects, William Henry Harrison was filled with deep pity for the
men and women of the forests who were being so rapidly
demoralized. And yet, like Tecumseh, William Henry
Harrison was a statesman and saw the immediate in terms
of larger issues. It was inevitable that the white man
should push onward. Skirmishes and terror and treaties
would not hold him back. But neither could a war on a
large scale, such as Tecumseh dreamed of. The Indians
were doomed in the northern continent of the Western

Hemisphere the day that Columbus discovered it. William Henry Harrison found himself the instrument of a force of which, in terms of abstract justice, he could not approve, but which he recognized, in the light of honest reality, as relentless and inevitable. The issue, if there was any in his mind, was further complicated by his honest belief that the British in Canada were inciting the Indians to revolt.

On this last score, his patriotism allowed him no other decision than the one that he made on the day Tecumseh departed from the Wabash country to go south and confer with his friends, the Creeks. The time to strike had come. Within a month after he made his pacific promise to Tecumseh, William Henry Harrison was leading an army toward the Prophet's Town on the Wabash below the mouth of the Tippecanoe.

A President Is Made

It was late September in 1811 when the army of a thousand men left Vincennes. Some of them were soldiers of the regular army under Colonel John P. Boyd. Some were volunteers from Kentucky. The rest were Hoosier militiamen. Through the flaming red and gold forests of early autumn they marched up the Wabash until they reached a spot one mile above the present city of Terre Haute, which William Henry Harrison decided to fortify. There they made camp and set up a log stockade, and there they remained for a month's drill. Then they went on.

Within a mile or two of the Prophet's village, Harrison halted his army and sent emissaries ahead for a parley. But the Prophet refused to parley. The army advanced then to a place within a hundred yards of the village before the Prophet changed his mind. At that point, he sent out messengers asking for a peace conference the next day. Harrison agreed and asked where his army might camp for the night. The Indians made vague gestures toward Tippecanoe Creek and vanished.

"I found the ground destined for the encampment not altogether such as I could wish it," the young general wrote

later to the secretary of war. "It was indeed admirably calcu-
lated for the encampment of Regular Troops that were opposed to Regulars but it afforded great facility to the approach
of savages. It was a piece of dry Oak Land rising about ten
feet above the level of a marshy prairie in Front and nearly
twice that height above a similar prairie in the rear, through
which and near to this bank ran a small stream clothed with
willows and other brush wood. Toward the left flank this
bench of high land widened considerably but became gradually narrower in the opposite direction and at the distance of
one hundred and fifty yards from the right flank terminated
in an abrupt point."

Not altogether such as Harrison could have wished
it then perhaps, that campground is certainly all that any
pilgrim might wish to find it today. A verdant oasis of
shade and peacefulness at the edge of the village of Battle
Ground, with its monument and cannon and the graves
of the soldiers shaded by tall hickory and poplar trees,
the triangle of land stands high above the surrounding
sun-beaten bottom land. Whatever their intentions on
the night of November 6, 1811, the Prophet's men offered the American army for its encampment one of the
most delightful spots in the whole Wabash valley.

Just what happened at Tippecanoe in the early
morning of November 7th, no one knows exactly, except
that a sentinel, Stephen Mars, seeing Indians creeping up
the bank of Burnett's Creek, fired a warning shot and
Governor Harrison, who was just on the point of issuing
orders for reveille, heard the shot and commanded his
men to take battle formation. Those who love to senti-
mentalize about the Indians say that Harrison's only
reason for rising at four o'clock in the morning was to
give orders for a surprise attack on the village and that

the Indians simply beat him to it. Those who, in the forties, wrote campaign biographies of the governor, say that he was betrayed, that his whole campaign at Tippecanoe was pacific in purpose, and the attack of the Prophet's braves was only another example of Indian treachery. The truth probably lies somewhere between these two extremes. It was only natural that the Indians, visited by a "pacific" party of a thousand armed men, should have been suspicious and watchful. It is quite possible that Stephen Mars was jumpy and, seeing scouting Indians in the dark, fired without stopping to investigate whether they were attacking or simply reconnoitering. And, once a shot was fired in that dark, tense atmosphere, it was inevitable that a battle should ensue.

The battle itself has been described as both glorious and inglorious. It was not such a crushing defeat as the Little Turtle administered to General St. Clair at the headwaters of the Wabash. Nor was it the complete victory that Anthony Wayne won at Fallen Timbers. The fighting raged for more than two hours, and there was much gallantry in evidence—and much stupidity.

In the beginning, there was confusion about Governor Harrison's horse. He had been riding a beautiful gray mare, but, in the first outburst of the conflict, he got astride Major Owen's bay horse. Major Owen, in turn, rode the governor's gray and was almost immediately shot down, mistaken, no doubt, for the governor himself by the Indians.

But there can be no question about the bravery of the governor and his men. He was everywhere, riding from one end of the battleground to the other.

"Where is the captain of this company?" he would shout.

"Dead!"

"Where are the lieutenants?"

"Dead!"

"Where is the ensign?"

"I am the ensign, sir!"

"Stand fast then, ensign, and I will relieve you in a minute!"

And all the while, Laulewausikau, the Prophet, stood on a rock a safe distance from the battlefield and implored the aid of the manitous, confident of victory.

A hundred and eighty-eight of the white men fell, either killed or wounded. But when dawn broke, the Indians fled. With them vanished the faith the red men had confided in the words of the Prophet along the banks of the Wabash and also the dream that his brother, Tecumseh, had dreamed. There was nothing left but an abandoned Indian village on the prairie and one abandoned old Indian chief with a broken leg, groaning in one of the tepees.

The Prophet himself fled to the refuge which a party of Wyandots offered him on Wild Cat Creek. But the Wabash country was no place for him after Tippecanoe. He soon set out northward for Canada, where he joined a band of Shawnees, "doomed," as George Catlin later described him, "to live the rest of his days in silence and a sort of disgrace; like all men in Indian communities who pretend to great medicine in any way, and fail; as they all think such failure an evidence of the displeasure of the Great Spirit, who always judges right."

Tecumseh, returning from the south after the collapse at Tippecanoe, was thwarted, but he was not defeated. Giving up his hope for a successful federation of Indian tribes, he, too, went to Canada, but not to an old age of silence and disgrace. He offered his services to the British in the War of 1812 and fought valiantly against the Americans until he was killed by a pistol shot at close range at the Battle of the Thames.

William Henry Harrison returned to Vincennes, confident that the Battle of Tippecanoe had brought to an end the Indian menace in the Wabash country. But the Battle of Tippecanoe was ultimately to mean far more than that to him. Thirty years later, glorified by eulogistic, political biographers, that dubious engagement by the Wabash was to carry him to the White House.

18

The Desolate March

ALTHOUGH it shattered their strength, Tippecanoe did not bring to an abrupt end the story of the Indians in Indiana. They lingered on, badly broken and disunited, but still a threat to the pioneers. The very next year a party of Shawnees fell upon the Pigeon Roost settlement in Indian summer, massacred most of the inhabitants, and burned their homes. Ten years later, they won their first battle in the white men's courts when three white men were sentenced to be hanged for the murder of innocent Indians at the headwaters of Lick Creek.

But by that time, even a legal victory could not save them from their doom.

It came finally in 1836 when the last of the Indian reservations about Lake Maxinkuckee, north of the Wabash, were surrendered to the United States in a series of treaties. All the chiefs signed the treaties except Menominee and his lieutenants. They refused and for two years more lingered on, bickering with the white settlers who were eager to move in.

Menominee was a minor Tecumseh.

"Brothers: I have not sold my lands. I will not sell them. I have not signed any treaty, and will not sign any. I am not going to leave my lands, and I do not want to hear anything more about it!"

Menominee's strength lay in his character. He was honest and peaceful. He was a religious man. He was constantly pleading with his followers to abstain from the liquor that the white men sold. Both the Baptist and the Catholic missionaries who worked in his tribe admired him and sang his praises. It was impossible to get something on a man like Menominee.

But Governor Wallace, father of the author of *Ben Hur*, knew how to handle Menominee. He gave General John Tipton orders; and, on a hot Sunday morning in the summer of 1838, General Tipton, with one hundred soldiers, marched into Menominee's village while Menominee and his tribe were in church. Drawing up in front of the church, the soldiers raised their muskets and fired a volley into the air as a warning, just as a farmer would fire his shotgun to scare away a flock of crows.

The warning was sufficient. The Indians were terrified. They tumbled out of the church and begged for mercy. One old squaw, the mother of a chief, fled into the forest, where she hid for three days without food. Only Menominee kept his courage and his dignity.

But Menominee had nothing else to support him, and there was no persuading a soldier like John Tipton to disobey orders. The Indians were disarmed. Squads of soldiers were sent out to round up stragglers. Within a few days, eight hundred and fifty-nine red men, women, and children were shoved into line and ordered to march. Where were they going? That was not their affair. They were simply to obey orders and keep moving.

It was September then. September is the season of dust and flies, and the heat lies over the land like a pall. The bite of mosquitoes and chiggers is worse in September than at any other time, and it seems that the thirst in

THE ONLY HOPE—IF IT COULD BE CALLED A HOPE
—LAY AHEAD, IN THE LAND OF THE SETTING SUN.

a man's throat can never be slaked. September is no month for forced marches, especially on the Grand Prairie west of the Wabash where there is no shade. But it was in September that the white men destroyed the Indians' homes and drove that straggling band across the blistering land to exile.

Many were already dying by the time they reached Logansport. The name of the town must have mocked them as they dragged through the dusty streets, thinking of the Logans who had made history for their race. But they pushed on. There were a few jolting wagons for the sick and the aged and the newborn; but only the very sick and aged and newborn could be persuaded to ride in them. There was no doctor in the company and, for weeks, no priest. By the time they reached Terre Haute, all the babies were dead or dying, exhausted by the heat. The rest could hardly walk.

At Terre Haute, they paused for consultation. The mother of one of the chiefs was desperately ill. Should they put her to death then and there? Or should they subject her to the tortures of further journeying? There was only one answer, for the white men were in command. To put the old woman out of her misery would be an uncivilized act. She traveled four days more before she died.

Westward the diminishing band was driven across the river and over the prairie like a giant snail, only eight hundred of them now, in single file, bareheaded under the blazing sun, choked with dust, stumbling, half naked, half starved, panting with thirst. But they had to push on. The guns of the white men were loaded. There was no Indian land left behind them. The only hope—if it could be called a hope—lay ahead, in the land of the setting sun.

Finally, west of the Mississippi, General Tipton turned his caravan over to a priest and a government agent and returned to the Wabash. His duty was done, and the story written by Tobacco's Son, Tecumseh, and the Little Turtle on the banks of the Hoosier river had come to its close.

19

Ma-con-a-quah

Ma-con-a-quah, however, remained in Indiana.

Ma-con-a-quah was an aged squaw who lived with her two daughters and a son-in-law on the banks of the Mississinewa, eight miles from its mouth where it empties swiftly into the Wabash at Peru. Ma-con-a-quah had been the wife of a Miami chief. But it was not because of her husband's title that she was allowed to remain. After all, Menominee, too, was a chief, but he had marched with the rest at the muzzles of General Tipton's guns. Nor was Ma-con-a-quah allowed to remain because of her double log house, the center of a farm as large and prosperous as any white man's. After all, Ma-con-a-quah's farm aroused the cupidity of many of her white neighbors and they would have taken it from her if they could.

Ma-con-a-quah was to remain on the banks of the Mississinewa, unmolested, as long as she lived, because a special act of the United States Congress protected her.

In September, 1837, a year before General Tipton started the Indians on their desolate march, two white men and a white woman arrived at Peru, Indiana, from the east. They were all in their sixties, and the long jour-

ney by carriage and on horseback had been very tiring.
When they reached the Bearrs Hotel, the woman, who
was the oldest of the three, declared that she could go no
farther; and her two brothers were forced to leave her
while they crossed the Wabash and continued their
journey in the company of an interpreter.

The road that wound up through the valley of the
Mississinewa, crossing and recrossing the little river, reminded them of their home in Pennsylvania; for the
hills were steep and the waters of the stream flowed clear
and swift among many tiny islands of pale-green grass
and reeds. But it was a wilder country than their Pennsylvania, and it had been many years since they had seen a
large Indian trading post like that of Chief Godfroy two
miles from the town of Peru. By the time they reached
the farm of Ma-con-a-quah, however, they were no
longer conscious of the scenery. They were thinking only
of the old woman they had come to see.

She received them stolidly, sitting on a bench in
front of her cabin. She was old and wizened and bundled
shapelessly in a red shawl. Even when they began to tell
her the story they had come to tell, her cold, sharp, expressionless face did not change; and when they had
finished, she remained silent and unmoved.

The story they told, through their interpreter, was
this:

Their name was Slocum—Joseph and Isaac Slocum. They
were born in Warwick, Rhode Island; but when they were
children, their parents had moved with them to a new home
in the Wyoming Valley, along the Susquehanna River in
Pennsylvania. That was in 1778. Their father was a Quaker
and, for that reason, had no fear of the Indians, for the Indians

knew he was not a fighting man. But, soon after they settled
in Pennsylvania, their oldest brother disobeyed their father
and went with some neighbors to fight the Indians. The
Indians, believing then that their faith in the Quaker family
had been betrayed, determined to take a bloody revenge.

They fell upon the Slocum cabin while the father was
away at work in the fields. They scalped a little neighbor boy
who was playing with the Slocum children. They stripped the
house of its provisions and took whatever furniture attracted
them. When they left, they carried off the youngest Slocum
daughter, Frances, who was a little girl of five with auburn
hair. With Frances Slocum, they also kidnaped a neighbor boy
named Wareham Kingsley.

For years, Joseph and Isaac Slocum said, they and their
father and brothers searched for the lost little girl; and after
their father was killed by Indians, the boys continued the
search. Each stranger who came to the Wyoming Valley was
closely questioned. Expeditions were made into the forest. The
brothers even traveled as far as western Ohio, following clues
that invariably proved false. When, after many years, Wareham Kingsley reappeared, the Slocums' hopes of finding the
little, red-haired girl revived. But Wareham Kingsley could
tell them nothing. He had been separated from Frances Slocum
soon after the Indians carried them from the Slocum clearing.

Then, one day but a few months before their appearance
at Ma-con-a-quah's door, they had received a letter from a
friend in Lancaster, Pennsylvania, that contained a clipping
from the Lancaster *Intelligencer*. The newspaper told of a
letter that had been discovered in the Lancaster post office by
the new postmaster. Its postmark was two years old, and it
came from a man in Peru, Indiana, who said that he had found
a white Indian woman near Peru whose father's name was
Slocum and who had been kidnaped years before from the
valley of the Susquehanna.

"That is why these men are here, Ma-con-a-quah," the interpreter explained to the old woman. "They think you are their sister, Frances Slocum."

Ma-con-a-quah sat unmoved. She remembered, two years before in a moment of strange loneliness and nostalgia, telling a young white man from Peru her story. But she did not betray her secret to the men who had come from Pennsylvania to see her. How did she know who they were or what they wanted? The white men these days were not to be trusted. Perhaps they wanted her rich farm, her pigs, and her cattle. And, even if they were her brothers, what did it matter? The brief period of nostalgia of two years ago had passed and she was happy once more, among her daughters and her grandchildren, living as she had always lived.

She looked up at the men and mumbled something in the Miami tongue.

"Ma-con-a-quah says she will come to Peru tomorrow to see your sister, if you want her to," the interpreter translated.

And that was all—until the next day when, Indian fashion, Ma-con-a-quah and her family came riding into Peru on their fat ponies in single file. A crowd gathered and followed them; and, when the procession reached the Bearrs Hotel, there was a large assembly in the street.

Dismounting, Ma-con-a-quah and her family marched solemnly into the hotel lobby and, meeting Joseph and Isaac Slocum and Mary Towne, their sister, presented them with the hindquarter of a deer, carefully wrapped in a clean, white cloth. Then, after seating themselves ceremoniously on the floor, they indulged in a long Indian silence.

At last, Ma-con-a-quah began to talk in the Miami tongue, which was the only language she knew.

Joseph and Isaac Slocum were right. She was their sister. She remembered her father. He wore a large, broad-brimmed hat. Her mother was a big woman and worked very hard. She remembered the day she was carried away by the Indians. She was frightened at first, but they were kind to her and she soon grew to love them. A chief adopted her finally, and when she was old enough she was married to a brave in the Delaware tribe. But he was cruel to her and she returned to her foster father's home. Later, she married a Miami chief, She-po-co-nah, and with him she saw the fighting between the Little Turtle and General Wayne. She-po-co-nah was good to her and she bore him two sons, who were dead, and the two daughters who sat beside her in the hotel. But She-po-co-nah lost his hearing in his old age and had to give up fighting. He built the farm on the Mississinewa, which was called Deaf Man's Village, and, when he died, the land became hers.

Finishing, Ma-con-a-quah waited for the interpreter to tell her brothers and sister what she had said. Her face was expressionless, her squatting, shapeless body very still. When the interpreter was through, she smiled for the first time and pointed to her hair, shaking her head. Her hair was gray now. There were no traces of its original color. But when she lowered her arm, she drew back a sleeve and bared an arm as white as any white woman's. Then, as final proof, she extended her hand. Half of one of the fingers was gone. The Slocums' eyes lighted. Years ago, they remembered, little Frances had maimed one of her fingers while playing with the tools in their father's blacksmith shop.

There was great rejoicing among the Slocums in the Bearrs Hotel that day, and the people waiting in the streets caught the infection and laughed and talked in a holiday spirit, crowding into the lobby until the air was stifling. But Frances Slocum had lost the exuberance of her white heritage, and she did not like crowded rooms. In the midst of the celebration, she vanished. It was not until they had searched almost everywhere that they found her rolled up in her blanket on the porch, fast asleep.

Looking down at their sister then, Joseph and Isaac Slocum and Mary Towne knew they would never be able to persuade her to return with them to Pennsylvania and take up the ways of white people.

By special act of Congress, Frances Slocum was allowed to remain in her log cabin on the banks of the Mississinewa, living in Indian fashion, until she died ten years later, in March, 1847. She was buried on a little knoll near the cabin, and her grave is marked today by a small stone monument that briefly tells her story.

20

Sycamore Island

THE young corn spreads its thin, green veil across the rolling land. The air is bright and clear, like a mellow white wine. The redbird whistles and the catbird calls. In the woods, the bellwort, the blue violet, and the trillium are in bloom; and, at the swollen river's edge, the redbud seems to float like a cloud of fire.

A small boy holds up two fingers, and a neighbor kid grins and nods. In a flash, they have their clothes off and are splashing in the waters of the Wabash, enjoying their first swim of the year.

When they come out on the clay bank, an old man is sitting there, his knees under his chin, his dreamy eyes looking out over the yellow river's sparkling waves.

"We'll go down to Sycamore Island, boys," he says, "as soon as the moon is full. They's somethin' thar I want to show you."

The boys stretch on the bank to let the sun dry them. They know that if they wait long enough, the old man will explain.

"Last time I seen it was thirty year ago, an' I've always swore I'd go agin, jist to be sure," he continues, at last, with an air of mystery.

"Me an' my brother was helpin' my pa plow up a

"THE BRAVES WAS A-FIGHTIN' WITHOUT MAKIN'
A SOUND."

piece of land south of here that spring, I remember, an' it was the day we'd been workin' along the river. Pa he told us not to drive the plow too near the bank, fur fear of a cave-in, an' we cut the teams around about fifteen feet from the bank. Noontime come an' we went over into a clump of woods to eat our dinner, an' when we come back, the land had fell into the river right up to where we'd turned the plows. Ten acres of the ol' man's best land fell into the river durin' that dinner hour. I tell you it give us quite a turn!

"But I was a-goin' to tell you about Sycamore Island. All our lives me an' my brother John had heared about what happens in the spring on Sycamore Island just down the river a ways, an' that year, it bein' so convenient an' all, we decided we'd see it fur ourselves.

"Well, we did!

"About midnight of a full moon, we got us a boat an' rowed down thar. 'Twasn't fur, but you couldn't see the clearin' till you was right on it, almost. First thing we noticed when we was in the middle of the river was a lot of lights on the island, an' I reckon we was skeered, 'cause we rested on our oars a minute an' thought about turnin' back. But the lights lifted, an' we saw it was only a cloud of lightnin' bugs. Then we rowed, cautious-like, right up to shore.

"Well, you won't believe it, boys, till you see it fur yourselves; but they was thar, all right—the three of 'em, jist like folks'd always said. Them two young Indian braves was all diked out in feathers 'n' war paint an' as nekkid as the day they was born. An' a-settin' on a log, a-watchin' 'em, was a beautiful Indian girl—nekkid, too.

"The braves was a-fightin' without makin' a sound. First they wrassled, an' 'en they started to it with knives, an' finally they both rech up an' snatched tommyhawks right out of the empty air an' set to with them. We could see their faces a-twistin' all out of shape, an' every once in a while the girl she'd jump up an' clap her hands an' holler, a-eggin' 'em on. But we couldn't hear a thing. Ol' Sycamore Island, fur all that fightin', was as silent as the grave.

"Finally, one of the braves he got his arm free an' come down on the other Indian's head with his tommy-hawk an' split it clean in two, as neat as a ripe water-melon. Then he stands thar with his foot on the dead man's body fur a minute, a-throwin' out his chest an' a-makin' a speech of some kind to the Indian girl. She seemed right took up with it all at first, but, after a while, she couldn't stand his jaw no longer and she run right into his arms. Well, he picked her up an' carried her away into the woods then, an' me an' my brother John we jist set thar an' stared at the dead Indian that was left."

The old man stops, and this time the boys cannot outwait him.

"What happened then?" they ask.

"Well, after a time, me an' John gits our spunk up an' we climb ashore an' go to whar the dead Indian is . . . an' you know what?"

"What?"

"He jist ain't!"

"He isn't there, you mean?"

"No, sir! They's nary hide nor hair of him! All they is left is jist that cloud of lightnin' bugs come back an' hoverin' 'round the spot, like they was the dead Indian's soul or somethin'. That's all!"

The old man gets up and rubs his rheumatic knee.

"Lightnin' bugs?" the boys asked suspiciously. "Lightnin' bugs in plowin' time?"

"Yes, sir!" the old man says. "They was ghosts, you see—lightnin' bugs an' all. They've been a-comin' to Sycamore Island in the Wabash ever since folks 'round here kin remember. They're the very last of the Indians in Indianny, I reckon. I seen 'em myself that time, an' I've got a hankerin' to see 'em agin. Me an' you fellers'll row down thar the first night we have a clear, full moon."

PART FOUR

Utopian Interlude

21

The Limestone Slabs

GEORGE RAPP stood on the bank of the Wabash River looking down at two slabs of limestone at his feet. He was not a tall man, but his steeple-crowned hat made him seem like a giant. Beneath the folds of his black silk cape, his shoulders were broad and heavy. His legs, in black hose, were sturdy and slightly bowed columns, supporting a body as solid and immovable as the water beech beside him. Under the broad brim of his hat, his brooding face was like the rest of him—plain and solid, the forehead massive, the nose long and fleshy, the chin square above a fringe of beard.

George Rapp was a German. Born in Württemberg in 1757, he had spent the first thirty years of his life as a simple vinedresser and farmer. But when he was thirty, a revelation came to him and he began to preach a new and unorthodox religious doctrine. For one thing, Rapp taught "the dual nature of Adam." Adam, he said, originally contained in himself both the male and the female nature, and the fall of man was simply the separation of the two and the creation of an individual female part. He believed also that the second coming of Christ was imminent, that it would happen in his own lifetime. For these doctrines there was no room in the official churches

of eighteenth century Germany, and Rapp and his followers were persecuted until they eventually fled to
America.

That was in 1803. They established a community of
equality in Pennsylvania. In the beginning, they did not
prosper, and the lean years led to a revival in their
religion which was responsible for their adding the doctrine of celibacy to their other beliefs. George Rapp and
his son set the example for giving up the married state,
although they at no time saw the need of husbands and
wives living in separate houses. Since they expected
Christ to appear soon, they wanted to meet him in a
spiritual, not a sensual state. They also hoped that by
stopping the increase of their numbers they might speed
the increase of their fortunes.

The hope was realized. By 1809, they had two thousand acres of land under cultivation and a large surplus
of grain for sale. By 1814, their Pennsylvania community was too small and remote for their expanding commerce, and they bought from the government a new and
undeveloped tract of thirty thousand acres fifty miles
above the mouth of the Wabash. In 1815, they traveled
down the Ohio and up the Wabash, eight hundred in
number, and founded the community of Harmonie.

On the day that George Rapp stood on the bank of
the Wabash looking at the two slabs of limestone at his
feet, the fortune of his community was so great that it
could hardly be reckoned. The Rappites had lived for
eight years in Harmonie, and the fertile valley had been
generous to a degree that excelled his fondest hopes.

"Thy will be done," he said, almost angrily; and,
turning his back upon the stone slabs at which he had
been staring, he strode down to the water's edge.

Men said harsh things about George Rapp; and, meeting him there on the riverbank for the first time, you might well have believed them. He was a man of stone, they said. He was dishonest. He was avaricious. He was a charlatan. In secret revels, he grossly violated the rules of temperance and chastity he had set up for his community. Yet he could not abide such violations among his followers. Before he came to the Wabash, they said, he had operated on his only son to cure him of rebellion against the Rappite law of celibacy, and, under his father's knife, the son had died. George Rapp was a man to avoid, said his enemies, tortured by envy of his success in the wilderness. He was a man to be driven out of the Wabash country, if possible. Seeing in the outward man a stolid, determined, unapproachable zealot whose religion was untempered by humor, humanity, or even ecstasy, you would have agreed and shunned him.

Yet, accepting the rumors about George Rapp, you would have rejected as impossible the two facts that were immediately and uncontrovertibly true. He had just risen from a devout and humiliating prayer before the limestone slabs, and his heart was filled with a deep and sentimental sadness.

Looking across the white shimmer of the water at the Illinois forest, George Rapp was remembering how, eight years before, he had first brought his followers in a fleet of broadhorns up the Wabash. It was spring then, and the country seemed like a paradise after the cold of the Pennsylvania winter they had left. The redbud was in blossom and the locust filled the soft air with fragrance. Against the blue sky, the tops of the gum trees seemed to float like pink clouds.

That sky . . . !

No wonder the cardinals and the mockingbirds sang so joyously! No wonder his dull Württemberg peasants forgot themselves and danced across the green carpet of cinquefoil in the open forest, like elves, when first they landed! What genuine thanksgiving they had put into their prayers on that first day!

"Die Bläue!"

He lifted his eyes to the speckless blue dome that arched above the river.

"Die ewige Bläue . . . !"

That everlasting blue! It still filled him with wonder each time that he looked at it. There was no sky in the world like this sky of Indiana.

Their lives had not been all thanksgiving and rejoicing in Harmonie, of course. When they broke ground in the bottom lands for the first time, they released the germs of malaria and many of the good Württemberg men and women died. Then had come the milksick and, with it, not only death but dissension and rebellious homesickness for the older land of Pennsylvania. The first crops had given them trouble, too. The soil was too rich for wheat. The stalks grew too long and broke with their own weight. Then, in August, came storms that destroyed the corn, uprooted the fine trees they had spared, and blew the shingles from the roofs of their houses. But, in the end, such hardships had only endeared the new town to them.

After all, they had made it with their own hands, lovingly and with great care, fashioning in the heart of the wilderness a little of the old world of Württemberg they had left so long ago. How generously they had spaced their roomy, comfortable houses, building first one of brick and then one of clapboards! With what tenderness

they had planted their flower gardens and planned the
community's labyrinth of shrubs and vines! Then had
come his vision of a church, thrice designed for him in
a dream, and every man had set to work making the
bricks that looked like huge Dutch biscuits and felling
trees until the strange building towered above the forests,
its roof supported by twenty-eight pillars of walnut,
cherry, and sassafras. Afterward, they built a fort and
community houses and more homes. And, all the while,
they had managed somehow never to neglect the tasks of
sowing and plowing and harvesting. How much they had
accomplished to the sweet German melodies their band
played for them while they worked in the fields! Their
hearts were quiet and their minds were filled with the
satisfying knowledge of work well done when they heard
the chant of the watchman making his rounds at night:
"Again a day is past and a step made nearer to our end,
our time runs away, and the joys of heaven are our re-
ward!"

"They will refuse to go!" George Rapp cried suddenly, clenching his huge fists at his sides. "They will refuse with their heads as well as their hearts. One hundred
and fifty thousand dollars is no price for what we have
done here! It is worth twice as much—three times—a
thousand times! The people will rebel. Edelmütiger Gott,
at least let me wait till my son returns before I tell
them!"

For Frederick, his adopted son, would give him the
strength that he needed—Frederick, who had transacted
the purchase of Harmonie eight years ago, Frederick,
who knew so much better than he how to speak in terms
of dollars and acreage and developments and deeds.

But the Lord had spoken. For eight years they had

lived in the valley of the Wabash and reaped its abundance. Now they must go and build a new home. They were growing too comfortable, too prosperous. Simple minds need the tasks of pioneering to protect them from idle and worldly thoughts. Another year or two in Harmonie and their prosperity would bring them only corruption. The Lord had spoken, and the Lord could not be denied. They must go.

"Thy will be done!"

George Rapp turned and walked back to the limestone slabs on the riverbank. Stooping, he ran his fingers over the smooth surfaces. He knew what men said of him, and secretly he admitted that many of their accusations were true. He was a charlatan, and with these stones he was about to practice the most spectacular and daring charlatanry of his career. But you cannot hold together eight hundred men and women in celibate and communistic life without diplomacy, and in diplomacy there must always be some deceit. The deceits that he practiced upon their ignorant and superstitious minds, however, were always for their own good. Their faith was not so strong as his own. They required constant and harsh discipline and an occasional outward sign.

Drawing down the heads of the surrounding weeds to protect the stones from the casual glances of passersby, George Rapp stood up with a heavy and reluctant heart. Then he folded his black, silk cape across his chest and climbed the bank among the willows toward the village.

22

Gabriel

Harmonie was deserted. The broad, dusty streets lay empty in the summer sun. There was no sign of life except an occasional sleeping dog and the murmur of old women's voices in the community houses.

That morning, George Rapp had led the brothers and sisters out into the wheatfields for the harvest. At the head of the celebration, he had ridden his fine horse. Behind him, on foot, came the band, and behind the band the brothers and sisters. The bobbing steeple-crowned hats of straw that the brothers wore had danced like sunlight above the pale blue of their smocks, and the women's white shawls had trailed lightly in the breeze like shreds of summer cloud. As they marched to the harvest, they sang the German words of the song the band was playing.

George Rapp, returning from the river, was grateful for his brief reprieve. He walked slowly through the streets, his footsteps hushed in the soft cushion of locust and catalpa buds that were strewn on the earth. As if he were bidding them farewell, he studied each of the solid brick and frame houses with their humped shingle roofs. He ran his hand affectionately along the picket fences built on the street side of the walk. He looked up at the black locust trees that he loved so well, noting each broken branch, each sign of decay. When he reached his own spacious house, he glanced at the sundial hung on the south wall and saw that it was five o'clock. The reapers would be returning soon for their suppers.

With a heavy tread, he went into his house. There, closing the door behind him, he knelt in the cool shadows of the parlor for one last prayer.

"Lord, give me strength . . ."

He was still praying when the first strains of band music reached his ears. He stood up and peered through the slanting yellow shutters. At the head of the street, the procession was already in sight, rounding a corner. The men and women were singing. George Rapp waited, his square jaw set, and when they were almost abreast of his house, he opened the shutters and stepped out on the porch, holding up his hand.

At once the music ceased, and the singing and laughter of the returning reapers was silenced. Stopping in the middle of the street, they looked up at him anxiously. They knew that the past few days Father Rapp had been in communion with God, and they were afraid. Too often such communion had brought down upon them new and harsher laws or great sacrifices.

"My children," George Rapp began, and his voice rumbled up from his deep chest like thunder, "let us praise the Lord for his goodness and mercy."

The Rappites stood like statues in the yellow sunlight. The only sound, during the silent prayer, was the mournful cooing of turtledoves in the giant hackberry above Rapp's porch. Then, suddenly, the prayer ended and George Rapp's deep voice once more broke the silence.

"God has been good to us here on the banks of the Wabash. For eight years we have prospered. Our vineyards have borne abundantly, and men say our wine is like the wine of old Hungary. Our corn and wheat crops have been bountiful. The six stones of our mill have turned without ceasing. In New Orleans, the fruits of our labors have been in great demand. Envying us, men have said cruel things of us and tried to destroy us, but we have remained pure in heart and the Lord has been our shield. Harmonie has become our home.

"I love it all as you do—these forests, these fields, our vineyards, our quiet valley, and the peaceful river. With you I have put my heart into the building of Harmonie. So, when I tell you that the Lord has commanded us to leave and build a new home elsewhere, you will understand that obedience comes as hard to me as it does to you. But it is foolish and sinful to doubt the wisdom of God."

He paused. The Rappites were stunned. He waited till the first signs of restlessness disturbed them. Then quickly he spoke again.

"I am selling Harmonie to a Welshman named Robert Owen. He will establish a community of his own in this village. We are going to return to Pennsylvania and begin again."

This time, when George Rapp paused, there was not silence, but a murmur of voices like the hum of bees. He watched their faces—the stolid, German faces of thick, sturdy men like himself; the round, pink and white, German faces of women like the woman he himself had once loved with the sinful love of the flesh. It was as he had feared. The faces were growing slowly troubled, then angry. He set his jaw harder. He loved these men and women. He must not allow his love to overcome his faith in the wisdom of God.

"Father Rapp!"

It was Brother Gottfried, the troublemaker. Brother Gottfried had once rebelled against the law that placed his infant in the common nursery—and it was an infant born after the adoption of the law of celibacy! They had exiled him to the forest, but now he was back among them and his spirit was not broken.

"Father Rapp, we will not go!"

A timid murmur of approval supported Brother Gottfried, and he was pushed forward by the crowd to be their spokesman. He stood out in front on his bandy legs, his blue smock fluttering in the breeze. Behind him, George Rapp saw Brother Gottfried's wife, Sister Frieda, come forward and clasp his hand. She, too . . . ! They had broken their vows again. He could tell by the brazen, defiant look in the woman's eyes. God have mercy on them!

"We will not go, Father Rapp!"

"It is the will of God."

"No!"

George Rapp held Brother Gottfried and Sister Frieda with his fiery, blue eyes. They trembled under his gaze. But they stood their ground.

"We refuse!"

"All right, then," George Rapp said quietly. "We shall have a vote."

"Yes . . . a vote!"

It was a chorus; and, with the true leader's intuition, George Rapp knew that his authority was teetering on the verge of destruction. In the twenty years of their communal life, in both Pennsylvania and Indiana, no vote had ever overridden his decisions; but if a vote was taken now, he would lose. God was right. They *must* leave Harmonie. The brothers and sisters were growing rebellious and worldly.

"A vote, then," he said, with outward calm. "But I have told you the will of God, and I warn you that he who disobeys the will of God suffers eternal damnation in hell."

They were silenced again for a moment, but Brother Gottfried, too, possessed the intuition of a true leader. He knew as well as George Rapp how the vote would go.

"The will of God!" he shouted contemptuously, turning to his comrades. "The will of God and the will of George Rapp are always one! How does he know any better than we what God wills?"

Before they could answer or Brother Gottfried could continue, George Rapp's deep voice rumbled over their heads once more.

"I have talked with the Angel Gabriel, and he told me God's will."

Even Brother Gottfried was abashed for a moment; and when finally he spoke again, his voice was without conviction.

"I do not believe you."

"Then follow me."

Stepping down from the porch, George Rapp led them up the street to the edge of the village, through the willows, and to the river. There, commanding them to halt, he stood before the tangle of weeds he had made over the limestone slabs and, lifting his hand, began to speak again.

"It happened here, two hours ago. After I left you in the fields, I came here to pray. I asked God to deliver us from his command. I prayed that we might remain in our comfortable homes in Harmonie. My spirit was weak. Like you, I was reluctant to obey. But, even as I prayed, the Angel Gabriel came and alighted on a stone slab that lay in front of me.

" 'The Lord has spoken,' Gabriel said, 'and you are to do his bidding.'

"Then, with the golden rod in his hand, Gabriel drew on another stone the plans for the new village we are to build in Pennsylvania; and when he rose into heaven again, I looked where he had stood and saw his footprints on the stone."

"Impossible!"

It was the voice of Brother Gottfried.

But George Rapp had parted the weeds above the limestone slabs and stood pointing.

"You may come and see the footprints for yourselves."

One at a time, the Rappites stepped forward and knelt before the stones. What they saw is still to be seen in the village of New Harmony on the banks of the Wabash—the imprint of two, large, high-arched, bare feet, perfectly traced in the hard rock, and a rectangular design. Silent and bowed with awe, the Rappites rose and returned to their places in the congregation. Last of all came Brother Gottfried and Sister Frieda. Doubting, Brother Gottfried put his fingertip in the hollow of the footprint and ran it over the swirling pattern left by the angel's skin. Then he, too, rose, convinced.

"God forgive me, Father Rapp!" he murmured.

With an ominous frown, George Rapp stared down at the rebellious man and his wife.

"God have mercy on your souls!"

"YOU MAY COME AND SEE THE FOOTPRINTS FOR YOURSELF."

The Rappites kept no records. George Rapp wrote no diary. Where the stones came from and who made the miraculous footprints is a secret that died with the old German leader years later in Pennsylvania. But the device was effective. The next spring, the Rappites departed.

Of their departure there is a written record. It is scrawled in German under a stairway in Community House Number Two.

"In the twenty-fourth of May, 1824, we have departed. Lord, with thy great help and goodness, in body and soul protect us."

The Lord's will, as George Rapp knew it, was done.

23

A Free and Equal Society

Bʏ April, 1825, the quiet, well-ordered German village of the Rappites had changed completely. The solid, brick and frame dwellings were still there. The great church still towered above the forests. The gardens bloomed, though rank and unattended. The black locusts, the blue gum, and the catalpa once more blossomed, and the finger of shadow continued to trace the passage of the hours across the face of the sundial on George Rapp's house. But the peaceful and orderly spirit of the town had fled before an invasion of newcomers from all parts of the globe.

Coming up from the boat landing one sunny morning in that April of 1825 was an eager, nervous, little man in a great, gray cape, who seemed especially curious about the sights of the town. He had seen it once before, in early winter; but it was only a half-deserted village then. It appeared to him now in a new light.

He walked slowly, his arms folded behind him, his quick eyes taking in everything. From time to time, in order to give closer scrutiny to an object that captured his interest, he paused and, tilting his chin skyward, adjusted his silver-rimmed spectacles on the end of his long and upturned nose. To the Rappite cemetery, with its moundless and unmarked graves, he gave several minutes of profound study. To the massive church, built of brick in the form of a cross, he devoted a meditative pause of half an hour. Finally, the old fort proved irresistible, and he picked his way over a carpet of white and blue violets in the yard and walked slowly all around it, feeling the brick wall with his hands, as if to test its strength. Then, suddenly, as if he would catch it by surprise, he swung about and peered across the yard at the former home of George Rapp.

It was a brick structure, too, almost as solid as the fort, and on its roof were two lightning rods. A slow smile crept over the little man's genial face. The old German had provided well for himself. They said there was a secret tunnel from the house to the fort—for the better execution of miracles, no doubt!

With this observation, the little man leaped spryly over the picket fence and was out in the lanelike street again approaching the cluster of community houses in the center of the town. But his way was impeded now by throngs of idlers. Lank Kentucky and Hoosier backwoodsmen in buckskins, clutching their long rifles, as if they were still in the forest, elegant ladies and gentlemen in silks and laces, posturing foppishly, long-bearded scholars, eager youths, and exuberant children, milling about between the fences, stirred up clouds of dust.

The eager little man threaded his way among them unnoticed, picking up scraps of their conversation.

"Well, I says to the ol' woman, if they've really got a paradise on the Wabash, like they say, you an' me'll git thar somehow. So we come . . ."

"Mais, monsieur, vous êtes trop gentil! Je trouverai un domicile à moi . . ."

"Human nature, of course, is a compound of animal propensities, intellectual faculties, and moral qualities. Once we recognize these . . ."

"But Rousseau points out . . ."

"Ach, Rousseau! Wer ist Rousseau?"

"Why, the Ballous lived just down the rud a piece from us in Rhode Island! Of course, we know them!"

"No; no work has begun yet. But once we get started, I tell you . . . !"

The little man in the gray cape reached the corner. The last time he had visited the village, he had stopped at a house advertising "Private Entertainment," which the landlord had told him was a device for turning away undesirable guests. But he had forgotten where the house stood.

"Can you direct me to the tavern?"

The man to whom he addressed his question was a gaunt scarecrow in a long, loose coat of yellow nankeen, over which his black beard and hair hung in silken curls. His tight pantaloons were buttoned down over his ankles, and the large pockets of his long waistcoat bulged with something that smelled strongly of fish.

"If it is Engleesh you are speaking, monsieur," the bearded man replied, with a marked foreign accent, "you must forgive me for saying it is the strangest Engleesh I have ever heard."

Smiling, the man in the gray cape repeated his question more slowly, and the deep eyes above the beard brightened.

"Mais si! The tavern! It is down this street—the beeg, breeck buildeeng! I will accompany you."

As they turned, they were jostled by a group of

backwoodsmen careening down the street in a cloud of alcoholic fumes.

"Say, look whar you're a-goin' at, will you! This-here is a free an' equal sassiety, an' we got as much right to the road as you have!"

"I beg your pardon," the little man said politely.

"Well, no harm done this time, I guess. But you'd ought to be keerful."

Behind the speaker, another backwoodsman held up a jug, winking and pointing.

"Bug juice!" he explained.

Walking on, the newcomer turned to his companion.

"Tell me, what do you think of the future of New Harmony?"

The scarecrow pulled at his beard thoughtfully.

"Frankly, monsieur," he said finally, "I have not made up my mind. It has been all confusion since I came here, with more people pouring in than there will be room for—and the wrong kind of people too often, like those we just met. Those ruffians will contribute nothing to a new social order, j'en suis sur!"

"But," interrupted the little man, "if the members were selected—hand-picked, you know,—the society would be worth nothing as an experiment. After all, it is just for such people as those we met that the society is designed. It is to make the world a better place for them —and to make them better for the world."

"Oui, oui, I understand that. The conception is excellent. But the execution worries me. Now—moi, monsieur—my name is Constantine Raffinesque—I came here to study the fishes in the Wabash. I have been working with Audubon down in Kentucky, and I came up here because I expected to find books and a laboratory and an order that I do not find in other wilderness settlements. But so far I have found only this madness and confusion."

"Perhaps when the society is organized . . ." his companion ventured; and the bearded man nodded emphatically.

"That is what I tell myself. When Monsieur Owen arrives, I say, everything will right itself. When he took over that cotton mill in New Lanark, Scotland, conditions among the workers must have been far worse than they are here, and there was no such intelligence as you will find already assembled in this community. Everybody knows the miracle Monsieur Owen accomplished in Scotland, and I have no doubt he can repeat it here. He is in Washington now. The whole government—the president and all—turned out for his addresses in the House of Representatives, where he was invited to describe his plans for New Harmony. Oh, yes, when Monsieur Owen arrives . . . !"

The little man smiled and held out his hand.

"He has arrived," he said. "I am Robert Owen."

The giant with the black beard was both embarrassed and delighted.

"Mais, monsieur, it is the beginning of the millennium, then!"

They were in the lobby of the tavern now, and Constantine Raffinesque introduced Robert Owen to the men gathered there.

"Messieurs—here is our leader, Monsieur Robert Owen, just arrived from Washington!"

The men rose and shook Mr. Owen's hand. One of them went out immediately to find Mr. Owen's son,

William, who had already established himself in the community. The others offered to look for lodgings for the leader.

"The town is filling up rapidly," they warned him. But the little Welshman shook his head.

"A room here in the hotel will be good enough," he said, "and if you gentlemen will excuse me, I shall go to it now and wash away the grime of my long journey. A boy at the landing is bringing up my trunks."

At the foot of the stairs, he paused and looked back.

"As soon as possible, I wish you would convene all prospective members of the community in the Rappite church."

He started up the stairs, but stopped once more.

"And that church, gentlemen—I think we should rechristen it. Shall we call it the Hall of Harmony?"

On the night of April 17th, the doors of the Hall of Harmony were thrown open and the people gathered— the whole motley society of crackpots, ne'er-do-wells, adventurers, savants, idealists, malcontents, and reformers, men, women, and children. The high, pillared room, where the Rappites had formerly held their solemn, silent services, echoed and re-echoed with their gay and hopeful chatter; and when Robert Owen himself finally appeared, there was loud applause.

A half dozen backwoodsmen, unable to find seats, had sprawled on the platform by the pulpit; but when they saw Robert Owen, they started to climb down.

He remonstrated.

"Do not disturb yourselves, gentlemen."

In amazement, they lolled back and stared up at him as he picked his way among them to the pulpit.

This was the true democratic spirit—even if he was a furriner. The little feller was all right!

"I am come to this country," Robert Owen began, "to introduce an entire new state of society; to change it from an ignorant, selfish system to an enlightened social system which shall gradually unite all interests into one, and remove all contests between individuals."

For more than an hour he spoke passionately and earnestly, and, at the end, his audience rose to their feet and cheered.

Three days later, on May 1, 1825, the Preliminary Society of New Harmony was formed. All the basic principles of Robert Owen's communism were included in the first constitution. Persons of all ages and descriptions—exclusive of persons of color!—were to be admitted, and all were to be of the same rank. Each member was to have, within a fixed amount in value, free choice of food and clothing from the community store, and, in return, each was to render his best services for the good of the society, according to his age, experience, and capacity. The children were to be located in the best possible manner in day schools and were to board and sleep in the houses provided for their parents. Everyone was to "enter the society with a determination to promote its peace, prosperity, and harmony, and never, under any provocation whatever, act unkindly or unjustly toward, nor speak in an unfriendly manner of, anyone either in or out of the society." Finally, Robert Owen was to remain the sole proprietor of the establishment for two years, at the end of which the members might choose one-half of the committee of control. At the end of the third year, the final step in self-government would be taken and the perfect community would be established.

Robert Owen called the Preliminary Society "the halfway house between the old system and the new."

24

The Boatload of Knowledge

THE Preliminary Society began auspiciously. The idlers settled down to work. The mill began to operate. Steamboats stopped at the landing, took on cargoes, left new members. Fences were torn down, removing the suggestion of private property, and new log houses were laid up. Pioneers undertook the study of Latin, and scholars played at pioneering. Elegant ladies learned to milk cows, and backwoods women learned to be elegant. The town hummed with eager activity, and on Thursdays and Fridays the townsfolk trooped down to Jacob Schnee's post office to receive the letters that came from the East by way of the corduroy road to Evansville and from the West and South by way of Mt. Vernon—letters whose grave misgivings and scandalized gossip the townspeople answered with enthusiastic and fanciful epistolary essays.

Unanimously the members praised their leader in those first days.

"He is a wonderful man—" William Pelham wrote to his son, "such a one, indeed, as the world has never before seen."

"I do not know how it is—" wrote Thomas Pears, "he is not an orator, but he appears to have the power of managing the feelings of all at his will."

"That feller," said the pioneers to each other in the streets, giving Robert Owen the highest praise of all, "I tell you, he's a *hoss!*"

Carried away by the reinfection of his own enthusiasm, Robert Owen soon grew restless, however. A simple utopia was not satisfying enough. He must have more men and women in New Harmony, and more brilliant minds. Within a month or so after launching the experiment, he was off again, leaving for the East to gather new recruits.

While he was gone, the town continued to grow and the impetus he had given it increased. The New Harmony *Gazette* made its first bow to the public—eight pages "on fine royal paper," so fine that it retains its quality to this day in the files of American libraries. In it appeared an official and enthusiastic "view" of New Harmony; the constitution of the society; Mr. Owen's addresses; essays on self-knowledge and taste; a plan for the abolition of slavery, "without danger or loss to the citizens of the south"; an article on "the Alcoran of Mahomet"; and—to prove that social revolution need not be all high seriousness—a sample of the editor's humor.

"How to Catch and How to Cure a Cold" was its title. "At this time of year colds are easily caught and difficult to cure. The following will be found effectual. —After a quick walk in the evening, sit in the draft, to cool; the consequence will be a severe cold attended with cough; the next day hoarseness, short breath, and much expectoration; in the evening, at seven, go to a well frequented tavern, and drink three or four glasses of strong punch or stiff rum and water; stay till eleven, walk home boosey, and go to bed; you need not get up the next day, but send for the apothecary, the following day for the physician, and the third day your friends will send for the undertaker. You will never feel the effects of an autumnal cold afterwards."

But, even in this lighter moment, it is obvious that the editor was mindful of his responsibility to society; for, in the end, it was the "strong punch" and "stiff rum and water" that did the victim in! The editor was no doubt in full agreement with Robert Owen, who abhorred the use of alcohol. The Welshman forbade the manufacture of liquor in his community, its sale, and its consumption.

But if he hated the demon rum, Robert Owen was not opposed to the social pleasures. Before he left in search of recruits, he instituted a program that made entertainment an integral part of his utopian scheme.

"Recreations are both pleasing and necessary," his admirer, Thomas Pears, was writing before the end of that first summer; "but we have Monday nights—parade and drill; Tuesday nights—dancing; Wednesday nights —public meetings for business; Thursday nights—unappropriated; Friday nights—concerts, etc.; Saturday nights—fire engine, debates, etc.; and so for every evening, playing at ball, cricket, etc."

The result of Robert Owen's campaign for recruits in the East was the "Boatload of Knowledge," a keelboat that came down the Ohio and up the Wabash in January, 1826, laden with more distinguished men and women than had ever before entered the wilderness in one group. Mr. Owen came overland, arriving a few days ahead of the keelboat; and immediately he called a meeting in the Hall of Harmony to tell the original members of the society the good news.

William Pelham, writing again to his son, described that happy day.

"I have the pleasure of saying that Mr. Owen is here; he arrived yesterday evening accompanied by a Russian lady whom he accidentally found somewhere below Steubenville on her way to New Harmony. An assembly of almost the whole population met in the Steeple house about seven. Mr. Owen entered and taking his stand in the pulpit expressed the pleasure and joy he felt to be among us. He said that he had left his company behind proceeding in a boat which contained more learning than was ever contained in a boat. He did not mean Latin or Greek or other dead languages, but real substantial knowledge."

That "real substantial knowledge" was the knowledge of men and women like William Maclure, the "father of American Geology" and a student of the Pestalozzian system of education; Thomas Say, the "father of American Zoology," who was to spend the rest of his days in New Harmony and is buried there; Charles Alexandre Le Sueur, a naturalist in the employ of the Jardin des Plantes of Paris, who had made part of the voyage around the world with La Pérouse; Madame Marie D. Fretageot, a Frenchwoman, who was coming to teach in the Pestalozzian manner; her two lovely wards, Miss Lucy May Sistaire and Miss Virginia Dupalais; Phiquepal D'Arusmont, another teacher, who was later to become the husband of Frances Wright; Professor Joseph Neef, who had once taught Admiral Farragut in a Pestalozzian school at Schuylkill Falls; Dr. Gerard Troost, a geologist from Holland; and Robert Dale Owen, Robert Owen's oldest son, who was later to become a nationally recognized champion of woman suffrage and free public education, and without whose keen and practical mind his father's communistic society at New Harmony would have collapsed long before it did.

The school children met the Boatload of Knowledge at the landing and escorted its passengers to the center of the village dancing and singing. Robert Owen was delighted. The community appeared to have progressed and prospered in his absence. Now that the distinguished recruits were safely landed, the prospect for the future seemed boundless. Again his enthusiasm carried him away from the task of slow and steady foundation building; and, within a week after the Boatload's arrival, he announced that the probationary period of three years for the Preliminary Society was unnecessary. The perfect and complete communistic society would be organized at once.

On January 25th, a constitutional convention was called and the "Community of Equality" was organized.

"Our object," the Declaration stated, "is that of all sentient beings, happiness.

"Our principles are:

"Equality of rights, uninfluenced by sex or conditions, in all adults.

"Equality of duties, modified by physical and mental conformation.

"Co-operative union, in the business and amusements of life.

"Community of property.

"Freedom of speech and action.

"Sincerity in all our proceedings.

"Kindness in all our actions.

"Courtesy in all our intercourse.

"Order in all our arrangements.

"Preservation of health.

"Acquisition of knowledge.

"The practice of economy, or of producing and using the best of everything in the most beneficial manner.

"Obedience to the laws of the country in which we live."

It was a magnificent dream, and once more the town hummed.

Old Joseph Neef wore blisters on his hands chopping down trees and notching logs when he was not teaching in the community school; and, in school and out, he all but wore blisters on his tongue trying to break himself of the habit of profanity acquired when he was an officer under Napoleon.

"Youngster, you must not swear! It is silly and it is vulgar and it means nothing!"

"But, Professor Neef, if—if it's vulgar and silly to swear, why—"

"Well, what is it? Out with it! Don't stand there stammering! What, in God's name, do you wish to say?"

"Then why do you swear yourself, Professor Neef?"

"Because I am a damn fool! But that does not mean you should be one!"

Young Robert Dale Owen was ubiquitous in his activities, keeping accounts, interviewing prospective members, finding houses for them, helping to build the houses if they were not to be found, writing plays, and taking over Professor Neef's classes whenever the professor's patience temporarily deserted him. Phiquepal D'Arusmont organized his own small school and proceeded to antagonize his students with his extravagance and conceit, until Robert Dale Owen decided he was "a wrong-headed genius." William Maclure, Madame Fretageot, Miss Sistaire, and Miss Dupalais set themselves up in style in George Rapp's old home across the street from Community House Number Two, where the Pestalozzian school was lodged. Dr. Troost and Thomas Say and Constantine Raffinesque worked in their laboratories. John Chappelsmith sketched exquisite pictures of fossils and dreamily studied meteorology, while his wife supervised his diet and his opinions and delivered lectures on entomology—whenever she could persuade Robert Owen to give up an evening's program.

"Liberty, equality, and fraternity in downright earnest," Robert Dale Owen called the Community of Equality, as he looked back upon it years later. "I made no opposition to all this. I had too much of my father's all-believing disposition to anticipate results which any shrewd, cool-headed business man might have predicted. How rapidly they came upon us!"

25

Discord in Harmony

How rapidly, indeed!

Within a few days after the Community of Equality was organized, the members were quarreling among themselves and a new community, called Macluria, was being formed on the outskirts of New Harmony. Within a few weeks, there was a second defection. "Feiba Peveli" it was called, its name inspired by a system worked out by Stedman Whitwell at New Harmony for the simplification of geography.

"Every state has its Washington, its Mt. Vernon, its Springfield," Mr. Whitwell complained. "But this confusion can be remedied by substituting letters for the latitude and longitude of places and compounding new names."

The first part of town names was to indicate the latitude, the second part the longitude. The letter "V" inserted into the longitude name indicated west longitude, its absence east longitude. An "S" in the other name indicated south latitude and its absence north latitude.

This is the key Mr. Whitwell devised:

1	2	3	4	5	6	7	8	9	0
a	e	i	o	u	y	ee	ei	ie	ou
or	or	or	or	or	or	or	or	or	or
b	d	f	k	l	m	n	p	r	t

If his system had been universally accepted, some of the results would have been astounding. New Yorkers might find themselves living in "Otke Notiv," assuming, of course, that they would accept the latitude and longitude of their city hall—40°42′43″N:74°0′3″W—as the latitude and longitude for the entire city; while London —at 51°31′N:0°0′0″W—would leave the Cockneys speechless as "Lafa Voutou"!

The offshooting of new communities was only a manifestation of the dissension growing within the older community itself. By the time the Duke of Saxe-Weimar arrived on a sightseeing visit in April, 1826, the dissatisfaction was obvious to everyone but Robert Owen. The duke was charmed to find an elegant society attending balls and concerts in the heart of the wilderness; but he was also highly amused by the vicious gossip, the constant complaints, and the meager fare that the rebellious and indolent communists provided for themselves. In that same month, the wife of Thomas Pears wrote to an aunt in Pittsburgh objecting to the division of families that had resulted from the overcrowding of the town.

"I assure you that Mr. Owen of New Harmony is a very different personage from Mr. Owen of Pittsburgh, Washington, etc."

Mr. Owen's great crime had been that he gave away his property too soon to unprepared beneficiaries.

The disintegration continued. The factories stood idle. Men and women brought their quarrels more and more into the open. Newcomers arrived and began to speculate in private property. A man named Taylor built a distillery at the outskirts of the town, and the backwoodsmen helped both to sell and to consume his products. A waggish utopian made a coffin and labeled it "The New Social System," and a mock funeral would have been held if a more loyal member of the society had not broken into the building where the coffin was concealed and destroyed it. Things went from bad to worse. Robert Owen tried to salvage what he could of the society by taking back the directorship into his own hands. But by April, 1827, he and William Maclure themselves were involved in a quarrel and posting defamatory notices concerning each other about the town.

Another month passed and Robert Owen was acknowledging defeat in the pages of the New Harmony *Gazette*. On May 26 and 27, 1827, he delivered farewell addresses to the citizens. In them, he admitted discouragement, but his tone was still hopeful. His last words were: "When I return, I hope to find you progressing in harmony together."

On June 1st, he left for England. The return that he promised was delayed two years. By that time, the last evidences of true communism in New Harmony had vanished.

26

The Seed Is in the Spirit

SEVERAL differences between Owen and Rapp make it obvious why the Rappites lived in harmony for nine years, whereas the Owenites were able to maintain new harmony but two. The German leaned heavily on the guidance of a mystical God, and he was unscrupulous at times in implementing what he considered God's will. The Welshman was devoted to pure reason and absolute religious freedom to such a degree that he inspired the fear and hatred of many devout souls in both England and America, and he had implicit trust in the natural goodness and wisdom of mankind for the working out of their own salvation. Rapp was cautious and phlegmatic, filled with the German's practical sense and, except in his religious flights, untroubled by imagination. Owen moved too swiftly. He was impatient. He could not wait for his social machinery to get under way naturally. He had to have his millennium at once. Rapp was hard-working and willing to pass his days in obscurity. Owen did not stick to his job, preferring to leave the community and make speeches about it before cultured and intellectual audiences in the East. Neither of the men had a sense of humor; but Rapp, with the unifying force of a religious faith to support his followers,

was better off without one, whereas Owen, struggling
to hold together a community of individualists and free-
thinkers, needed one badly.

But Rapp's experiment was not altogether a success,
nor was Owen's altogether a failure. Today there is nothing left in New Harmony, Indiana, of Father Rapp's
long regime except the buildings he constructed. On the
other hand, the Owenites left few physical marks upon
the town, but the culture and tradition they established
have persisted in the quiet and lovely little village on the
Wabash for more than a century. Because of them, it
has attracted, through the years, many of the best minds
in the country; and its history is unequaled by any other
town of its size in the reforms and social movements it
has inaugurated.

In New Harmony, women were first given equal
social, legal, and political rights with men; the movement for the abolition of slavery received one of its first
impulses; one of the earliest American dramatic clubs
was formed; the first woman's literary club was organized; the first effort to prohibit liquor traffic was attempted; Josiah Warren originated a system of "time
stores" and "labor notes" that foreshadowed the great
co-operatives of England and the Scandinavian countries; the first kindergarten, the first free school, and the
first coeducational school in America were established,
and the first serious effort was made to incorporate
manual training into a public educational system; the
first workingmen's library was opened; and the headquarters for the first national geological survey of the
country of the Old Northwest was established under the
direction of David Dale Owen, another of Robert
Owen's distinguished sons.

Modern New Harmony is at its best scenically in early June, when the streets and walks are covered with a carpet of golden blossoms dropped from the golden rain trees. The seed for the first of these trees was sent by William Maclure to Thomas Say in 1828 and planted at the gate of the Maclure mansion. For that reason, the natives usually call them "gate trees," although the name which the Chinese originally gave them was "The Tree of the Golden Rain." They shade the streets of New Harmony in great numbers today, and that village is the only place in America where the trees grow in abundance.

But at any season of the year New Harmony is beautiful, nestling peacefully in the "cutoff" hills on the banks of the quiet river; for its beauty is a beauty of tradition and of the spirit. There the descendants of the Owens, the Pelhams, the Fretageots, and of the other Owenite settlers still live, maintaining the faith in intellectual and spiritual independence which their forefathers established for them, amid the ivy-grown mansions that the Rappites built. There, under the able and enthusiastic direction of Mr. Ross F. Lockridge, a newly organized state commission is beginning a program of restoration and preservation which should one day make the town one of the most interesting historic spots in the country. There, too, can be found the spirit of Indiana's kindliness and humanity and hospitality. And there the Wabash is at her lovely best.

PART FIVE

She Comes In Free

27

Kentuckian

GEORGE BOONE came of the Kentucky stock that Daniel Boone fathered. He stood almost seven feet high in his bare feet. His shoulders were like an ox yoke balanced on top of his spine, and his heavy arms hung long at his sides, weighted by hands as big and brown as hickory-smoked hams. But his feet were what you saw first. Folks said that in the early days there was always a county missing in Indiana. George Boone was standing on it.

When he was eighteen, George Boone made up his mind to spark a girl named Sally. He was still a growing boy at that time—only six feet six or so—and his one butternut suit of store clothes was a trifle too small. He admitted himself that it stretched over him as tight as an eelskin dried on a hooppole. But he thought it looked right nice, just the same. Fortunately, it was too early in the fall for shoes, and Sally could hardly be surprised to see him arrive at her cabin barefooted.

Sally's folks had mush and milk for supper that night, and George Boone liked mush and milk. What was more, Sally looked prettier than ever. It promised to be a good evening.

But the very first time the milk pitcher was passed

to George, he was so busy looking at Sally that his big paw missed the handle and the pitcher fell and milk ran all over the table.

" 'Tain't nothin'," Sally's mother said. "It'll rub off when it gits dry."

"Worse accidents has happened at sea," said Sally's father philosophically.

But Sally stuck her fist into her mouth, jumped up, and ran into another room.

After that, nobody said anything. George Boone wanted to go home. He tried to get up and go home. When Sally's father went to bed, he knew he really ought to go home. But he kept hoping Sally would reappear. So he just sat.

When ten o'clock came, Sally's mother broke the silence with a yawn and said, "It's so late, Mr. Boone; why don't you jist warsh yer feet an' spend the night here?"

George's face brightened. He wriggled his big toes in delight at the prospect of bundling with Sally.

"Why, I don't keer if I do, ma'am," he said.

Sally's mother filled a pot with warm water for him and then modestly left the room. The pot was big, but not quite big enough. George had to slide his feet into it sideways. But he got them in, heels and all, and sat dreaming of Sally. After a while, when he stopped dreaming and tried to take his feet out of the pot, he discovered they had swollen and would not budge. He tugged and he strained. Sweat broke out all over him, and he heard his store suit rip at the shoulders. Finally, he realized it was hopeless.

"How much did this-here pot cost, ma'am?" he called to Sally's mother.

"One dollar," came the answer from the other room.

Without another word, George Boone reached for the ax, broke the pot, laid a dollar on the table, and bolted out the door.

George Boone never won Sally's hand, but, after Indiana became a state, he got himself elected to the state senate. There, his big frame and big voice were an advantage instead of a handicap. He could outfight as well as outshout any other member of the senate.

Once he was debating with a member of the opposition who stood only four feet ten and whose voice was no louder than a katydid's. As soon as George began his speech, the little senator tried to interrupt him.

"That's a lie!" he squeaked.

Ignoring him, George roared on.

"That's an infernal lie!"

The katydid senator hopped over the rail and, running up to George, hit him on the back with all his might. Undisturbed, George continued to address the chairman. The katydid worked himself into a fury and rained blows on George's back, but George's speech rumbled on, uninterrupted. When at last he had rounded out his peroration, George turned to the little senator behind him.

"Hey thar, senator," he said, "what you up to?"

"I'm a-fightin'!" shrieked the katydid.

"A-fightin'?" George drawled, looking puzzled. "Who you a-fightin'?"

The katydid turned purple.

"You!"

George beamed benevolently and laid one of his big hands on the little senator's head.

"Well, now, senator, you'd ought to let me know about it, seems like."

George Boone was a simple and a practical man. When he thought about slavery, he merely thought about the black people he knew who worked in bondage. If they laughed, he reckoned slavery was a pretty good thing. If they were oppressed, he thought they ought to be taken away from their masters. It was the same with land ordinances and taxes and elections. George Boone reduced all public issues to the terms of his own particular observations. The development of Indiana meant to him simply clearing his land in peace, getting justice done to his neighbors, and, if possible, getting himself elected to public office. Most of the pioneers in the Wabash country were like George Boone.

28

New Yorker

JOHN PAYNE was an immigrant from New York State. He cleared a tract of land for himself some miles back from Rising Sun, just over the line in eastern Indiana, and settled down to recreate in the wilderness the eastern home he had left.

Hunters in the forest back of Rising Sun soon beat a path to John Payne's cabin door. John Payne's wife was a neat, jolly, pink-cheeked, motherly sort of woman, who kept the cabin as clean as the hunters kept their rifles. There was always a cloth on her table and plenty of food. The hunters liked John Payne, too. He wasn't much of a one for sashays and palaver; but, in his forthright way, he always made them welcome. John Payne's cabin was the best place in the forest for a square meal and a smoke and a quiet hour of rest.

John Payne had six daughters. Each of them had flaxen hair and bright blue eyes, and when they were little they seemed to be all over the place, laughing and singing and prattling merrily all the time. They weren't ill-behaved. They were just full of healthy energy and happiness, and the hunters liked nothing better than to coax them up on their knees and tell them stories of the old days when there were Indians and the forest was full of panthers and bears.

"They're my jewels," John Payne's wife used to say. "If I have nothing else to be proud of, I can always look at my daughters and be happy."

"You've got aplenty to be proud of, ma'am," the hunters would say politely, casting approving eyes about the scrubbed little cabin and helping themselves to some more fried sausage and another ear of corn.

When John Payne's daughters grew up, each in turn eloped and was secretly married—but invariably they eloped with the most desirable and promising young bachelors in the country.

It wasn't because John Payne was a wealthy man, although he was making a go of things all right. It wasn't because Mrs. Payne gave promise of being an ideal mother-in-law, although indeed that was what she later proved to be. It wasn't even because the girls themselves were so well brought up, so good-looking, so smart, so beautifully dressed. It was because John Payne was a shrewd and ambitious man. That was why his daughters all married so well.

"You're a-doin' right well with those daughters of yourn, John Payne."

"M—m—m," John Payne would answer, in his laconic eastern way; and that was all.

But when the last of them had eloped and was successfully married, he revealed his secret.

"I married them off on the buckwheat straw principle," he said.

"The buckwheat straw principle? What's that?"

"Well, it's like this. If you leave your buckwheat straw in an open field where your cattle run, they'll never nibble so much as a bite of it. But just build a rickety fence around it, let the cattle break through, and then dog them out a couple of times, and you'll find they'll break down the strongest fence you can put up, just to get at the straw and eat it up clean.

"Now, that's the principle I went on with my daughters. Whenever I saw a particularly desirable young man bringin' one of my daughters home from a huskin' bee or a house warmin', I'd meet him at the door and say, 'Young man, I don't ever want to see you keepin' company with my daughter again!' Well, 'twouldn't be long till the two of 'em would elope and get married and I'd have another first-rate son-in-law!"

That was the buckwheat straw principle, and John Payne knew how to apply it to other problems besides the marrying off of attractive daughters. The forests back of Rising Sun were gradually cut down and John Payne's farm spread wider and wider. Then other settlers came and looked at John Payne's farm and decided they would like to live near such a man. John Payne prospered. By his labors and by his connections with the in-laws of his six well-married daughters, he became a man of influence and importance.

Like George Boone, John Payne had no ideas about the larger issues of slavery. But the tradition he inherited and his natural instincts were "agin" it. He had got along pretty well in New York State without slaves. He had made his way in Indiana without the aid of slave labor. He saw no need for a race in bondage. He liked to use his own hands and build and expand his estate by himself. It was more satisfying that way.

Unlike George Boone, John Payne had no natural flair for politics, although it was impossible for him to live in Indiana long without acquiring such a flair in some degree. But John Payne had a vote, and he never failed to exercise it. If you work hard and make a go of things, you want to see that honest men are elected to office to protect the results of your industry.

John Payne's kind came later to Indiana than George Boone's and there were not so many of them; but they planted their feet firmly wherever they stood and refused to budge.

29

Interloper

JESSE B. THOMAS was born in Maryland and came to Indiana by way of Kentucky, but he might have originated anywhere. His grain was finer than George Boone's and John Payne's, but it was not so straight. He had read law and he knew a few tricks that gave him an advantage over men like George and John. He would not have been overwhelmed by George Boone's big voice and big frame, and John Payne's buckwheat straw principle would not have fooled him.

"You can't talk a man down," Jesse B. Thomas often said, "but you can whisper him to death."

That was how Jesse worked. His acquaintances called him "tricky." He was not exactly dishonest. He was just "tricky." He always knew which way the wind was blowing, and he could build fires without smoke. People voted for Jesse B. Thomas and afterward wondered why. It was because Jesse B. Thomas always knew the kind of man they wanted to vote for, and, for a time, he was that man.

When he was in the territorial legislature in 1805, he voted for an "Act concerning the introduction of Negroes and Mulattoes into this Territory." The act said that any slaveholder could bring slaves over fifteen years old into Indiana Territory and, after thirty days, enter into an agreement with his slaves as to the number of years they would remain slaves. If the slaves would not agree to their own slavery, their owner had sixty days left in which to take them back where they came from.

That was the kind of legislation Jesse B. Thomas liked to vote for. It did not provide for slavery in Indiana Territory, and yet it did not provide for the exclusion of slavery. It simply provided for "Negroes and Mulattoes." You could argue about it either way. Among your constituents, you could make it appear either a proslavery act or an antislavery act, whichever was the more acceptable.

When Jesse B. Thomas voted for this act, the people of his county largely favored slavery. But when the year 1807 came around, and he was up for re-election, they had changed their minds. They wanted the territory to be absolutely free. They would have no truck with a man who voted even for acts providing for "Negroes and Mulattoes." But that did not trouble Jesse greatly. He went to all the barbecues, kissed pioneer babies, praised the women for their cooking, and, whenever he was asked what he thought of slavery, he spoke fervently of the glory of this great country.

He was re-elected.

When the legislature convened, there was a new issue before it. Should Indiana Territory be divided into two parts? At that time it included all of what are now Indiana, Illinois, and Wisconsin and a part of Minnesota, Michigan having been detached as a separate territory in 1805, and Ohio having been separated when the Indiana Territory was formed in 1800. Governor Harrison's an-

swer to the question was in the negative. The Illinois
region was the source of most of the proslavery sentiment
in Indiana Territory, and Governor Harrison was a proslavery man. But Jesse B. Thomas's constituents were
now antislavery people. Jesse B. Thomas thought and
thought about it. Then he said, "I am opposed to
slavery, but I am ready to support Governor Harrison
in the matter of the division."

That got him the speakership of the House.

Not long after this, Jesse B. Thomas was a candidate
to become the territory's delegate to the national Congress. The only way he could win would be to combine
the support of the eastern Indiana counties, which opposed slavery, with the support of the western Illinois
counties, which favored slavery. The task looked impossible, but Jesse B. Thomas was the man for it.

He had already stated flatly that he was opposed to
slavery. He now said, "I am still opposed to slavery, but
I favor the division of the territory so that the Illinois
people may come in as a slave state if they want to. I shall
work for a division of the territory when I am elected to
Congress, and if the Illinois voters do not trust me, I
will give them my bond."

Apparently they did not trust him, for John Rice
Jones demanded that he give his bond and he gave it.

The result was that he was elected.

Having given his bond, Jesse B. Thomas kept his
pledge this time, and early in 1809 the territory was
divided into two parts—Indiana and Illinois—with the
Wabash River as the southern dividing line. This reduced
the country called Indiana to the boundaries that it has
kept ever since.

A man like Jesse B. Thomas is more successful in a

new country than in an old country. Perhaps that is why he left Maryland and went to Kentucky, why he left Kentucky and came to Indiana. In a new country, communications are slower and the people's political memory is shorter. They have too many other things on their minds for them to be constantly checking on the unfulfilled promises of their legislators. At all events, after he got the territory divided, Jesse B. Thomas got for himself an appointment as a judge of a court in the new territory of Illinois; and that was the last the older region of Indiana saw of him.

Years later, the Indianians heard that he had been elected to the United States Senate from Illinois. But they weren't much interested. By that time, they had a plentiful new crop of Jesse B. Thomases on their hands in Indiana.

30

Virginian

THOMAS RANDOLPH was a Virginian. He went to William and Mary, graduated with high honors, served a year in the Virginia legislature, practiced law for a while, and then came to Indiana.

In the new territory, Thomas Randolph became one of the ablest lawyers of his time. But because he was a proud and austere man, few people liked him. They admitted he was brilliant. They respected his courage and his integrity. But something in the haughty curl of his broad mouth, beneath that long, patrician nose and those steady, hazel eyes, kept them at a distance. They called him a Virginia aristocrat. Thomas Randolph was of the Pocahontas blood.

Thomas Randolph owned slaves; he believed in slavery; he gave his brilliant talents to the cause of slavery in Indiana; and, although he was ultimately defeated, he never changed his mind about slavery. The story of Thomas Randolph in Indiana is like the story of the Old South in the United States—a story of proud defiance, of inevitable frustration, and of defeat that never touched the spirit.

Governor William Henry Harrison and Thomas Randolph were intimate friends. With Waller Taylor, they formed the innermost clique of the proslavery group that gathered frequently in the high-ceilinged, oval parlor of the Harrison mansion in Vincennes. When the other proslavery men were present, their talk was heated and strongly partisan; but when only Governor Harrison, Waller Taylor, and Thomas Randolph sat round the punch bowl, they discussed old times in Virgina, horses, tobacco, women, and occasionally literature, transcending the personalities and petty squabbles of the market place.

For example:

Benjamin Parke was one of their men. He was a valuable, an invaluable lieutenant in the proslavery party. His loyalty was so strong that when William McIntosh criticized Governor Harrison, he published an advertisement in the *Indiana Gazette:*

"Circumstances have recently occurred which authorize me in pronouncing and publishing, WILLIAM M'INTOSH, an arrant knave; a profligate villain; a dastardly cheat; a perfidious rascal; an impertinent puppy; an absolute liar; and a mean, cowardly poltroon.—B. Parke."

Yet when the governor and Taylor and Randolph read Mr. Parke's advertisement, as they sat around the punch bowl in the Harrison parlor, they only laughed— as they would have laughed at the musical baying of one of their favorite hounds. You would never have guessed that they had any personal interest in the quarrel of Mr. Parke and Mr. McIntosh.

After all, Mr. Parke had come to Indiana from New Jersey. He was not a Virginian. And, as for McIntosh— well, he was a Scotsman!

Mr. McIntosh, however, became so offensive after a while that Governor Harrison had to sue him on a charge of slander. Thomas Randolph took his friend's case and won $4,000 damages. That should have quieted Mr. McIntosh, but it didn't. One day, he came up behind Thomas Randolph in the streets of Vincennes and stabbed him in the back with a dirk. Randolph had only a pocket knife with him and could do nothing but slash the Scotsman across the face before he fell. The wound in his back almost killed him.

Governor Harrison appointed his friend attorney general for the territory in 1808, and Thomas Randolph served ably. In his office, he did much to advance the cause of slavery in Indiana; but his methods were always honest. There was nothing "tricky" about him. Men did not like him, but they knew where he stood.

That was why he failed to be elected a delegate to the national Congress in 1809. Men knew too well where he stood on the slavery issue, and by 1809 he was standing with the minority. Thomas Randolph refused to compromise. He believed in slavery as he believed in God, and he would not sacrifice his principles for personal gain.

"I still favor the introduction of slavery into Indiana," he told his constituents, "but I believe it is the imperative duty of a representative to be controlled by the wishes of his constituents. If a majority of the people of this territory are opposed to slavery, I shall feel compelled to vote against it."

Such honesty makes voters distrust a politician.

Even so, Thomas Randolph had a good chance of election. General James Dill and Captain Samuel Vance were the political bosses of Dearborn County. Dill was an Irishman who had a smooth tongue and wore a white flannel suit in the summer, with a flower in his lapel. Vance was the clerk of the courts and controlled the patronage of the county. Thomas Randolph was related to both Dill and Vance by his second marriage.

But Thomas Randolph was of the Pocahontas blood. He was a Virginia aristocrat. When he went to a house-raising or a husking bee, he tried his best to mingle affably with people like George Boone and John Payne; but he could never make himself lend a hand in their labors. Manual work, in his opinion, was for niggers. Standing by and watching his opponent, Jonathan Jennings, pitch in and help, Thomas Randolph could almost see his votes melting away. But he could not prevent them. It was all right for Jonathan Jennings to work with his hands if he wanted to. He came from Pennsylvania. But Thomas Randolph could not see how manual strength and dexterity qualified a man for the legislature. His own knowledge of national and international affairs was far superior to Jonathan Jennings's. He hoped that the voters would realize that when they went to the polls.

But his hopes were in vain. His superior talents ran second to Jennings's strong, friendly, democratic hands. Even Dill and Vance and Governor Harrison himself were of no avail against them. Thomas Randolph lost the territory by twenty-six votes.

He contested the election, naturally: it was so close. But Congress voted Jonathan Jennings in. Then Thomas Randolph accepted his defeat as a gentleman should.

When his opponents failed to accept their victory as gentlemen should, however, and gloated in scurrilous, anonymous letters in the *Western Sun*, Thomas Randolph was driven to action. He asked the editor, Elihu Stout, for the names of the letter writers, and then invited them to cross the Wabash with him and partake of his company and the amusement he wished to afford them.

That, of course, meant a choice of pistols or swords.

The first man Thomas Ranholph challenged was one Dr. McNamee. Unfortunately, Dr. McNamee was a Quaker and, instead of accepting the challenge, he had Thomas Randolph arrested and put under bonds to keep the peace.

Already, in Indiana, men like Thomas Randolph had become an anachronism.

Of this story, there is left only one more valiant and frustrated act. It was the last act of his life and it can be told briefly. When Governor Harrison set out on his campaign against Tecumseh's brother, the Prophet, Thomas Randolph, who had once been the attorney general of Indiana Territory, enlisted as a private. He was felled at Tippecanoe by an Indian bullet, and his friend, the governor, buried him on the field.

31

Pennsylvanian

THERE was a very beautiful young lady over in Charlestown, Indiana, named Anna Hay. Furthermore, in Charlestown the sentiment was against slavery. A young lawyer who wanted to get ahead and who could not open his mouth without talking free soil and even abolition would do much better there than in Vincennes, which was dominated by men like Governor Harrison and Thomas Randolph.

These were the considerations that made one young man pack all his worldly goods into his saddlebags, mount his horse, and prepare to ride away to Charlestown.

There were a few men in Vincennes who agreed with the young man on the slavery issue, however, and they came to tell him good-bye.

"When you get to Clark County," one of them called after him, "look us up a good candidate for Congress!"

The young man wheeled his horse about and came back.

"Why wouldn't I do?"

That was Jonathan Jennings at the age of twenty-five in the year 1809. He was a pleasing young man of medium height, with blue eyes, fair complexion, and sandy hair. He had come to Indiana from Pennsylvania, although he was a native of New Jersey. His father was a Presbyterian preacher, and both his parents had degrees in medicine. Jonathan Jennings himself studied in the Presbyterian school at Cannonsburg, Pennsylvania, and later read law and was admitted to the bar in Vincennes. He had been brought up to believe that slavery was wrong; and his antislavery convictions were as much an essential part of him as proslavery convictions were a part of Thomas Randolph.

When Jonathan Jennings asked his friends why he would not do as a candidate for Congress, they were surprised; but they found themselves immediately nodding their heads. Come to think of it, he would do! He was the very man!

So Jonathan Jennings rode to Charlestown, Indiana, married the beautiful young lady named Anna Hay, announced himself a candidate for Congress in opposition to Thomas Randolph, made the unequivocal statement that there should be no slavery in Indiana, and set out to get himself elected.

Knox County was hopeless: Harrison dominated it. Dearborn County seemed as good as lost: Randolph's relatives, Dill and Vance, were in power there. But the Whitewater country was settled now by Quakers from the South who had fled slave territory because they hated it, by many newcomers, like John Payne, from New York, and by others from New Jersey and Pennsylvania: Jonathan Jennings could count on them.

Jonathan Jennings could count on himself too. His Presbyterian training had taught him to do that. Let them call him "a beardless boy" and "a cold potato." He was not ashamed to strip off his coat and help roll logs and throw the maul or pitch quoits. He could take an ax and carry up a corner of a log house with any man. With a scythe, he could keep ahead of a dozen mowers.

"Wherever Jennings goes, he draws all men," General Dill wrote lugubriously to his friend, Thomas Randolph, on the eve of the election.

And so he did. He drew twenty-six more votes than Randolph in Indiana Territory and went to Congress at the age of twenty-five.

But that was not the end. Two years later, Jonathan Jennings increased his lead when he beat Randolph again. Then the proslavery party set Waller Taylor against him; but Waller Taylor, too, went down. In 1814, one more Virginian—Judge Elijah Sparks—tried to dislodge Jonathan Jennings from office. But, by that time, elections were child's play for Jonathan Jennings. He could have outrun Elijah Sparks with both hands tied behind him and one leg chained to a stump!

When his fourth term expired, there were more important things for Jonathan Jennings to do than to run for a seat in Congress. It was 1816. Indiana was to have a constitutional convention to decide whether it was ready to become a state. More important to Jonathan Jennings than the affairs of the nation, which Thomas Randolph had understood so well, were the affairs of Indiana. He announced himself a candidate to become a delegate to the state convention.

Men like Randolph and Harrison and Taylor had not worked in vain in the cause of slavery. The Wabash shores were thickly populated by men who owned and naturally favored the owning of slaves. In the eastern part of the territory, the sentiment was just as strong against the institution of slavery and these antislavery men were in the majority; but what the slaveowners along the Wabash lacked in numbers they made up in wealth and political genius.

That was why Jonathan Jennings came back to win a seat in the state convention. The doctrine upon which he had been reared by his Presbyterian father and mother needed his talents as it had never needed them before.

On a warm day in June—a day so warm that the delegates soon deserted the limestone statehouse in Corydon, Indiana, the new capital, for the shade of an elm tree at the edge of town—the battle began. James Dill was there in his white flannels and with a flower in his lapel. James Noble, who was later to become the state's first senator, was there also, and Benjamin Parke, as violent and vindictive as ever. David Robb of Gibson was there with Frederick Rapp, the adopted son of old Father Rapp of the Harmonists in Posey. William Hendricks was there, too, another product of the Cannonsburg Presbyterian school, who six years later was to be elected governor of the new state, polling exactly 18,340 of the 18,340 votes cast! Only William Henry Harrison and Thomas Randolph, of all the men who had fought the battle of slavery in Indiana, were absent. Harrison had returned to Ohio, yielding his post to Thomas Posey, another ardent proslavery man. Thomas Randolph lay buried at Tippecanoe.

There were many articles to be considered for the new constitution, of course; but there was one that took precedence above all others:

"There shall be neither slavery nor involuntary servitude in this state."

In the sweltering heat, the delegates wrangled and

argued and plotted and delivered orations for three weeks, while the people waited for news of their fate.

With Jonathan Jennings in the chair, the cause of slavery seemed like a lost cause from the start. But there are several ways to skin a cat, and John Johnson, a Virginian, knew all of them.

"Gentlemen," he said suavely, "we have adopted a clause which reads: 'No alteration of this constitution shall ever take place.' Now, I move that it be amended to read: *It is the opinion of this convention* that no alteration of this constitution *ought* ever to take place.' "

The delegates wondered why John Johnson bothered to make such an insignificant suggestion. It seemed innocent enough, and they were on the point of adopting it as a gesture of goodwill toward the defeated forces of slavery, when Jonathan Jennings pointed out that the amended wording would leave the slavery issue open, even though slaves were prohibited by the constitution. *"In the opinion of this convention"* and *"ought . . ."* Did the delegates not see that others after them might hold other opinions?

Defeated in this ruse, John Johnson was again on his feet.

"Let us strike out the words 'involuntary servitude,' gentlemen. If we prohibit slavery, they are unnecessary."

But that was too obvious. Jonathan Jennings did not have to point out to the delegates that the indenture of servants might very easily become slavery without being called slavery. The remonstrance was so noisy that he did not even have to call for a vote.

"There shall be neither slavery nor involuntary servitude in this state."

The wording stood, and on the twenty-ninth of

June, 1816, a few months before a family named Lincoln moved into Indiana from Kentucky, the convention announced to the world that Indiana had a state constitution and she had come in free.

"She has come in free! She has come in free!"

For months thereafter, the word rang through the streets of the villages of Indiana, from Evansville to Fort Wayne, from Vevay to Terre Haute. It was the phrase with which men greeted each other in the forests, the song children sang about the cabins, the theme of Hoosier talk along the Wabash from its source, where the news was received with rejoicing, to its mouth, where men heard it with a frown.

"She has come in free!"

Jonathan Jennings became the first governor of the new state and, later, served eight more years in the national Congress. But the journey he undertook at twenty-five with that question, "Why wouldn't I do?" never won him more enduring honor than that which he earned in the little town of Corydon when he set the people of the Wabash shouting:

"She has come in free!"

32

Yankee

IN THE 1820's, the high windows of the Harrison mansion stared blankly down at the Wabash. The house was deserted and falling into ruin. Rats gnawed at the paneling in the empty, oval parlor where once William Henry Harrison, Waller Taylor, and Thomas Randolph discussed politics, women, tobacco, and literature over a bowl of punch. On the lawn, where the governor had conferred with Tecumseh and fêted the Virginia ladies and gentlemen of his acquaintance, the grass grew high and rank, and great dead branches dangled from the elm and locust trees, broken by the storms of many summers.

In the 1820's, the charm of the Vincennes of French days was fast fading, too. The neat, whitewashed, and verandaed houses were falling into decay and rapidly disappearing. Around the few that remained, clustered the hastily constructed log cabins of new settlers and, here and there, the pretentious brick houses of the newly rich. In the center of the town, there was a new brick schoolhouse, but it was empty, for want of a master; and, on the bank of the Wabash, there was a modern steam mill, equipped to grind corn, saw timber, and card wool and cotton, but it, too, stood idle, for want of trade.

Vincennes was not dying, however. It was only

changing. Having lost—first to Corydon and then to Indianapolis—its aristocratic position as capital of the country, it was adjusting itself to the coarser, if more virile role of a transportation center and national crossroads. There was an atmosphere of newness and opportunism in the hundred-year-old town.

Evidence of the new life was most apparent on the water front where flatboatmen and keelboatmen fought noisily for positions to take aboard the products of the freshly cleared lands. Traders bought corn from the farmers of the Wabash valley at harvesttime for twenty-five cents a bushel, paid the rivermen another quarter for freight in the spring, and sold the grain in New Orleans for seventy-five cents or a dollar. For wheat, they paid slightly more and reaped still better profits. But corn and wheat were not the only cargoes that the rivermen fought for. Corn ferments and makes strong whisky. The Wabash country is also good hog country, and hogs make pork and lard. A typical cargo list for a single flatboat in 1823 reads as follows:

"39 kegs of lard; 100 kegs of butter; 680 bushels of corn and wheat; 40 barrels of whisky; 88 barrels of flour; 103 barrels of pork; 32 oxen; and 16 hogs."

Besides the keelboats and flatboats, an occasional steamboat nosed in under the hill that once was crowned by George Rogers Clark's fort. The *Florence* was the first to appear on the Wabash, clumsily paddling her way against the river's current as far as Terre Haute in 1823; and after her came the *Highlander* and the *Tippecanoe*. These boats brought from New Orleans such staples as salt, sugar, coffee, and tea, as well as the frills and furbelows that the Wabash folk were beginning to fancy in addition to their everyday homespun.

The other evidence of the change taking place in Vincennes was the size and prosperity of her two taverns, the better of which was a large, two-story, frame building at the corner of Second and Perry streets. Its public room and wide porches swarmed with guests—river pilots and steamboat captains in elegant clothes; fantastic keelboatmen; gamblers; preachers; hunters and traders in coonskin caps and deerskin moccasins; politicians; peddlers; circuit-riding lawyers; and curious, but slightly intimidated, visiting Englishmen. In the public room and on the porches, they boasted and gossiped and bargained and cursed and argued and told tall stories, drinking Gargantuan quantities of white, Wabash corn and spattering the cedar shavings on the floor with streams of brown, Wabash tobacco juice.

To Colonel Hyacinthe Lasselle, the innkeeper, their custom meant a fortune and many friends. To the colonel's wife, it meant fashionable clothes and social prominence, but also ceaseless toil and responsibility and perhaps frequent nostalgic memories of the days when she was Julie Busseron and led the happy, carefree life of a French belle in the comfortable, puncheon home of her father, Major François Busseron.

In most of its aspects, this was a different Vincennes from the Vincennes of Major Busseron and Father Gibault, or even of William Henry Harrison. But in one aspect it was the same. In spite of the success of Jonathan Jennings at Corydon ten years before, the labor on the water front and in the two taverns was still largely slave labor. As late as 1830, a local census gave Vincennes thirty-two slaves.

One of these chattels of former days, held in defiance of the constitution that brought the state in free, was the Lasselles' Polly. Polly was a mulatto girl whom Hyacinthe Lasselle inherited from his uncle Antoine. She was neat, polite, and intelligent; and Hyacinthe and Julie Lasselle treated her as a member of the family. But she was none the less a slave.

Her bondage made little difference to Polly. She was well housed and well fed. Her work was not heavy. She loved her master and mistress as a father and mother. Jonathan Jennings's constitution meant nothing to her. She had no desire to be free. She was very happy with things as they were.

But in the town of Washington, Indiana, near by, there was a man who was very unhappy every time he thought of Polly's condition. His name was Amory Kinney and he came from Vermont. In Vermont, black people were as good as white people. Furthermore, law was law. Amory Kinney had read law with Justice Samuel Nelson, later of the United States Supreme Court, and he respected what he knew almost as much as he respected what he believed. The law said that the Lasselles' Polly was free. It was wrong of the Lasselles to hold her, even with her consent.

Amory Kinney lived in Washington but his law practice was in Vincennes. When he came to the city, he stayed at the Lasselle Tavern. It hurt him to see Polly in illegal bondage there, but there was no choice for him but to see her. At the other tavern, he would have seen other Negro slaves, and, anyhow, the Lasselle house was the more comfortable of the two. But there was something in Amory Kinney's blood that made him try to make amends for his compromise with principles. If he was going to accept the services of a slave in a free country, he had to do something to ease his conscience. So, when he entered the public room of the tavern, he went out of his way to be kind to Polly, treating her with ostentatious respect and deference. You might have thought that Polly was Madame Lasselle herself.

"Who is that nigger lover?" an elegant gentleman of Virginia ancestry would ask another at the bar.

"Oh, he's one of those new Yankees that are coming into the country."

"Well, we ought to ride him out on a rail!"

"Now, lookie here, you gentlemen . . ."

It was the drawl of a Kentuckian beside them, breaking in over the cultured, though ominous, tones of their Virginia voices. The Kentuckian pushed back his coonskin cap and glowered at them. He was in town to sell his hogs and buy a gallon or two of blue ruin. Most of the blue ruin was already inside him.

"Now, lookie here, you gentlemen! This is free soil we're on, an' if a feller wants to cotton up to a coon, they ain't nothin' kin stop him. I ain't no nigger lover myownself, but I come up from Kaintuck an' settled in Indianny to git shut of slavery, an' I don't want to hear no talk out of you all about ridin' law-abidin' citizens on a rail!"

The gentlemen of Virginia blood reached for their pistols, and then, on second thought, moved quietly on down the bar, leaving the Kentuckian to deliver his oration to empty air. And, all the while, Amory Kinney sipped his rum in silence and thought his own thoughts and minded his own business, Yankee fashion; and when Polly thanked him for the shinplasters he shoved across the counter in payment for his drink, he said, "You're welcome," just as if she were white.

Amory Kinney had no ulterior motives, no designs on Polly. He was a distinguished lawyer and a man of excellent character. It was only Polly's illegal position in the Lasselle house that made him go out of his way to be kind to her. He had to make amends somehow to his Puritan conscience for witnessing a wrong without attempting to right it. But, as Amory Kinney rode back and forth between Washington and Vincennes, he thought more and more about Polly, until finally he realized that merely being kind to her was not enough. He could not wait for the wrong gradually to right itself in this new and changing country; he would have to right it himself.

So he talked the matter over with his friend, John W. Osborn, an Englishman who had fought in the American army during the War of 1812 because he was convinced of the justice of the American cause. John W. Osborn was not a lawyer, but he had money; and since Amory Kinney was a Yankee, it was only natural that he should talk with a man with money before he launched a crusade. With the promise of Osborn's support, Amory Kinney next called upon two fellow lawyers: Moses Tabbs, a Marylander, and George MacDonald, a wise old gentleman from New Jersey. Tabbs and MacDonald were quite ready to join Amory Kinney in Polly's behalf.

Habeas corpus proceedings were instituted against Hyacinthe Lasselle, and he was haled into court, where Amory Kinney insisted that Polly was as free as the judge himself. Hyacinthe Lasselle answered that Polly was his slave by purchase before the Indiana state constitution was adopted and, as such, she should remain his slave until either he or she died. That sounded like good sense to the court, and the case was dismissed.

But the court could not dismiss a man like Amory Kinney. He was a Vermont Yankee and he had, after long deliberation, decided upon action. A few weeks later there was a murmur of surprise in the public room of the Lasselle tavern when the news came that Polly's case was to be carried to the supreme court at Indianapolis. Men were not familiar with Vermont Yankees in Indiana at that time.

"What kind of a feller is this Amory Kinney?" the drinkers asked each other.

"Oh, him! Why, he's one of these new Yankees that's a-comin' into the country these days."

"Nigger lover?"

"Must be. Can't see no other reason why a feller'd put himself to so much trouble over a darkie."

"Abolitionist?"

" 'Twouldn't surprise me. Yankee, you know."

When the supreme court decided that Amory Kinney was right and Polly was free, the drinkers in Lasselle's public room were speechless. They were hornswoggled!

For a time, Hyacinthe Lasselle considered appealing Polly's case to the Supreme Court of the United States; but finally he gave up the idea, bought Polly a new dress, instead, and sent her off to her relatives in St. Louis, where she reckoned she might be happy. There was no beating a man like Amory Kinney, and Hyacinthe Lasselle knew it.

After that, Amory Kinney's rum tasted much better in Lasselle's public room—even though the atmosphere was sharply hostile; even though Polly returned from St. Louis eventually and greeted her former master and mistress with great joy and affection; even though, when she served Amory after her return, she gave him the puzzled and injured look of a sick child that has been allowed to eat too much candy.

Yes, Amory Kinney's rum tasted much, much better. By winning Polly's freedom, even though she did not want it, he had removed all legal basis from the continuance of slavery in Indiana. His Yankee conscience was clear.

33

Hoosier

THESE were the men who settled the Wabash
country—Kentuckians, New Yorkers, Pennsylvanians,
interloping opportunists with no tradition behind them,
Virginians, and ultimately Yankees—and decided that
Wabash soil should be free.

They were not always divided among themselves
according to their backgrounds. Many of the Southerners
came to Indiana because they found the institution of
slavery abhorrent; many of the Northerners, like Benjamin Parke, worked for the introduction of slavery into
the state. Strangely enough, some of the best Democrats,
like James Whitcomb, who was elected governor in 1843
and 1846, were from New England, while some of the
ablest Republicans, like Abraham Lincoln, were from the
South. Perhaps that is why all Hoosiers are politicians at
heart: their pioneer ancestors so often were members of
fighting political minorities in the regions whence they
migrated.

These were the ingredients poured into the Wabash
melting pot in pioneer days. The slavery issue was not
settled by them with the constitution of 1816, nor even
with the case of the Lasselles' Polly. There were still three
slaves in the state as late as 1840, and Article XIII of the

new constitution of 1851 excluded the immigration of Negroes into Indiana. Even during the war of 1861-1865, the Wabash was a political, if not a military, battleground. But from these ingredients, after a half century, was ultimately distilled the Hoosier.

Physically, the Hoosier is likely to be tall and rather lean. At one time, there was no taller civilized man in the world. Dr. B. A. Gould of the United States Sanitary Service, studying statistics of the Civil War, discovered that "the Indiana men are the tallest of all the natives of the United States, and these latter are the tallest of all civilized countries." The Hoosier's height was probably the result of his diet; for the cereals of the north central states are richer in proteids and show a larger number of heat units than the cereals of any other region of the world. In recent years, however, with standardized breakfast foods on every table and the consumption of corn, wheat, and rye no longer limited to the region in which they are grown, the Hoosier has lost the distinction of unequaled height.

The character of the Hoosier is not easy to describe, for he is a compound of many contradictory qualities inherited from both his southern and his Yankee ancestors.

His friendliness and hospitality, however, are universally recognizable. He is easy to meet and quite ready to talk about himself. His eagerness to share his possessions as well as his private life sometimes appears naïve to the outsider accustomed to the self-protective reticence and suspicion of more thickly populated regions. But the Hoosier is not naïve. He inherits his tradition of cordiality from lonely pioneer days when every stranger was at once a welcome friend and a helpless supplicant; yet, from those same early days, he inherits a talent for quick and accurate appraisal of character. You may think that the Hoosier lays himself wide open on short acquaintance; but the chances are that he knows all there is to know about you long before he tells you a single significant thing about himself. If you think he is an easy mark, just try to skin him once—and see what happens!

The Hoosier is sentimental. His poetry and his flourishing fraternal societies, as well as his speech, are proof of that. And, in such a mellow and generous land as his, it is inevitable that he should be sentimental. But he is humorous also, and over his most saccharine effusions he is likely to sprinkle the salt of shrewd wit. Alone in his isolated cabin, the pioneer had to fool himself to keep from going crazy; but he also had to know when he was being fooled, in order to stay alive.

The Hoosier is fond of good living. No man eats more heartily than he, and no man has better food to eat. Anyone who has put his feet under a Hoosier table will agree. Fried chicken such as can be found nowhere else, even in the South; perch and pickerel and fiddler catfish in a thick crust of brown batter; hickory barbecue that must be eaten out-of-doors to be fully appreciated; rich burgoo; buttered hominy; hot, flaky biscuits; dry, crisp porkchops; well-seasoned succotash stewed in rich, peppery juice; succulent roasting ears; buckwheat cakes with thick sorghum molasses; and blackberry "mountain pie" under a high crust of golden meringue—they specialize in these dishes in Indiana. And everyone who has ever tasted them comes back for more.

The Hoosier is many other things: shrewd; industrious; quick-tempered; ambitious; conservative in politics, but willing to experiment; emotional in religion; and inordinately proud of his land. He is no longer of pure pioneer stock. Since the state was founded, there has been a good admixture of Irish and German blood in his veins. In some sections of the state, the Pole and the Italian have appeared in appreciable numbers. But it is because of these additions to his family, and not in spite of them, that the Hoosier is sometimes called "the typical American"; for he has somehow managed to Hoosierize them all.

As for the origin of the name "Hoosier"—no one is quite sure. Some have tried to trace it to the pioneer greeting from cabin windows when strangers knocked at night. The pioneer asked who was there, and from his question the word "Hoosier" was developed. But that explanation is rather farfetched; for the similarity between "Who's *thar?*" and "*Hoo*sier" is very faint. Others have discovered that a company of hussars once made a nuisance of themselves in Kentucky and the word "hussar," or "husher," was thereafter applied to all boisterous and objectionable outsiders, its application eventually being limited to the hard-drinking and rowdy Indiana men across the river. But such an isolated and largely hypothetical source is not satisfying.

Jacob Piatt Dunn, the historian, seems to know more about it than anyone else. He says that "hoosier" was a slang word once used in the South to denote a "jay" or "hayseed." It came originally from England, where "hoose" is still the common name for a disease of calves, known here as strongylus micrurius, which "causes their hair to turn back and gives them a wild, staring look." Any boy who has worn a stocking cap, the modern equivalent of the coonskin, will understand the condition of the average Indiana pioneer's hair; and any man who has experimented with the kind of Indiana "corn" that is preserved in jugs can explain the "wild, staring look."

Whatever its origin, "Hoosier" is now the name for all Indiana folk alike, of Yankee or of southern stock or of more recent European background—and they all respond to it proudly.

PART SIX

Abe Lincoln: 1816-1830

34

"This-here Is Mighty Fine"

"PAPPY, air we still in Indianny?"

The dark, thin boy leaned against a beechtree trunk that was as broad as the side of a cabin and wiped his knife blade on the bark. He had pushed back his coonskin cap, and, below a shock of black hair, his gray eyes were apprehensive. This was the afternoon of their third day in the wilderness. The time before that—the time elapsed since they left the cabin on Knob Creek in Kentucky—he could no longer measure. But he knew that three days had passed since they borrowed the oxen and sled at Posey's farm on the Indiana side of the river and began to cut their way through the spicewood and sumac and matted grapevines. It seemed to him that surely they were lost.

In Kentucky, there had been roads to follow and frequent cabins where they could ask for water and inquire about the trail. In Kentucky, they had ridden horses—he and his father on one, his mother and sister on the other. But the roads and the cabins and the horses had been left behind in Kentucky. Ever since they set out from Posey's Indiana farm, there had been nothing but this trackless, uninhabited tangle of trees and vines—endless columns of trees, standing so close together that the dead ones could not fall to the earth but only leaned, like wounded soldiers, in the arms of those about them; impenetrable vines that hung, like cloaks, from the highest branches or grew so rank upon the ground that the boy could have lost himself among them.

"Air you shore, pappy?"

He waited anxiously for his father's answer, stabbing the knife into the tree.

It was not that he was impatient or tired of the journey. But, in his boy's way, he was beginning to worry. The man named Jesse Hoskins, who had set out from Posey's to guide them, had turned back yesterday. They were on their own now, in the new land.

"Pappy, air you shore?"

Pappy straightened up over the young poplar he had just felled and, leaning his ax against his leg, blew warm breath on his big, red hands. Above them, he winked at the woman who sat in the ox-sled with the boy's sister.

"You cain't be shore of nothin' in this-here world, son," he said solemnly. "An' once a Linkern plunges into somep'n, they ain't nobody kin tell whar he's a-goin' to come out at."

The boy was thoughtful for a moment. Then he shrugged. After all, he did not care much where they came out at. The journey could go on forever, as far as he was concerned, as long as his father and mother and sister were there in the sled at night for him to snuggle against while he gazed, wide-eyed, at the stars festooning the tops of the trees and dreamed for one brief moment before he surrendered to a sleep too deep for dreams. The days, too, would take care of themselves, as long as his father and mother and sister were there. He could go on forever cutting away small vines with his knife, shouting at the stubborn oxen like his father, and stopping from time to time to turn a cart wheel or hang from low branches by his knees or make strange noises in his throat just to hear his mother's laughter and his sister's admiring squeals. If his pappy was lost, then they were all lost together—and what did it matter?

"Well," he said, "maybe we'll come out at one of them-air big lakes up north I've heared about, an' 'en we kin make us a boat."

The man laughed, and the woman in the sled smiled down at them.

"Quit a-plaguin' the boy, Tom," she said gently to her husband; and then she turned to her son. "We're still in Indianny, Abe. It's a big state—bigger'n all outdoors, purt'near. Don't you worry about us a-gittin' lost."

Tom grew serious and reassuring.

"No, son. Pigeon Crick ain't fur away now, an' we'll be thar afore you know it."

Within an hour they were there. They came out of the forest suddenly upon a low hill where the undergrowth was not so thick and the trees grew sparsely. Tom Lincoln's ax marks were still clean and white in some of them, and there were the piles of brush he had gathered a month before, laying out his claim.

"Thar she is!" he said proudly. "Now, what did I tell you?"

Without answering, Abe dashed forward and stood at the top of the hill. It was not a high hill, and the gray, winter forest rose like a mist from the surrounding swamps. But Abe did not need a view. With an inward eye, he created at once the hills that rolled away southward toward the river and the deep and solemn wilderness toward the north, and he peopled them with the deer and bear and possum and panther that were there in great numbers, and with Indians, too, who were, actually, no longer there.

This, then, was what they had traveled so many miles for—this vast and unexplored world, so vague and exciting in the winter shadows! This was his new home! Thrusting out his narrow chest, he claimed the land for the kingdom of boyhood.

Then, as he turned to call his sister to share the discovery with him, the day suddenly darkened and the whole sky turned black and was filled with the beating of wings. Startled, he shouted to his father above the din.

"What is it?"

Tom Lincoln, watching the birds with a hunter's calculating eye, waited until they passed and the white daylight once more flooded down upon his weather-beaten face.

"Pigeons," he said then; and, pointing to small branches snapped at the trunks of the trees and hanging broken and scarred, he added: "That's what they do when they roost at night. They's so plaguey many of 'em!"

But there was no time for talk. The afternoon was advancing, and the raw chill of December night was already in the air. In another moment, Tom was clearing ground and giving orders to his son, while his wife and daughter unloaded the sled of its light burden of bedding and pots and pans.

Between two convenient trees, fourteen feet apart, Tom Lincoln laid a pole and from it stretched the framework of a slanting roof to two forked stakes driven firmly into the ground. That done, he began to cut more poles, and Abe dragged them to the clearing and helped lay up the walls between the trees and at the ends of the shelter. Last came the thatching of the roof with leaves and brush, and then a fire was laid and lighted before the open face of the camp; for it was already long past night-fall and supper was overdue.

"This-here'll keep the snow offen us till I kin git round to fixin' up somep'n better," Tom said.

They were squatting about the fire, eating corn-dodgers. As his father spoke, Abe felt his mother's hand contract involuntarily over his own. Nancy Hanks Lincoln had lived with Tom Lincoln for ten years. Nancy Hanks Lincoln knew that many months—perhaps the whole winter—would slip by before her husband would "git round to fixin' up somep'n better." But Abe under-stood nothing of his mother's anxiety. To him, the little, makeshift, three-sided hut of poles and brush was as good as a castle.

"This-here'll do," Tom said again.

"This-here is mighty fine," Abe agreed.

35

A World Is Made

ABE was splitting firewood in front of the camp. It was only the second day after their arrival in Indiana, but already Tom Lincoln had found an excuse to go off and leave to his wife and children the burden of getting settled in the new home. Abe swung the big ax over his head and sank it into the logs with a sharp and accurate "plunk" that punctuated the murmur of his mother's and sister's voices in the hut. From time to time, he would stop and blow on his red hands or whistle a little tune off key to catch his breath; and it was during one of these pauses that he saw a flock of wild turkeys at the edge of the clearing only a few yards away. At once, he dropped the ax and ran quickly and silently into the shelter.

"Mammy, give me the gun!" he whispered.

It was his pappy's second rifle—a big gun, too big for a boy of seven to handle; but his mother took it down, loaded it, and handed it to him.

"Jest be keerful, Abe," was all Nancy Hanks Lincoln said.

Laboriously and importantly, Abe pushed the long, heavy barrel through a crack between the poles and, without taking aim, pulled the trigger. The next thing

he knew, he was sprawled on the earthen floor in the middle of the hut and his mother was standing over him
laughing, while, behind her, Sally was dancing in the glee-
ful manner of elder sisters who must somehow compen-
sate for their sex.

Abe got up, rubbing his shoulder and grinning
sheepishly.

"I reckon you must 'a' loaded 'er backerds,
mammy!" he said.

Out in the clearing, the flock of turkeys was gone,
but Abe could see from the doorway a little heap of
feathers. His heart leaped. He had hit one! In an instant
he was dashing joyfully to the spot at the edge of the
clearing where the dead bird lay.

The bronze feathers were still quivering, and a tiny
stream of blood trickled across the snow from the young
turkey's breast. Abe stood still, unable to move, the joy
suddenly gone out of him. The bird was a painfully beautiful and delicate thing, lying in the snow; and he wanted
only to restore its life and freedom. But there was nothing
he could do. He remained where he was, motionless, unable even to look away until he saw that the last, faint
quivering of the gold and amber feathers had ceased.
Then, without touching the turkey, he turned and
walked, heavy-footed and sick, back to the woodpile.

"Did you hit anything, Abe?"

It was his sister—as ready now to admire as she had
been to gloat.

Without looking at her, Abe nodded.

"Whar is it, then?"

He jerked his head in the direction of the forest.

"Over yander."

Sally bent down and tried to look into his eyes, but he evaded her.

"Why didn't you fetch it back?"

Without warning, the threatening tears flooded his eyes and his voice rose, harsh and angry.

"If you want it, you kin git it fur yerself!" he cried; and, turning, he ran blindly into the forest where she could not see him.

He never hunted again. From that time on, he always grew sick at the sight of anything trapped or cornered or defeated. He learned to fight. He had to. It was not long till they knew him in Spencer County as a dangerous antagonist. He could lick anybody his own size for miles around—and, within a few years, there wasn't anyone else in the county his own size! But he fought only when he had to, or when he saw that a fight was the only means of restoring peace.

But hunting and fighting were not the only outlets for a Hoosier boy's energies in those days any more than they are now. Time was never heavy on Abe's hands. Six acres of ground were cleared that winter round the Lincoln camp, and, when spring came, there was plenty of plowing and planting and hoeing to be done. Best of all, though, during that first year, was the exciting process of getting acquainted—the social adventure that most delights a Hoosier's heart.

"Howdy, mister."

"Why, howdy, son! What's yer name?"

"Abe Linkern."

"Then you must be that new boy I heared tell about."

"I reckon maybe I am. I live over in that-air new

clearin' near Pigeon Crick with my mammy an' pappy an' sis. We come from Kaintuck."

"Well, you ain't much different 'n most, then. My name's Grigsby."

"Seems to be a heap o' Grigsbys round these parts."

"They shore is now, ain't they? Quite a run of 'em, seems like."

"Well, I come to see if you all had any young'uns here my size, er if you had a book with pitchers in it. I cain't read yit, but I'm a-goin' to larn."

"Come to think of it, son, they *was* two er three young'uns 'bout yer size round this-here cabin, last time I counted. I reckon you'll find 'em out back sommers if you'll jest step around an' look."

"You ain't got no books, then?"

"Son, childern is a whole lot easier to git in these parts 'n books is, I'm afeared."

"Well, much obleeged to you. I'll go look fur them childern o' yourn. You all come an' see us sometime."

"Much obleeged to you, son. We'll do that, now."

So he met them—the Grigsbys and the Brooners and the Gentrys—everyone within the radius that his long, spindly legs allowed him.

"You seen that new Linkern boy from over 't Pigeon Crick?"

"Likely little feller, ain't he?"

"Smartest young'un I've laid eyes on in a blue moon."

"Feller told me he could outwrassle any boy in the whole county."

"Shore kin, now! An' outargufy 'em, too! You'd ought to git him to talkin' sometime. Land o' Goshen, you never heard the like!"

Spring came to southwestern Indiana and brought the lady-slipper and the wild honeysuckle, the blossom of the haw and wild plum and crabapple, and the song of the bluebird and the mockingbird; and Abe Lincoln knew all the hills and creeks and forests from Gentryville to Rockport and from Boonville to Anderson's Creek Ferry, and the folks who lived thereabouts.

And then came summer, with its long, hot, lazy days under the deep and mellow Hoosier sky, and Abe had friends to play with. Those were days of swimming in the creek and fishing for mud cat, of playing Andy-over and run sheepy run and the game of Indian in the tall ironweed, or just long, empty days of lying under a willow tree, chewing sourgrass or slippery elm and wriggling bare toes in the cooling breeze.

By this time, Abe had pets as well as friends—a pet cat and a pet pig, a set of turtles for swapping, and a June bug on a string. He had a pet crow, too, that could talk if only his pappy would take the time to split its tongue. And, of course, he had a pet coon, with rings around its tail.

"Whar'd you git him at, Abe?"

"Oh, I don't know. I jest found him, like, I guess."

"Aw, come on, Abe! Whar'd you git him at?"

Stooping, Abe takes the coon's little, black hand and strokes it gently. It is softer than anything he has ever touched before, and already the coon has learned to trust him and not draw away.

"Come on, Abe! Tell me how you got him. I won't tell nobody. Honest!"

Abe looks up at his friend and grins. There is plenty of the selfishness of the "keep" in Abe, but the selfishness of the "git" is something he has never known. If there is another coon to be had, he will help his friend to catch it. He stands up; and then, because he likes a little mystery, he only says, "Foller me," and starts off down the road.

He walks slowly at first, not only to prolong the suspense and tease his friend, but also because he likes the feel of the warm, deep dust seeping up between his naked toes. But when he turns off the road, he slithers quickly through the powdery jungle of dog fennel and the tumble, Jimson, and iron weed, until, at last, he and his friend are near the creek.

Abe raises his hand.

"S-h-h!" he says.

Silently, he bends the weeds and saplings down and peers through the thick tangle toward the creekbank. His friend is behind him, watching over his shoulder, and all at once, simultaneously, the two boys are stuffing their fists into their mouths to keep from laughing aloud. They have seen what they are after.

"He's a-goin' fishin'!" Abe whispers; and again they bend over in silent, agonizing laughter. For a coon that's a-goin' fishin' is about as comical a sight as any boy can ever hope to see.

There he is—old Mr. Coon—running along the bank, as solemn and intent and as spry as a little, old man. He is inspecting crawfish chimneys; and, when he finds one that suits him, he pushes it over and, with great deliberation, runs his arm down into the hole. At once, he begins a rhythmical pump-pump-pump, all the while looking off into space with the abstracted and innocent expression of a small boy swiping cookies from the jar behind his mother's back. Then his serious, little face suddenly brightens. You can almost imagine he is smiling. His hand has touched something in the hole and, in another moment, he has it out on the ground—a succulent crawfish.

"Now, watch him!" Abe whispers. "He always warshes it afore he eats it."

And, sure enough, away the fisherman canters to the water's edge with his crawfish and sets to washing it, in his droll way, just as a washerwoman scrubs clothes between her hands.

This is too much for Abe and his friend. They burst into uproarious laughter, frightening the coon. The coon scampers away and climbs a tree, where he disappears into a hole in the trunk.

Abe's friend is suddenly sober.

"He's got away, Abe!"

Abe shakes his head, still laughing.

"Naw, we've got him fur shore now! You foller me."

He is already running toward the tree, peeling off his deerskin shirt. He ties the shirt about the tree trunk, with a good, firm knot of the sleeves. Then he turns to his friend.

"Now, you git yer pappy to come an' chop down that-air tree an' you've got yerself a coon. He won't cross that shirt. You kin count on that. He'll still be thar tomorrow, er even the next day."

"I'm much obleeged to you, Abe," the boy says.

"Aw, 'tain't nothin'! 'Tain't nothin' at all!"

That was summer.

In the early fall came the harvest and the corn-shucking and quilting bees; and when the corn was all shucked, there were adventurous trips to the mill seventeen miles away near Posey's farm.

" 'Tain't nothin' but a little-bitty hand-horse mill," Tom Lincoln would say contemptuously. "I reckon 'tain't worth makin' the trip fur."

"Aw, pappy!"

"Naw, sir! A feller kin eat the meal as fast as it's ground."

"But, great day, pappy, we ain't a-aimin' to eat it at the mill! We're a-goin' to fetch it back fur corn-dodgers fur this winter!"

Nancy Hanks Lincoln would hear the argument and come out into the clearing.

"Now, Tom!"

Then Tom would grin and wink at his wife and Nancy would rumple her son's black hair, looking out at the blue haze of autumn that was already settling on the hills.

"You jest rest easy, Abe. Of course, yer pappy's a-goin'. The winter will soon be here."

"You a-tellin' Abe to rest easy agin, Nancy? Why, that's about all the boy's done all summer, fur's I kin tell!"

But they went to the mill, and they came home by way of Rockport and Abe met a man named John Pitcher who, in the next dozen years, was to do as much for him as any man ever did in all his life, a man who was to lend him books and encourage him in his reading and speechifying.

That fall, Tom got around to "fixin' up somep'n better" than the little, open-faced camp, and he and Abe built a new house, a four-sided cabin this time. Old Thomas and Betsy Sparrow, who were Nancy Hanks Lincoln's uncle and aunt, but who were known as "gran'pappy" and "gran'mammy," came up from Ken-

"PAPPY, AIR W

"TILL IN INDIANNY?"

tucky to live in the open-faced camp, bringing Cousin
Dennis Hanks, who was seventeen and who, in later
years, always referred to his first Indiana home as "that
Darne Little half face camp."

That fall, there were rails to split—walnut and oak,
because they weathered the best—and logs to notch and
nuts to gather and hogs to butcher and cure. It was a
busy fall and the winter that followed was consequently
luxurious compared with the one that had gone before.
Abe celebrated his ninth birthday in the February of that
winter; and, as he thought about the two houses and the
six acres of cleared land, where hardly a year before there
had been only trees and brush, of the paths leading off
through the forest to the homes of nine new families in
the neighborhood and the ones who were already there
when he and his mother and father and sister arrived, and
as he looked at his mother and father and sister themselves, sitting before the fireplace, with a grease lamp
flickering from its curved handle above their heads, it
seemed to him that, in his one year in Indiana, he had witnessed the creation of a world.

36

A World Is Destroyed

But before another birthday came round to him, Abe Lincoln was to see his safe and comfortable, new world destroyed.

The tragedy came first only as a whispering in the late summer of 1818—a message or two brought through the shadows of the tall trees to the doors of the cabins on Little Pigeon Creek as swiftly and as silently as the wind of death itself. Abe watched his father lean across the rail fence before the cabin and talk to Peter Brooner, the hunter, to one of the Grigsbys, or perhaps to a buck-skin-clad "furriner" he had never seen before. Fearfully, he crept close and listened to the low and anxious voices above him.

"First the stock," the visitor would be saying; "three of his best heifers in one night. An' 'en the ol' woman herself come down with the same thing. Only a week an' she was gone . . ."

"The milksick . . ."

He heard Gran'mammy Sparrow whisper the word to his mother as she scraped the hoecake from the blade by the fireplace and laid it on the table.

". . . One of the Lamars the other day an' 'en that Roby boy. Didn't hold out a week, neither of 'em!"

"It starts with a coatin' on the tongue, they say."

"The milksick . . ."

"Ain't a yarb doctor in forty mile of here, I reckon."

"We'd be smart to git outen the country—back to Kaintuck maybe. . . ."

But they didn't "git." There was no place for them to "git" to, and, anyhow, their help was needed. So Abe and Sally were told to stay close to the cabin and not to play with any children who might come running through the woods, and for long days at a time both women were gone.

"The milksick . . ." the children would whisper to each other. "Miz Brooner's got it now, an' mammy's a-goin' to set with her."

"The milksick . . ."

"One of the Gentrys now . . ."

"It starts with a coatin' on yer tongue, an' you git cold . . . cold . . ."

"The oldest Turnham gal tuck down with it yestiddy, they say."

"The milksick . . ."

Nobody knew what it was or what to do for it. They only knew that it came without warning among the cattle and the people alike and took its victims quickly. They tried lobelia and they tried calomel, which were supposed to cure anything, but they did no good. They mixed a double handful of cherry-root bark, a double handful of yellow poplar-root bark, a double handful of sarsaparilla, a double handful of red sumac roots, and a handful of bitter root. They boiled them in two gallons of water until there was only a half gallon. Then they simmered it down to a pint and mixed in a gallon of hard cider and a couple of ounces of madder and drank it by the teacupful. That was a cure for yaller janders. It might take care of the milksick, too. But it didn't. They tried dewberry root and cranebill root and witch-hazel root. They tried brandy, when they could get it, and loaf sugar and forty-rod whisky. But nothing helped.

"Sally, you stay to home today an' bile us a squirrel an' make us some corndodgers fur supper an', Abe, you mind the chores, like a good boy. Gran'mammy an' me has got to go out agin."

Then, one day, in the open-faced camp next door, Gran'mammy Sparrow could not leave her bed, and the next day Gran'pappy Sparrow was ailing. They had already buried Mrs. Brooner on a hill a half mile south-east of the clearing, so Mammy was free to stay at home and tend her own kin.

"The milksick . . ."

The whispered word haunted the little cabin, and Abe and Sally saw their parents' faces grow gaunt and gray, until one morning the axes rang once more at the edge of the clearing, as they had rung when first they arrived, and the children heard the whipsaw whine. That day, Sally did the cooking again, while Abe took over the men's chores on the place.

"They're a-goin' to bury Gran'mammy an' Gran'-pappy on the hill next to ol' Miz Brooner, Sally."

"Don't talk about it, Abe."

"But, Sally . . . !"

"Git me another armful of wood, will you, Abe?"

"Ain't you skeered, Sally?"

"You git me another armful of wood this minute, Aberham Linkern, an' take keer you don't step over that-air broom, er we'll be a-havin' it in this cabin!"

"The milksick, Sally? Oh, Gawd, we cain't have the milksick here! Not Mammy ner Pappy ner you ner me! Not we-uns, Sally!"

They buried Gran'mammy and Gran'pappy Sparrow on the hill that afternoon, and once more life was resumed.

But only for a day.

"Abe, call yer pappy! Run an' fetch him!"

"Mammy!"

Not Mammy, sure!

She lay there on the bearskin in the corner, with the blanket drawn up to her chin. It was a warm, bright day—Indian summer—but his mammy was cold. He could see the shudder run down her body stretched so long under the blanket, a shudder that began with a twitching across her tight, wide mouth, then plucked at her chin, like an invisible hand, and at last shook her whole frame.

"Mammy!"

"Run, Abe, boy!"

Not Mammy! It couldn't happen to Mammy! He was out the door and dashing across the clearing. He couldn't see where he was going. But he could hear his pappy's voice, talking to Cousin Dennis. It couldn't happen to Mammy! They couldn't take her! She couldn't . . . !

"What is it, boy? What's a-gittin' at you now, son? You're a loony, you are! I never seen a loonier one ner you, I swear!"

"Pappy!"

He couldn't get the words out. His breath was gone, and his lungs were constricted with fear and grief. Above him, his father's face was remote and alien.

"Come on, son! Don't stand thar a-blubberin'! What's eatin' you?"

"Pappy!" he cried at last. "It's Mammy! She's got it!"

You lived with death intimately in those days. Young or old, you were spared none of its tedious and obscene drama. You sat with it all day, helplessly, wondering what it was and whence it had come. You ate with it only a few feet from your table. At night, you slept with it, hearing it fumble at the throat of the one you loved in the same room, in the same bed. You could never escape it, shut it out, or forget it for a single moment. You could neither glorify it nor pretend that it was not there. And when, at last, it had finished and gone, you lived on, in the same shameless intimacy, with what it left behind, until you did what you had to do and found yourself finally standing bareheaded above a mound of wet and yellow earth that you had dug yourself, taking your leave in silence and without a ceremony.

It was hardly a week after Nancy Hanks Lincoln's first chill that the axes rang once more at the edge of the clearing and the whipsaw whined again. This time, Abe, hunched like a sick and forlorn bird on the rail fence, himself whittled out the pegs that were to hold the wooden box together. He did not yet believe the thing that had happened to him. He would not realize it for a long time. He would brood over it the rest of his life.

When the box was finished, they laid the body of Nancy Hanks Lincoln in it gently and, with as little noise as possible, they fastened the lid with the wooden pegs that her son had carved. Then, on a sled, they dragged the box slowly over the rough, brown field and up the hill, where they lowered it into the shallow trough they had dug beside the graves of Nancy's aunt and uncle and Mrs. Brooner.

Peter Brooner was there to help and Natty Grigsby and little Allen Brooner, standing beside Abe at the east side of the grave, and one or two others of the neighborhood were there too. But not many could come. Each had his own sick to care for, and they were all afraid, hiding from the mysterious and invisible thing that was destroying their homes. For only a moment, the little group on the hill stood silent and bareheaded, with the sharpening October wind blowing through the dead leaves above and the squirrels chattering down at them. Then they left the unmarked grave and returned to their homes.

When it was over, just the four of them remained in the Lincoln clearing where there had been seven—Tom Lincoln, the father; young Dennis Hanks; Sally, who was twelve and the only woman left in the family; and Abe, who was not yet ten. In the cabin, they stood silent for a moment, listening to the echoes of the voices that had once filled it; and then, separately, without speaking, they turned to the tasks that lay ahead of them in the long and empty winter.

37

A Man Needs a Woman

ABE LINCOLN lay on his back on a pile of brush and leaves in a corner. He lay as still as he could, for when he stirred, clouds of dust rose from the pulverized leaves and choked him. His sister, Sally, had asked him several times to go and fetch her some more firewood, but he had pretended not to hear. He did not want to hear. He did not want to move. He wanted to do nothing at all—unless it was to close his eyes against the thin, stooped figure of his thirteen-year-old sister, against the littered floor and the mean and barren cabin, against life itself. He was tired and very lonely. Perhaps he was sick, too, from the stagnant water he had been drinking for months from puddles and pools.

"What we a-havin' fur supper, Sally?"

Sally did not look up from the pot she was stirring. "Squirrel."

"Biled er fried?"

"Biled."

"Biled squirrel," he murmured, without even the conviction of contempt. "First thing you know, Denny Hanks'll 'a' kilt all the squirrels in Spencer County, an' 'en you an' me'll starve to death!"

Sally turned on him.

"Then whyn't you go out an' try to kill somep'n different yerself, Abe Linkern, 'stead o' jest a-layin' thar all day a-doin' nothin'?"

Abe opened his mouth to answer her, and then he closed it without speaking.

He was sick of everything, just as he was sick of squirrel. Ever since his mother had died a year ago, nothing had been right. The cabin was an empty place, and his father and Dennis and Sally went about their chores drearily, the two men hunting every day and neglecting the cleared ground, and Sally cooking the game they brought her—first in the skillet and then in their one, cracked, earthen pot. At mealtime, they sat about the table, without knives or forks, gnawing stolidly at the meat, which was all they had. It was true that there had been very little more when his mother was alive; but his mother's presence in the cabin had been warm and vital and reassuring, giving their frugal lives a kind of security and purpose. Now, they only existed.

It wasn't the filth and the hunger and the cold that troubled Abe, anyhow. It was the fear that they were allowing his mother's memory to grow shadowy and unreal. His father and Sally seldom spoke of her; and, when they did, it was with constraint, as if it were an effort for them to remember her. He was not old enough yet to know that there are griefs that lie too deep for words; and, for that reason, he wondered whether anyone else thought of her almost constantly, as he did. After all, when the Baptist preacher came to visit them, it was he who had asked him to preach a sermon over the grave on the hill.

"Sally, when you reckon pappy'll be a-gittin' back?"

"Most any day now, I guess."

Abe thrust out his lower lip. The past few days a
new fear had been growing in his heart.

"You reckon Denny's right," he said finally, "about
what pappy's up to down thar in Kaintuck? You reckon
pappy's really a-sparkin' him a new wife?"

Sally continued with her work.

"Well, I don't know what pappy's a-doin', but if
they's another woman down thar he kin git hitched to, I
hope he's a-gittin' hitched."

Her words congealed the fear in Abe's heart and
made him acknowledge its existence for the first time.

"A man needs a woman in this country to take keer
of him," Sally went on, "a growed woman an' not jest a
little gal like me."

Abe closed his hands at his sides into angry fists.

"I don't want no new mammy in this-here cabin!"
he said. "I'll hate her! If she's an angel outen heaven, I'll
hate her!"

"Abe!"

But Abe paid no attention to his horrified sister.
Turning his face to the wall, he swallowed the dust that
rose from the dead leaves and clenched his teeth.

At that moment, nevertheless, his father was talking
to Sarah Bush Johnston down in Elizabethtown, Kentucky.

" 'Tain't as if you'd never seen me afore, Sarey.
'Tain't as if I was a stranger to you. You've knowed me
fur a long time. Me an' Nancy Hanks was happy together an' I ain't a-sayin' she hain't tuck somep'n with
her 't I cain't never give to you—still an' all, I ain't never
fergot you, Sarey, an' I'll be good to you an' yer children.
I give you my word I will."

Sarah Bush Johnston looked at the man who had come back to her out of her youth and wondered what she ought to say. Tom Lincoln had courted her once before, years ago, before he married Nancy Hanks; and, although she herself had married and been widowed since and had three children of her own, she had never forgotten him. He had proved himself a poor husband for Nancy, but he was a good man. He neither drank nor swore, and that was something.

"They ain't no time fur proper sparkin', Sarey. I cain't play a waitin' game. I'm more'n forty year old an' I need you right now. Them two childern of mine up in Indianny needs you, too. We're all in powerful need of you."

It was probably the two children that decided her, for Sarah was born for motherhood; but there was still an obstacle in her way. She looked at Tom Lincoln squarely.

"I'm a-owin' debts here in 'Liz'bethtown, Tom."

Tom Lincoln's earnest face broke into a slow smile.

"Well, now," he drawled, "if that's all . . ."

From an old debt of his own, he collected the money and paid what Sarah was owing, and on December 2, 1819, they were married and set out for the cabin on Little Pigeon Creek.

38

A World Remade

"ALL that I am or ever hope to be I owe to my angel mother," Abraham Lincoln is reported as saying many years after he had left Indiana. All that he was; yes. It was Nancy Hanks Lincoln who bore him, and it was from her, rather than his father, that he inherited the strain of greatness in him. But it was his stepmother, Sarah Bush Lincoln, who first brought hope into that clearing on Pigeon Creek—hope and, with it, ambition, into the life of the ten-year-old boy.

The material things that Sarah brought into Abe's starved and barren world required a wagon and a team of four horses. There were pots and pans and skillets that were to mean such food as Abe had never before tasted. There were knives and forks that were to "larn" him manners. There were blankets and quilts, a feather mattress and feather pillows that would give him the first winter night of warm sleep he had ever known. There were chairs and a clothes chest and a bureau that cost forty-five dollars in Kentucky: furniture that you could sit upon decently and stand up to, like a civilized being, instead of a savage.

Sarah swept out the dirty cabin, and into a pile by the door she threw the brush that had been their beds.

"Burn· it!" she commanded her new husband.
" 'Tain't fitten fur the pigs!"

She brushed Abe's hair back from his forehead and
made him wash his neck and ears. She mended clothes
and, from the cloth she had brought with her, made new
ones. She scrubbed and she cleaned and she cooked and
she washed and she tidied things up; and, when she had
finished, she turned to her husband and said:

"Now, Tom Linkern, you're a-goin' to start to work
on this-here cabin soon as it gits warm. You're a-goin' to
fix us up a cabin that's fitten fur humans to live in, a
cabin with a winder to let in light an' a puncheon floor
an' a loft with pegs in the wall to reach it by. First warm
day, Tom Linkern, you're a-goin' to start to work."

There was a force in her that Nancy Hanks Lincoln
had lacked, a force that made easygoing and indolent
Tom Lincoln do things for her that Nancy, in her two
years of Indiana life, had never been able to make him do.
When the first warm day came along, Tom Lincoln set
to work.

There was something more in the character of Sarah
Bush Lincoln—a yearning and an eagerness which told
her that what she was and what she had were not the best
that one could be and have in this world. She had passed
her thirty-first birthday and it was too late for her to
learn to read and write, but she saw that the quick and
hungry mind of her new stepson ought to be tutored and
trained so that someday it could take him beyond the
narrow limits of the world of Little Pigeon Creek in
Indiana.

"That-air boy's a-goin' to have more schoolin'," she
said.

Abe had already had one year of school with

Andrew Crawford for a teacher; and he had learned "spellin', readin', writin', and cipherin'" to the single Rule of 3 no further." In Master Crawford's "blab school," he had learned also to take off his cap when he entered a cabin and to try to say "how-de-do" instead of just plain "howdy." For the past year or two, moreover, on trips to and from the mill—alone now, because he was old enough—he had stopped at the cabins along the way and borrowed such books as he could borrow. These books he had spelled out laboriously and memorized.

All this, Tom Lincoln thought, was enough.

"Too much book-larnin' 'll spile the boy," he said. "I cain't git him to do his work proper now, what with his nose always between the kivers of one of them-air books er else him a-wantin' all the time to make a speech er recite a pome he's larnt by heart."

But Sarah would not listen.

"Abe's a-goin' to git an eddication."

And Abe did—such, at least, as was open to him in a new school started by Azel W. Dorsey in a cabin four miles away.

In Master Dorsey's school, he studied Webster's *Spelling Book* and Pike's *Arithmetic* and the Bible, and he tried his best to sing with the other pupils when the songbook was passed around. His voice was high-pitched and scratchy and made everyone laugh. But it was good-natured laughter. They knew better than to make fun of him. He was well on his way to his towering height of six feet four inches, and his long arms and legs were as tough and strong as hickory hoop. poles.

"Git Abe Linkern to take a-holt an' it'll come," they said, when they found a task too heavy for them. "Git old Abe!"

He towered above them in every other way, too; and they depended upon him when the problems of Pike's *Arithmetic* seemed insoluble or a two-dollar word turned up in the speller. Abe could outcipher, outspeechify, and outspell, as well as outwrassle, all of them.

But he was never high-and-mighty about it. He was always modest and good-natured and ready to help.

There was that little Roby girl he liked so well, little Anna Roby with the pretty curls. It was a Friday afternoon and the usual week-end spelling contest was just coming into the home stretch. Everyone had been spelled down but Abe and Anna, and the whole class was sure that Abe would win. But Abe knew better. There wasn't anything he wouldn't do for a girl like Anna Roby. He had made up his mind to misspell the next word that was read out to him.

But it was Anna's turn first.

"Defied," old Azel Dorsey read from the spelling book and peered above his spectacles at Anna.

Anna blushed, and Abe's heart sank. She was going to spell herself down before he had a chance to give her the victory.

"D—," she said, "d-e-f—"

The room was very still, and Anna's cheeks grew rosier.

"D-e-f—"

Her lips pursed hesitantly over the letter "y," and Abe, behind the schoolmaster's back, shook his head violently.

"D-e-f—" Anna began again; and, by that time, Abe had the solution. Still unnoticed by Master Dorsey, he put his finger solemnly over one eye.

Anna brightened.

"—i-e-d!" she finished victoriously; and Master Dorsey turned to Abe with another word, which Abe gallantly misspelled.

Azel Dorsey, in Abe's one year of schooling with him—the last year of schooling he was ever to have, simply gave Abe the tools for learning. The real education he got by himself. He read and reread *Robinson Crusoe, Pilgrim's Progress, Sinbad the Sailor,* and Aesop's *Fables,* the books that Sarah Bush Lincoln, unable to read herself, had brought with her from Kentucky. Then he set out and borrowed more books. He walked seventeen miles through the forest to Judge Pitcher's office in Rockport and borrowed them. He borrowed them from David Turnham and from Josiah Crawford, Master Andrew's brother. He walked to Gentryville and Boonville and possibly to Evansville and to New Harmony on the Wabash, where there were more books at that time than you could find anywhere else in the state of Indiana.

Books! He was hungry for them and devoured everything that he could find within a radius of fifty miles of the cabin on Little Pigeon Creek. Still there were not enough. He was always walking, walking, through the forest, in quest of them; for he started to read them as soon as he had his hands on them and, usually, by the time he was home again, he had finished his first reading and there was nothing left for him but a second and third reading until he could go and borrow more somewhere.

Unlike many omnivorous readers, he did not admire everything he read. He had taste and judgment. The first book he ever owned—Parson Weems's *Life of Washington*—he considered too flattering, biased, and unreliable. He was "real put out" over the acquisition of that book, anyhow. Originally, he only borrowed it from Josiah

Crawford; but when it got rain-soaked in the chink in
the cabin wall where he kept it, Josiah refused to let him
return it and made Abe work for him a couple of days
pulling fodder to pay for it.

"Abe was the awfullest plagued boy I ever seen,"
Mrs. Crawford said, when she told the story of Abe's first
book years later.

He must have been. He wrote a poem about Josiah
Crawford, calling him "old Blue-Nose Crawford," and
recited it for weeks everywhere he went in Spencer
County. Poor Josiah remained "Old Blue-Nose" among
his friends until his dying day.

"My pa larnt me to work," Abe explained, "but he
fergot to larn me to like it."

"That-air young'un's too all-fired fresh!" his pa
would say sometimes; and, more than once, he sent the
boy "a-windin'" with a blow from his fist.

"The Old Man Loved his Childern," Dennis Hanks
later testified, "but I have Seen his father Nock him
Down of the fence when a Stranger would call for Information to Neighbour house."

Abe had a strong streak of mischief in him—that
Hoosier vein of malicious humor which just misses mean-
ness because of the hearty laughter that goes with it and
continues even when the joke backfires and makes the
joker its butt. Once, when he was not invited to the in-
fare of the Grigsbys' double wedding, he secured the aid
of a confederate, got the brides and bridegrooms mixed
in their beds, and then wrote a Rabelaisian poem about
the confusion, called it "The Chronicles of Reuben," and
dropped it in the road in front of the Grigsby "mansion."
That brought about a free-for-all fight; and, when Abe

emerged victorious, he went about for a while boasting, "I'm the big buck of this lick!"

"You'll come to a bad end, Abe Linkern," his sister used to warn him, "if you don't quit a-laughin' an' a-jokin' all the time."

But to ask a Hoosier boy to quit "a-laughin' an' a-jokin'" is to ask him to cease living; and to ask a boy like Abe, who had got hold of *Quinn's Jests* and Scott's *Lessons in Elocution*, was to ask the impossible. Even if he had tried, his friends would not have let him stop entertaining them.

"Come on, Abe, spell us a while with one of them yarns of yourn."

"Git up an' give us a speech, Abe!"

The boss was out of sight, and the rail splitters would be leaning on their axes, addressing the boy who had been hired because, when he had a mind to, he could do more work than any three of them. Even if he had tried, Abe could not have resisted them. His pa had larnt him to work, but he had forgotten to larn him to like it; and, anyhow, no Hoosier can refuse an invitation to make a speech or spin a yarn. So, without hesitation, he would climb upon a stump. There, with blue and narrow shins exposed below pants that were too short and with his great arms waving like a windmill, his lank and comical figure would infect the men with good humor even before he began to speak. And when he spoke, he could make them cheer or laugh or cry, as he willed.

A speech in defense of Henry Clay (Only Hoosiers under the age of six months are unresponsive to political argument!); the appeal of Brutus after Caesar's death (Behind every Hoosier's eyes, there is a ready reservoir of tears!); a tall and lengthy yarn of none too delicate flavor (The Hoosier likes 'em tall and long and ribald!) ; or an imitation of the new brimstone peddler at the Old Pigeon Hard-Shell Baptist Church (The Hoosier takes his religion, like his politics, straight and hard-hitting!) —all these were in the boy's repertoire, and more.

When he was seventeen, Abe won his first law case. One of his neighbors had accused another of stealing a goose. The case was taken to the schoolhouse, where it was to be tried by lawyers before the county squire. But Abe got there first.

"Give us a speech, Abe, while we're a-waitin'."

"Heared any new yarns lately, Abe?"

Abe untangled his long legs from the bench he was sitting on and went up to the schoolmaster's platform.

"I'm reminded," he began, "of the summer the squirrels got into my pappy's corn patch an' did all his shuckin' fur him afore he could shift his chaw to his other cheek an' say 'Skedaddle!' If this ruckus you're here to settle tonight keeps up much longer—what with all the scrappin' an' ear chawin' that's been goin' on lately between the friends of the litigants—why, they soon won't be a whole ear left in Spencer County!"

He drawled the words out in his high and screechy way, and the men and women, who a moment before had been tense with animosity, began to titter.

"An' what's the cause of all this to-do, anyhow? Why, I'll tell you! It's nothin' but a o-l-d g-r-a-y g-o-o-s-e!"

His voice rose to a shrill crescendo; and someone in the back of the room shouted, "That's a-tellin' 'em, Abe!"

"Fur many a year, we've lived in peace an' plenty round old Pigeon Crick, an', 'ceptin' fur a man a-bitin' another man's nose er ear off now an' 'en in a moment of fergetful playfulness, ain't nary a one of us has carried a real grudge agin his neighbor since I kin remember.

"But now somep'n has come among us an' divided us into two camps. We ain't a-speakin' to each other like we used to. We ain't a-hangin' over one another's fences an' a-swappin' gossip like we used to. I ain't heared a real, honest-to-God, knock-down-an'-drag-out, repytation-blastin' jaw-fest among good friends in a coon's age!

"An' what is it 't's come among us? Why, you know! 'Tain't nothin' but a o-l-d g-r-a-y g-o-o-s-e!"

They were all laughing by this time; and when their laughter ceased, Abe turned to the two men involved in the case.

"Now, lookie here, you fellers! You're a-fixin' to have you a law trial; an' when it's over, one of you will have the goose an' the other won't. But that ain't the pint at all. The pint is that, no matter what's decided, you're both a-goin' to lose. Because you're a-goin' to ruin yer one-time friendship an' put the whole community at outs furever.

"An' all because of a . . ."

Everyone joined in the chorus.

". . . o-l-d g-r-a-y g-o-o-s-e!"

At that point, the squire and lawyers came in, but they were too late. Already the litigants were crossing the room toward each other with outstretched, friendly hands; and a half dozen young bloods in the back row had started clapping and singing:

> "Fly in the buttermilk, shoo, shoo, shoo!
> Fly in the buttermilk, shoo, shoo, shoo!
> Fly in the buttermilk, shoo, shoo, shoo!
> Skip to my Lou, my darlin'!"

What had begun as a "law trial" was now well on its way to being a "shindig," with roast goose as a starter for a feast.

Soon after that, Abe pleaded another case, which was even more important to him, because, in it, he himself was the defendant. He had built himself a scow down on the Ohio and, whenever he could, he would take passengers to and from the passing steamboats that were unable to land at the mouth of Anderson's Creek. He earned his first dollar in this way, and the business was very promising until another ferryman, John T. Dill, grew jealous and got the law on him for operating a ferry without a license.

The trial was in Kentucky, before Justice Samuel Pate.

"I know the state of Kaintuck runs to the low-water mark on the Indianny shore, yer honor," Abe acknowledged; "an' I know I been a-rowin' my boat into Kaintuck's waters. But I ain't a-settin' passengers clean over the river, so, therefore, by rights, I ain't a-operatin' a ferryboat."

Justice Pate rubbed his head, looked quizzically at the gawky riverboy who seemed to know so much about the law, pondered the case for a few minutes, and then decided for the defendant.

But by that time, law and oratory and politics and even books were only secondary interests with Abe Lincoln. He was now in that stage which even the modern Hoosier boy must survive. He wanted to go on the river.

39

Down Around the River

MAYBE Anna Roby had something to do with it.

"Annie, will you go to the Taylors' house-raisin' with me?"

"Why, Abe, I don't know as I kin."

"Why not, Annie? Has somebody else ask you first?"

"Maybe so an' maybe not."

"Aw, Annie, quit a-teasin' me! What makes you act like that all the time?"

"Like what?"

"You know what!"

"I don't know what you're a-talkin' about, Abe!"

"Yes, you do! You're always a-puttin' me off an' tormentin' me. Sometimes I figger you jest don't like me at all."

"I do like you, Abe. I think you're an awful nice boy—an' smart, too."

"Annie . . ."

"What?"

"Annie . . ."

"Abe, don't you tech me!"

"Annie Roby. . . . Thar! I done it! That's what I been a-wantin' to do all summer!"

"Abe . . . !"

"Thar! I love you, Annie Roby! Kin you understand that? You're the first gal I ever loved. I don't know no sashay ways of sayin' it. I jest love you. That's all!"

"Aberham Linkern!"

"Say you love me, too, Annie!"

"You let me go, Abe Linkern! You're too ugly fur any gal to love! You're the ugliest boy I ever knowed! I couldn't never love you!"

And, within a year, she was married to one of Abe's best friends, Allen Gentry.

Abe had no taste for the blue ruin, the bug juice, or the moral suasion that was consumed in those days in great quantities. His "innards" weren't made to accommodate the stuff. So there was no danger of Anna Roby's rebuff driving him to drink. But, working for James Taylor as a farm hand and ferryman near the mouth of Anderson's Creek, he was tempted to escape from his sorrow in the life that the rivers offered.

It was the age of the "half horse, half alligator men," the keelboatmen, like Mike Fink, who swaggered and fought and bragged their way up and down the rivers with regard for no law but that of their knives and their guns and their own two fists, fantastic men whose solemn faces grew even more solemn and truculent when they boasted of shooting off the tails of little pigs that ran wild in the bottom lands, of being weaned by wildcats, of having to sleep with both eyes open to keep from killing their own tempestuous selves in their beds.

It was the age of the coming of the steamboat, too, those new, smoke-belching, water-churning, sugar-candy contraptions that scared the daylights out of the Indians and made the keelboatmen gnash their teeth in futile, jealous rage. Abe knew the names of all the boats that passed on the Ohio—the *Eclipse*, the *Western Engineer*, the *Independence*. He knew the *Highland Laddie*, Captain M'Cullum, that plied between Louisville on the Ohio and Terre Haute on the Wabash, and the *American*, Captain Wilson, that was not so fast but boldly pushed farther up the river. He knew the other Wabash and Ohio boats—the *Josephine*, the *Belvidere*, the *Triton*, the *Wabash*, and the *William Tell*.

He not only knew these boats, he could recognize their whistles before he saw them coming round a bend; and, with the solemn fervor of youth, he was arguing constantly with his friends about the advantages of low pressure and the new hog-frame design and slanting paddles set toward the stern to catch the second swell. Sometimes, in his ferryboat in midstream, he rested on his oars and gazed southward down the broad and yellow stretch of water, until his dreams carried him past the mouths of the Green and the Wabash and the Cumberland and the Tennessee to the greatest river of them all.

Too ugly, was he!

Well, the world was big and full of opportunities, even for a boy who was too ugly for any gal to love!

"I reckon they's nothin' grander in this world," he would say to himself, "nothin' grander ner bein' a steamboat man!"

At last, in the fall of 1828, the chance came to him to realize at least a part of his dream. James Gentry offered him the bow oar on a flatboat he was sending down to New Orleans loaded with meat, corn, and flour.

"You're a steady boy, Abe, an' I want you to go

along and look after my son, Allen. The two of you together kin take keer of yerselves, I reckon. Will you
do it?"

Would he do it!

His heart was pounding so fast that he knew Mr.
Gentry must be able to see it under the buckskin shirt
drawn tight across his narrow chest. But he pretended to
hesitate, thrusting out his lower lip, as if in study.

"How much kin you offer me, Mr. Gentry?"

"There'll be eight dollars a month in it fur you,
Abe, an' yer return passage on one of the best steamboats
on the rivers."

"Well, now, Mr. Gentry, I reckon I kin go."

They left from the landing at Rockport in December, just the two of them. Allen Gentry was twenty-one,
and Abe Lincoln was nineteen. As they swung the clumsy
craft about in midstream and headed her down with the
current, Abe stood up in the bow for one last look at the
high, yellow bluff where the pioneer village sprawled. It
was the first time he had ever left home, and there was an
odd, smothering sickness in his heart. But he was nineteen, and ahead of him lay an unexplored world where it
did not matter that he was the ugliest boy Anna Roby
had ever seen.

For several days they drifted lazily on the broad
breast of the Ohio. They passed Green River and then the
mouth of the Wabash, which was to them like a great
lake with large and confusing islands that gave the rivers
numerous channels. They saw Cave-In Rock on the Illinois shore and steered for the Kentucky side as they read
the sign above the entrance—"Wilson's Liquor Vault
and House of Entertainment." Tales of the murders

committed by the Wilson gang in that den of vice had already spread as far as Little Pigeon Creek.

"Let's git a hump on, Allen," Abe said; and the two boys dipped their oars deeper into the brown water.

When they reached the Mississippi at last, they had constantly to keep "a hump on"; for the great river was not only crowded with traffic, it was also a master of treachery, with its hidden snags and false currents and writhing, shifting twists and turns. Still, no accident befell them until, almost at the end of their voyage, they tied up for the night at the plantation of Madame Duschesne in the sugar country below Baton Rouge.

That night, it seemed to Abe, he had hardly got his eyes shut for a good sleep when he heard Allen Gentry yell.

"Abe!"

Abe leaped to his feet.

"Right here, Allen!"

He had done the wrong thing. In an instant, great, shadowy figures loomed all about him in the dark, over-running the flatboat, and rushed him.

"Niggers!" he muttered. He could tell by the smell.

Quickly, he raised his arm in defense, but one of their hickory clubs came crashing down and caught him across his right eye.

Then they lost their courage and ran.

Snatching up a club of his own, Abe went after them, almost blind in the dark with the blood streaming across his eye, but swinging fiercely right and left. He chased them up the levee, his long legs stretching out fast beneath him, his long arm reaching out with the club and tingling with a satisfying shock each time it connected with a black head.

When at last the marauders had vanished, Abe and Allen went back to the boat and, untying her, let her drift downstream until they reached a more secluded spot.

"I reckon they won't bother us here," Abe said, when once more they were tied up to shore; and, closing his swollen eyes, he went to sleep with a wet rag tied across the gash that was to leave its mark on his forehead the rest of his life.

They were several days in New Orleans, the biggest town Abe had so far seen; and the eyes and ears of the Hoosier boy were once more busy, as he wandered with his friend through the crowded, foreign streets, listened to the French and Creole and Spanish that the people spoke, and watched, in bewildered amazement, the hustle and confusion among the steamboats, keelboats, arks, flatboats, and seagoing vessels that jammed the port for two miles below the levee.

They returned, as James Gentry had promised, on one of the most luxurious steamboats on the Mississippi; and when they got back to Rockport, there was no longer much that mattered to Abe but the rivers.

The river . . .

"What's yer worry, Abe?" William Wood, looking up from his desk at the youth in the doorway, would say.

"Uncle Billy, I want you to go to the river and give me a recommend to some boat."

"Yer age is agin you, son. You ain't twenty-one yet."

"I know that, uncle, but I want to git a start."

"No, Abe; I cain't give you a recommend till you come of age."

The river . . .

"What's the matter, boy?"

Judge Pitcher's voice would be anxious. He had great hopes for Abe Lincoln. He had read an essay the boy wrote once on the evils of drink and he had sent it off to a temperance paper in Ohio and they had published it.

"What is it, Abe? Now, there's those newspapers on my table that've been a-waitin' fur you fur more'n a week. There's a Cincinnati paper an' the Louisville *Journal* an' the *Telescope* that Billy Wood told me to give you. What's the matter, son? You still a-moonin' over that Roby gal?"

"No, judge; I'm all over that. But the pilot of the *Decatur* over on the Wabash is a-lookin' fur a new cub. She runs between Terre Haute an' Shawneetown, an' I know a feller 't could git me the job if only I could git a release from somebody that's responsible fur me."

"Land o' Goshen, boy! You cain't afford to waste yer talents on the rivers—not with that foul-mouthed, whisky-guzzlin' passel o' varmints! That's not fur you, Abraham Lincoln!"

"But that's what I want to do, judge. I want it worse 'n I ever wanted anything in my whole life."

The river . . .

"What's eatin' on you, son?"

"I want to go on the river, pa."

"After you're twenty-one maybe, boy. You jest keep on clerkin' in Colonel Jones's store over 't Jonesboro a while longer. It's a good job, an' the colonel likes you, even if he does say you like yer pay more'n yer work. Then, maybe when you're twenty-one . . ."

Well, when he was twenty-one then . . . after February 12, 1830 . . . maybe . . .

40

Twenty-one

By the time his twenty-first birthday came around, Abe Lincoln was too busy at something else to think about the river. For weeks, he had been sawing tree trunks into slices thin enough and round enough for wagon wheels and shaving down poles to the size of axles. For months, he had been helping his father turn what little they owned into cash; and whenever there were enough shinplasters in the drawer of the cabinet he had made, they went out and bought another yoke of oxen.

"The milksick is jest as like as not to come agin, boy," his father argued, although it was really his own natural restlessness that was urging him on, "an' we got to git a hump on afore it catches up with us. We're a-goin' to a new country whar, I hope, the milksick ain't."

"We're a-goin' to Illinois," Abe told his friends dully, and with many misgivings.

And, three days after his birthday, they set out.

Sarah Bush Lincoln and her two daughters rode in the cart, which was loaded with all that was left of their household goods. Dennis Hanks walked on ahead. Abe and his father took the middle yoke of oxen, carrying long staves, and young John Johnston and Squire Hall,

Matilda Johnston's new husband, brought up the rear, followed by Abe's pet dog.

Abe's only sister, Sally, lay buried in the Old Pigeon churchyard, having died two years before.

Natty Grigsby rode over from his cabin on the day of their departure to accompany the caravan. Walking his horse beside his friend, Abe, he went as far as the settlement called Lickskillet, where he told them all goodbye and turned back. After that, they were unaccompanied in the forests, headed northwest, toward Vincennes on the Wabash River, where they would cross over into Illinois.

41

"Mr." Lincoln

A SWARTHY, little man stood in the gateway of one of the high picket fences, smoking his pipe. It was a warm day, late in February, and the early Indiana spring was already in the air. Behind the man, a neat, two-story house of whitewashed puncheons glistened in the sunlight. There was a pile of rotting manure under the fruit trees in the yard, and the smell it gave off in the spring warmth seemed to tease the little man's nostrils and remind him pleasantly of the abundance his garden would yield that year; for he smiled cordially as the stranger in the half-boots and linsey-woolsey pants and jacket loped up to him.

"Kin you tell me whar I'll find St. Louis Street?"

"St. Louis Street? Bien, sur, m'sieu. C'est par ici. You are on it right now. Vous comprenez?"

The young stranger doffed his coonskin cap, grinned, and thanked the Frenchman. Then he strode on down the narrow street. It had been a whole year since he had heard that lingo—just a year ago this season, when he and Allen Gentry had wandered the streets of New Orleans together. He wondered if the Frenchman re- membered George Rogers Clark and Hamilton and his hair buyers. It wasn't likely, but no doubt the French-

236

man's father had lived in Vincennes during those stirring days when Fort Sackville fell.

Abe's head was full of history as he walked on down St. Louis Street toward the Wabash River; for, as soon as he arrived in Vincennes, he had shaken off his garrulous, gawking family and set out to enjoy the sights by himself. He had visited the spot where Fort Sackville once stood and seen the site of old Father Gibault's church, which had been torn down only five years before. He had seen the river, which had borne men into the Northwest for almost two hundred years. And now he was going to see what was for him the most important sight of all.

His steps lagged timidly, as he caught his first glimpse of the river through the willows at the foot of the street. They had told him it was in the last cabin on the street, and there it was. As he read the puncheon sign —*Western Sun and General Advertiser*—he came to a full halt. He wished Judge Pitcher could be with him to help him. After all, he was only a long-legged, back-country galoot who had no business taking up a great man's time. But he gathered his courage finally and rapped on the puncheon door under the sign.

The door creaked open and a man in shirt sleeves stood before him. He was a stern and forbidding man, with great sidewhiskers, a firmly set mouth, and steady, penetrating eyes. But when Abe looked a second time, he saw that the mouth was twisted slightly with ironic humor and the eyes were friendly.

"I'd like to see the printing press," Abe said timidly, "an' I'd like to meet Mr. Stout, too, if he kin spare the time."

"I'm Mr. Stout," the man said. "Come in."

Abe caught his breath. Judge Pitcher and David Turnham and William Wood had seemed like big and important men to him, but here was one whom everybody in the Wabash country knew by name, a man whose editorials he himself had read for years. Elihu Stout! Elihu Stout had come to Vincennes in 1804 with a printing outfit and established the first newspaper in the Northwest, calling it the *Indiana Gazette*. His first office burned down, but he re-established the paper in 1807 as the *Western Sun*. Now, in 1830, it was the *Western Sun and General Advertiser*. Elihu Stout! After Governor Ray, this stern, quiet man in shirt sleeves was perhaps the most important man in Indiana. And that engine behind him was his printing press—the first printing press Abe had ever seen.

Abe overcame his awe at last.

"My name's Lincoln, Mr. Stout—Abe Lincoln. I'm on my way to Illinois, but I had to stop an' see you an' that printin' outfit. I couldn't go by without doin' it. But I won't take no more of yer time."

But Elihu Stout saw something more than a raw, backwoods boy before him. He shook the boy's hand and led him into the office, insisting that he had plenty of time. He showed him the press and how it worked. He explained the methods by which his news was gathered and how he decided what was important and what was not. He drew up a chair and began to talk, drawing his visitor out.

What did Mr. Lincoln think of Henry Clay?

"Mister . . . !" Abe had never been called that before! And what did he think of Henry Clay? Why, he could write Elihu Stout's editorials for him on Henry

Clay! There wasn't a greater man than old Henry Clay
in the whole country!

And what of John C. Calhoun and that Yankee fire-
eater, Daniel Webster? What of all this talk in the
Senate about the right of secession? Should it be "Liberty
first and Union afterwards" or should it be "Liberty and
Union"?

There was already only one answer to that, of
course. The Union must be preserved!

When they understood each other, found out where
they disagreed and where they saw eye to eye, Elihu
Stout took one of his newspapers fresh from the press
and gave it to his visitor.

Sitting by the door in the office, with the fragrance
of early spring and the river in his nostrils, Abe read the
damp, printed sheet avidly, every line of it. He read
Webster's speeches on the Foote Resolution and Hayne's
replies. He learned that the election of James W. Ripley
in Maine was being contested. His mind struggled to
comprehend the speed of the new B. and O. Railroad train
that had run from Pratt Street in Baltimore to the Car-
rollton Viaduct at the rate of "fifteen miles per hour"!
He saw that a female academy was being opened in Har-
rodsburg, Kentucky, down in the country where he was
born. Perhaps wistfully, he paused over the announcement that the steamboat *Tippecanoe* and the steamboat
Highlander were about to start a regular packet service
as far up the Wabash as Terre Haute and Lafayette. He
pored over Dr. Beecher's sermon on Intemperance and
compared it with his own effort of a few years before.
He even read the notices of the terms of the circuit
courts and the marriage announcements, which appeared
in a column headed "Hymeneal."

When he had finished, he sat for a moment looking out over the sparkling river. Then he got up reluctantly and gave the paper back to Elihu Stout.

"I'm very much obleeged to you, sir," he said.

"It has been a privilege to meet you, Mr. Lincoln. I hope you'll drop in again if you ever come back this way."

"I will, Mr. Stout. I shore will."

And, with that promise, Abe took his leave and went out into St. Louis Street to find his family and cross the Wabash into Illinois. His fourteen formative years in Indiana were ended.

PART SEVEN

Growing Pains

42

"I'm as Good as You Air"

IN many ways, the life of the Lincolns in Indiana remained typical of most of Hoosierdom until the middle of the century. But after Abe's departure for Illinois in 1830, not many Hoosiers were thwarted as he was in their efforts to "git an eddication." Yankees were beginning to settle in the country, and with the Yankees came "book larnin'." Most of the early Hoosier schoolmasters were Yankees; and, although the pioneer boys were attracted to the schools chiefly by their ambition to lick the teacher, it was inevitable that they should absorb some knowledge and acquire a thirst for more, whether they licked him or not.

George Cary Eggleston, writing about the boyhood of his famous brother in and about Vevay, remarks upon the universal thirst for education in the forties; and an Englishman, passing through Indianapolis in the fifties, quotes with amazement a census showing that only 32 of the 1,920 children in the town were not attending Sunday school. As it was explained by some authorities —though rather imaginatively—the very dialect of the pioneer bore witness to his eagerness to improve himself. Hearing the educated man pronounce the word "curse" as "curse," instead of "cuss," he attempted to change his own pronunciation and ended by saying "furse" when he meant "fuss." Likewise, realizing that he should say "get," instead of "git," he felt safer saying "set" for "sit" and "pet" for "pit."

A log schoolhouse was built in almost every community, with benches arranged around an open fireplace in the center of the room and the master dominating his class from a platform, with a good supply of rods on his desk. Most of the first schools were "blab schools," in which the pupils were required to study aloud, so that the master could be sure they were actually studying and not just dreaming of the swimming hole or yesterday's coon hunt.

The result of the grammar schools was a demand for high schools and seminaries and, later, colleges. Vincennes University had existed since 1806. Indiana University, opening its doors in 1823, became the first state university west of the Alleghenies. Soon after came the sectarian institutions, springing up all over the state: Wabash and Hanover, founded by the Presbyterians; Franklin, by the Baptists; DePauw, by the Methodists; Notre Dame, by the Catholics; Earlham, by the Quakers; and Butler, by the Christians.

By the middle of the century, when the state adopted its second constitution, Robert Dale Owen had preached the gospel of free public education so widely and thoroughly that the provision for schools took precedence over many other articles in that document and established a tradition in the Wabash country. "Book larnin' " is esteemed there today with almost Oriental fanaticism. Any man who has taught school, if only for a year, or even a month, is likely to carry the title of "professor" the rest of his life, regardless of his later achievements and occupations, and boys and girls who show promise in the schoolroom are encouraged by the whole community to carry their studies as far as they can.

The men and women who have grown up in Indiana schools have repaid the region's debt to the early Yankee schoolmasters in a curious way. No figures are available; but a census of the faculties of the schools and universities in twentieth century New England would show that the Hoosiers are playing a large and important role in modern education in the East.

Learning inspired a desire for finer living, and the prosperity resulting from the clearing of the land made finer living possible. The pioneer cabins of squatters, like Tom Lincoln, eventually began to disappear, and in their places rose the dignified houses that are the old homesteads of many Hoosiers today. Yankees and Pennsylvanians preferred small and concentrated farms that allowed them to live close together and to be self-supporting. They built their homes modestly but solidly, and they tilled their small, neat fields with great skill, producing almost nothing for the market, but making of each of their estates a complete and self-sufficient community. The Southerners, on the other hand, lived more expansively. Their homes were high-ceilinged and high-roofed, standing usually on knolls far back from the roads and approached through avenues of trees. They were fond of sports and politics and consequently lacked the time and energy necessary for the establishment of self-sustaining homes. The result was that they bred cattle for the market, they butchered more hogs than they could eat, they raised crops on a larger scale; and, with the money they received, they bought their clothes and household articles, instead of making them for themselves.

But one obstacle prevented these old homesteads from ever developing completely the expansive, leisurely, and graceful culture of the South or the highly intellectual society of New England. It was the servant problem, which arose, in part, from the Hoosier's distaste for taking orders.

"I'm as good as you air," he said; and when he was forced to take employment as a cook or a waiter or a stableboy, he made it obvious that it was only a temporary shift and insisted that he live in the house on an equal footing with his master.

"I'm as good as you air, an' someday I may be President of the United States."

That is still a part of the Hoosier creed.

43

The Prairie House

THE National Road reached Indiana in 1827. It was surveyed by Jonathan Knight, and he did his job so well that the Hoosier stretch of road, running from Richmond through Indianapolis and then across the Wabash at Terre Haute, is only two miles longer than the state is wide. The roadbed was eighty feet in width and the bridges and culverts were made of stone. A track thirty-five feet wide was macadamized in the middle of the bed. For many years, it was the finest road in the world.

By 1850, however, this was no longer true. Congress had given part of the road to the state, and the state in turn had leased it to a private company. The company converted it into a plank road, laying sawn boards about three inches thick across it and nailing them to sleepers that ran along the roadside. A plank road, though slippery when wet, was a joy to travel on when it was new. The elastic boards rose and sank under the passing traffic, like the springs of a fine carriage. But when the road began to wear out, it was full of chuck holes and dangerous traps. Then the planks were replaced by corduroy— the unhewn trunks of trees laid side by side and held together by a slip nailed across each end. The sensation of riding over a corduroy road was something like the modern sensation of riding on a flat tire—only much worse.

A half hour before midday on a hot Sunday in June, 1853, a handsome wagon, drawn by two fine horses, drove off the National Road and into the yard of the Prairie House at the outskirts of Terre Haute. It was a covered wagon, but not the clumsy, creaking covered wagon of the usual westward-pushing pioneer. It was much too elegant.

Climbing down from his seat, the driver went into the lobby of the Prairie House and asked for accommodations for himself and his wife and nine children.

"You a Yankee, Mr. Beste?" Mr. Bunting, the proprietor, asked, glancing up from the name the stranger had written in his register.

"No, I'm an Englishman."

"An Englishman? But you don't talk like an Englishman—or an Irishman, either, for that matter! You don't drop yer h's an' say ' 'ot' when you mean 'hot.' "

Mr. Beste smiled wanly and remarked that perhaps Mr. Bunting was acquainted with a different kind of Englishman.

Mr. Beste was eager to be shown to his rooms. He had spent the past three days driving his wagon through the heavy traffic on the plank and corduroy road from Indianapolis, a distance of seventy miles; and he had suffered sleepless nights and lean rations in the roadside inns, having chosen his stopping places indiscriminately, not realizing that the signboard of an inn on the National Road did not always indicate a true inn. Many hospitable farmers, reluctant to turn away strangers who knocked at their doors, were forced to put up inn signs to keep from being eaten out of house and home by persons seeking free meals and lodging. Furthermore, Mr. Beste had been unwell during the last day of his journey, and one of his daughters was quite sick. He was fearful and feverish and eager to get to bed.

The Beste family were given a suite on the first floor of an ell at the rear of the hotel. They intended to spend only one night in Terre Haute, because they had been told that the Wabash valley had an unhealthful climate. But, having already exhausted their resistance by traveling long after they should have called on a physician, they were destined to stay in the Hoosier settlement several months. For them, the delay was a misfortune; but for future inquirers after the ways of the Hoosiers in the 1850's, it was a happy accident. Mr. Beste kept a diary. Rare and out of print today, it is one of the richest and most entertaining of nineteenth century travel books.

Although he was an admirer of the sturdy, honest Hoosier character and the sweep and luxuriance of the Hoosier scenery, Richard Beste was not altogether pleased with his surroundings. The heat troubled him more than anything else, and he frequently complained of it and his sleepless nights in the Prairie House.

"You go into your bedroom and find it swarming with bats, locusts, beetles, mosquitoes, etc. You send as many of these out as you can; and, shutting the window, you undress and throw yourself on your bed, in the vain hope that you will soon be asleep. Before many minutes, you feel as if you were in a well-heated oven. You jump off the bed, take off the bottom sheet, and then lie down on the bare mattress; from the beginning, the pillow has been discarded. In a few minutes, the heat obliges you to change from place to place on the mattress at least twenty times; and, at last, you throw it on the ground after the pillow, and lie upon the straw paliasse.

But the straw paliasse is not much cooler than the wool or hair mattress; and, as a last resource, you open the window, quite convinced that you would rather be eaten alive by insects than suffocated. You open the window, and in rush all your old enemies again, thicker than ever. You resign yourself to the mosquitoes, and listen to them,—buz! buz! buz! But presently a new enemy appears in the shape of an enormous stag beetle, and flies round and round the room; but being too heavy to remain long on the wing, every two or three minutes it tumbles down. . . ."

One of Mr. Beste's daughters eventually discovered that the proprietor of the hotel slept with his head on the window sill, to keep cool.

Considering that Terre Haute in those days was only a village and there was another hotel in the center of town, Mr. Beste found the size and prosperity of the Prairie House impressive. All the rooms were filled. But the roomers were, for the most part, not the transients of the National Road, but local people who had been driven to hotel quarters by the servant problem. The Hoosier women, just emerging from the pioneer era, were much too ladylike for Mr. Beste's taste, reluctant to do their own housework and spending their days in idle gossip and constant rocking in the hotel's rocking chairs. These chairs, however, fascinated Mr. Beste's daughters, and by the time they left Terre Haute, they were well on the way toward becoming rocking chair addicts themselves. Had they stayed longer, they might also have acquired the universal feminine habit of chewing burgundy pitch—one of the precursors of modern American chewing gum, or "chaw-wax," as it is still called in some parts of Indiana. As for Mr. Beste's boys—

they immediately adopted the male custom of sprawling whenever they sat down, throwing their legs over the arms and even the backs of chairs; and Mr. Beste himself soon confessed a secret pleasure in putting his feet on a desk or table, Hoosier-fashion.

The hotel itself knew no servant problem. The place was overrun with servants. The first one to appear came through the passages at six, ringing a hand bell to awaken the guests. At six-thirty, he came around again, announcing breakfast.

And what a breakfast—!

"There were ranged down the table and cut into slices, hot and cold bread of different sorts, including cornbread (a little of which was rather nice with plenty of molasses and butter), little seed cakes, pancakes and fritters, milk, butter buried in large lumps of ice, molasses, preserves and blackberry syrup in large soup toureens. Besides these things, there were hot beefsteaks, roast and boiled chickens, and various sorts of cold meat. To drink, we had tea, coffee, and, occasionally, chocolate, with hot, cold, and iced milk, and white and brown sugar."

As a Negro in Indiana might say, they had everything on that table but *quit* and *don't*!

"At dinner, there was roast beef always, and, in general, the following dishes:—chicken pie, veal pie, beefsteaks, roast lamb, veal and mutton cutlets, boiled ham, pigeons, roast veal or roast pork. As vegetables, we had generally elderly peas and beans, hominy (a sort of dry bean resembling haricots), and potatoes. Once, we had sweet potatoes, which were red and tasted like common potatoes diseased; and, another time, we had a vegetable called squash; and always boiled ears of green Indian corn. Several times, we had soup made of land turtles, which was good. Our sweets were generally custard pie (there

are no tarts in the United States, everything there is 'pie'), or
sometimes cherry pie, squash pie, apple pie, and occasionally
blackberry pie. Sometimes, too, we had stewed pears or roast
apples. Then followed cheese and dessert; at which, latterly,
there were large bowls of iced cream and watermelons, which
they called 'cholera bomb shells'; and, in spite of their terrific
name, they were eaten with avidity. Nuts and almonds were,
also, always on the table."

The servant who annoyed the Bestes the most was
the waiter who was sent round twice a week. Without
knocking, he would poke his head in at the bedroom door
unexpectedly, as if to detect the guests in crime, and ask:
"Got any spoons?"
The charge per person for this fare, lodging, and
attendance was five dollars a week!
When Richard Beste was able to leave Terre Haute,
he turned his fine wagon and horses over to a grandson of
William Henry Harrison for future sale and chose the
Wabash and Erie Canal as the most comfortable means
of traveling back to the East. His English pride was hard
pressed to explain away his disappointment in the journey, for the canal was at that time the property of
English owners. Connecting the Maumee and Wabash
rivers below Fort Wayne and running the full length of
the Wabash, the canal was begun in 1832 as a link between the Great Lakes and the Mississippi. But it was no
sooner started than the railroads began to appear, doom-
ing it as an important method of travel. When, a few
years later, the state was unable to pay off its bonds, it
turned the canal over to a group of its English creditors.
The boat on which the Bestes journeyed from Terre
Haute was constructed like a river steamboat without

"THEY HAD EVERYTHING ON THE TABLE BUT
Quit AND *Don't!*"

an engine room. There was, of course, no hold. The passengers' baggage was piled on the roof of the deckhouse. On the deck, at the stern, were the kitchen, stewards' rooms, and offices. Forward was the large saloon, which was a sitting room during the day and the sleeping room of male passengers at night. Adjoining it was the ladies' saloon, used as a dormitory at night; and beyond it, a small cabin containing four small staterooms. The boat was drawn by three horses that plodded along a path about fifty yards ahead.

Once more Mr. Beste and his family were troubled by the heat, the mosquitoes, and what they considered the bad manners of the Hoosier "lady" passengers, who bickered over their rights in the crowded dormitory. A male passenger who insisted on shooting at birds from the roof of the deckhouse all day long was another source of annoyance.

But, as they progressed northward, the scenery changed constantly and prevented their being bored. Above Covington, where the canal passed through a sandstone country, they found it especially attractive. Lafayette, at first, disappointed them. It did not appear so large and prosperous as they had expected. But, at Lafayette, an elegant lady and gentleman came aboard at the last minute, promising more congenial companionship than they had so far enjoyed. From Lafayette northward, the countryside was wilder and sparsely settled, giving Mr. Beste the notion that it was more salubrious and making him feel better at once.

"I never saw more magnificent timber than shaded the valleys through which we passed. Great sticks of plank oak shot up straight from the bottoms without a knot or branch, until their heads spread out some scores of feet above, like the tufted summits of the Italian pine."

At Fort Wayne, the ground was considerably higher, but equally fertile; and the Englishman was fascinated by an old blockhouse on the riverbank, the first he had seen in America. But, a few miles farther north, where the Wabash Canal joined another that ran south to Cincinnati, he lost all interest in his surroundings; for there he parted with his two sons. In spite of the petty annoyances of traveling in the strange land, Richard Beste was fully aware of the advantages it offered. He wanted his sons to escape the curb of the British law of primogeniture. He wanted them to have an equal chance of prospering and improving themselves. He was sending them to a college in the new land. He was eager that they should become Americans.

44

Morgan!

O<small>N</small> the twelfth of April, 1861, the news
reached Indiana that Fort Sumter had been fired upon.
On the fifteenth of April, President Lincoln asked the
state for five thousand volunteers. In less than two weeks,
not five, but ten thousand were ready.

From every farm and settlement they came in
greater numbers than were called for—the tallest men
to fight in the Union army and the only ones whose
marksmanship equaled that of their Confederate foes.
They were mustered in; they drilled; and eventually
they tramped away southward, many of them never to
return. Those who remained at home took up the work
of the departed soldiers and, in their spare time, did what
they could to aid the cause, the women organizing hospitals and canteens, the old men and boys banding together into companies of home guards. During the next
four years, the Wabash mules and horses were worked
overtime and the Wabash soil yielded double its rich
abundance to supply the fighting army. The river itself,
flowing southward toward the scene of the conflict, became an instrument of the Union cause. Overnight, elegant steamboats were converted into fighting craft and
transports, and towboats graduated to the dignity of

rams, while their pilots and captains forsook the luxury of peacetime navigation for the sterner glories of commissions in the United States Navy.

Such was the prompt and generous response of the Hoosiers to the crisis that threatened the Union in '61; and, through the dreary years of deadlock, their enthusiasm and loyalty did not falter. And yet, in the South and even in the North, there were many who doubted the fundamental loyalty of Indiana and hoped or feared, as their own loyalties inclined them, that the Hoosiers would eventually come to the support of the Confederacy. No one knew exactly the strength of the Knights of the Golden Circle, the numbers of the "Stars" and the "Copperheads." Fires were seen blazing in the hills along the Wabash at night. Meetings and rallies were held in open protest against the war. Such able and influential men as Daniel W. Voorhees and Thomas A. Hendricks were accused by their political enemies of affiliating with the Order of American Knights. Rumor everywhere was rampant; for the Hoosier, after all, had deep ancestral roots in the South and his history showed no great affection for the Negro.

In 1862, the Hoosiers sent a Democratic legislature to Indianapolis; and in July of that year, their loyalty received its first test.

At noon on July 17th, Captain Adam Johnson, a Confederate officer of Kentucky, seized a ferryboat on the Ohio, some fifty miles above the mouth of the Wabash, and, with only thirty men and two stovepipes mounted on wheels, crossed the river and captured the little Hoosier town of Newburg. Captain Johnson's men made prisoners of the seventy-five Union soldiers who were patients in the Newburg hospital and then, not

knowing what else to do with them, magnanimously
paroled them. But they knew what to do with the plunder they collected in the homes and stores of the village.
They carried it back with them into Kentucky, pausing
only long enough to proclaim the village officially captured in the name of the Confederacy.

The "capture" of Newburg was nothing more than
a border raid, of no importance in the vast drama of the
war. Two men were killed at Newburg, however, and
their deaths were of considerable significance. Both were
citizens of the town. Yet they were not killed by Johnson's soldiers, nor did they lose their lives during the
attack. They were shot after the Confederate raiders had
departed. Their fellow citizens shot them down in the
streets; for, during the raid, those men had been seen
pointing out property for seizure.

The casualty list at Newburg might have been a
warning to those in the South who believed that Confederate troops would receive a warm and sympathetic
welcome on Hoosier soil. But if the significance of that
brief casualty list was recognized, it was not heeded; for,
a year later, gray soldiers once more crossed into Indiana
and the South's longest invasion of northern territory
was on.

For forty years, the village of Corydon, once the
state's capital, had slept in its quiet valley where Big
Indian and Little Indian creeks unite. During court
weeks, the streets were crowded with the carriages and
wagons of farmers and their families, come to the county
seat to trade and barter and to disentangle their legal
broils. On Sundays, too, the town bestirred itself, as the
Presbyterians, the Methodists, and the Christians gath-

ered in their finest clothes for worship. But at other times Corydon drowsed peacefully, content with the classic beauty of the name that William Henry Harrison had bestowed upon it years before and the departed glory of which the old, square, limestone capitol and the Constitutional Elm were symbols.

On the night of Wednesday, July 8, 1863, however, the town was alive with unaccustomed weekday activity, as it prepared to play one more brief role in the nation's history. Men, women, and children were busy in the houses, ripping open feather mattresses, digging holes in cellar floors, rummaging in cubbyholes and rafter rooms, seeking everywhere the secret places of their homes where valuables might be hid. In the streets, other citizens of Corydon stood talking in low, excited tones; but, every once in a while, a silence would fall upon them as they listened for distant hoofbeats or the rumble of cannon.

"Morgan!" they whispered to each other, in unbelieving horror. "John Morgan!"

The name itself was enough. But occasionally a courier came riding into town, weaving his way through the droves of mules and horses and the caravan of wagons and carriages, bearing the aged and the sick, that pushed endlessly northward in frantic quest of safety.

"He's across the river now! The guards at Mauckport have fallen back!"

On the courthouse lawn, the local home guards were gathering. Colonel Jordan and Major Pfrimmer were wheeling their horses back and forth, up and down the line.

"They've burned their boats behind them! The road is full of refugees!"

"Keep the refugees moving north, major. We'll hold the rebels back! Keep them moving!"

They came in swarms and droves, women and children mostly, on horseback, on muleback, in carriages and wagons, walking.

"Keep them moving!"

More couriers galloped into the courthouse square.

"There's five thousand men with Morgan!"

Six thousand!

Ten thousand!

"Keep them moving, major! We'll hold the rebels even if it's Lee's whole army! Keep the refugees moving north!"

The citizens of Corydon on the street corners huddled closer together.

"Morgan!"

"General Morgan—and Basil Duke is with him!"

"Duke and Morgan!"

One more courier came riding in from the south. His horse's flanks were steaming. He stopped only long enough to shout his message to the men in the streets.

"They're coming! They're on the road from Mauckport now!"

Then he rode on.

At dawn, the last of the refugees had fled through the town, the valuables were all hidden, the citizens of Corydon were locked and barred in their homes. The streets were deserted, except for the company of home guards under the trees in the courthouse square.

"Give the order to march. We'll form our line on the hill south of town."

Three hundred of them—old men and boys, with sabers, pistols, squirrel rifles, axes, corn knives—they marched out to the hill and, stripping down the rail fences, threw up a barricade across the ridge.

"Remember how they held them at Bunker Hill, boys!"

And they remembered—three hundred of them against Morgan's four thousand!

At ten o'clock in the morning, the first gray-clad riders appeared on the road below.

"Don't fire, boys! Remember Bunker Hill!"

They waited, each man and boy breathless; one of them, an old man with a weak heart, already dead from the excitement, although they did not know it then. In the hot July sun, they waited, no one daring to bat away the insects that hovered over them in a cloud, to wipe the sweat from his face, to scratch, to cough, to whisper. A move might be fatal.

Then the attack came. Up the hill, a line of gray moved swiftly, like a ripple over the sunburnt field. A thousand of them? Ten thousand? They did not know. They only waited—old, watery eyes sighting down the barrels of rifles that years before had killed bears and Indians; young, sharp eyes, widening eagerly, having never before drawn a bead on anything more deadly than a turkey or a squirrel. But when the order came to fire, they were ready. And when the smoke cleared, they saw that the ripple of gray had crested and was breaking, was falling back.

A cheer went up. They had held them! They had stopped Morgan!

And for another hour they held them, until, at last, John Morgan brought up his artillery and began to shell the town behind them. Then they thought of their mothers and sisters and children and began a retreat that ended in Colonel Jordan's surrender.

Eight Confederates killed and thirty-three wounded. Three home guards killed, two wounded, and one dropped dead. The Battle of Corydon was over—the only pitched battle north of the Mason and Dixon's line, besides Gettysburg, officially recorded by the War Department in the Civil War!

The three hundred home guards were made prisoners of war. At the outskirts of the town, the editor of the Corydon *Democrat* and the county auditor met the gray army to intercede for their fellow townspeople.

"You must ride at the head of our column, then, as hostages, until the town is invested."

The man who spoke had just ridden up from the hill where the artillery was still firing. He was a giant, deep-chested, broad-shouldered, astride a great, bay mare. His blue eyes flashed as he spoke. His blond mustache and imperial were streaked with dust and black pomatum.

"Morgan!"

The name ran in a whisper through the disarmed home guards, like the shiver of an October wind through a shock of corn. This was the man whose army they had held for an hour!

General Morgan stopped in Corydon only long enough to catch a little nap at the Kintner Hotel and to allow his men to forage for food, clothing, money, and horses. Then he moved on, northward.

They cut telegraph wires as they marched and destroyed the bridges and railroads they crossed. They left behind them only such horses and mules as were spent and useless. They did not burn or murder. But they took everything they could lay their hands on. And, as they marched on, they were an army swallowed up and invisible, reappearing mysteriously where rumor said they were not and failing to appear where rumor said they were. The only warning of their approach was their thundering song—"Here's to Duke and Morgan, drink them down!"—but it never came soon enough. Before them lay terrified uncertainty and suspense; behind them, silence and emptiness.

General Hobson, who finally crossed the Ohio with Union troops in pursuit, never knew where his quarry was. Governor Morton, who issued proclamations from the frightened city of Indianapolis, could not guess from which direction the capital might be attacked. All that either could depend upon were rumors, and the rumors were not dependable.

"Ten thousand of them, guv'nor! I saw 'em myself. They've taken Salem an' Vernon an' Versailles! They'll be here in a few hours!"

"Indianapolis has fallen, general! I jest heared it from a feller that come from there! They've released those six thousand Rebel prisoners in the capital and thrown the arsenal open to 'em. Indianny's captured for sure! A Confederate army of twelve thousand men in Indianapolis!"

In the meantime, Morgan continued to march and forage and plunder and raid, while the song thundered more and more deliriously.

"Here's to Duke and Morgan, drink them down!"

He might, indeed, have taken Indianapolis and held Indiana, for a time at least. He might also have turned quickly upon his pursuer, General Hobson, and cut the

Union troops to pieces. But he chose, for some strange reason, to do neither. Instead, he allowed his men to scatter widely over the Hoosier countryside and plunder as they pleased, until eventually he lost control of them.

By the time he reached Vernon, Indiana, his magnificent army of crack Kentucky cavalrymen had degenerated into a straggling band of looters, drunk with a carnival spirit. From their saddles hung bolts of calico which, when night came, they burned as torches, knowing that more could be found in the morning. One soldier, for two days, carried a bird cage with three canaries in it. Another rode with a silver chafing dish strapped to the pommel of his saddle. Still another carried seven pairs of ice skates slung about his sweating neck. Hams, flour, blacksmith tools, lace dresses, shoes, hats, moneybags—the rich spoils of Indiana were gathered up, then scattered, then gathered up again.

Some historians say that by the time he reached Indiana, John Morgan was no longer the fearless and expert commander that he had once been. He had grown soft and uxorious. His new, young wife had spoiled him, weakened his decisiveness and determination. Others say that Morgan was disappointed in the reception the Knights of the Golden Circle gave him on Hoosier soil and his discouragement forced him to give up his original plan of conquest. A third explanation is that he was only working in concert with Bragg and taking orders from headquarters. No one knows. All that is known is that Vernon was the crest of the invasion. There the invaders' morale crumpled and they began to straggle southward, until at last they crossed into Ohio, where eventually they were overtaken and captured.

But Morgan's capture is another story. By the time

the last of his army had been dispersed or imprisoned, the Hoosiers had returned to their homes and collected what was left of their scattered property. Morgan's raid was something that they would long remember, but, at the moment, their minds were filled with other thoughts. Vicksburg had just fallen, and Lee had lost at Gettysburg. Morgan had come and gone, and Indiana had stood the test. The worst of the Civil War was over.

45

Hello, the Boat!

THE waters of the Wabash wind placid and undisturbed through the fields and woods of Indiana today, and it is hard to imagine the rush of riverboats to the service of the Union in '61 or the jam of commerce that crowded the river both before and after the Civil War. Yet the boats were there in countless numbers, making the Wabash an important artery of river traffic for more than a century.

In the spring of 1826, the *Highland Laddie* brought Joseph Neef and his family to New Harmony, anchoring before the town on a stormy Sunday night; and, a few weeks later, when news came from Terre Haute that the *Highland Laddie* had left that town to proceed up the Wabash to the Big Vermilion and thence to Grounendyke's Mills, the editor of the New Harmony *Gazette* caught his first glimpse of what was to come.

"It is truly gratifying to contemplate the rapid improvements of this country," he wrote. "Three years ago this place was for the first time visited by a steamboat, the *Florence*—she arrived once that year; two years ago, the *Ploughboy* visited us twice—last spring we had two arrivals, and this season we have had five from below."

Within another year, there were many new names on the river—the *Josephine*, the *Decatur*, and the *Belvidere*, the largest of her time. Then came the *Cincinnati*, the *Cumberland*, the *Triton*, the *Wabash*, and the *William Tell*, which was christened by George Rapp himself. In 1831, only eight years after the first black smudge of steamboat smoke had clouded the sky above Wabash willows, the New Harmony *Disseminator* was boasting that in one month thirty-six boats had arrived at the town from below and twenty-seven from above, while "about 1700 flatboats have descended the Wabash this spring." In the late sixties, it was not unusual for twenty boats to be moored at the New Harmony landing in a single week and for even more to crowd the larger ports of Vincennes, Terre Haute, and Lafayette.

By that time, steamboating was a business in real earnest. From the Mississippi and its tributaries, you could reach hundreds of northern towns via the Wabash. You could go as far as Indianapolis on the west fork of the White; to Petersburg, Indiana, on the east fork; to Danville, Illinois, on the Vermilion; to Lafayette and Delphi and Logansport on the Wabash; and, with a little land travel added, to Fort Wayne and points north. Journeying thus in ease and elegance, you spared yourself the uncertainty and discomforts of the new railroads, the fatigue of horseback riding, and the dangers of the stagecoach; and, what was more, you saw the country and its people as you went.

"Hello, the *Ollie Sullivan!*" they called from the shore; for the classical names of the packets were giving place to more intimate and affectionate titles. "Hello, the *Aggie!* Hello, the *Clara Scott!*"

"Hello, the *Sam Parker!*" they called. "The *James*

Gray. The *Hoosier!* The *Buckeye!* Whatcha loaded with?"

Then the captain—no matter what his home port, his destination, or his cargo might be—would step to the rail of the texas and wave his arm in response.

"Fruit and lumber!" he would cry; and his eyes would twinkle with merriment at the old jest of Wabash rivermen. "Fruit and lumber—pawpaws and hooppoles!"

You saw the boat nose into the bank in the heart of the corn bottoms where a farmer had collected his stock and produce for shipment. You heard the farmer and the captain haggle over the price. Then you watched the fine cows and hogs and mules of the Wabash valley driven aboard and marveled at the abundance of Wabash crops.

You saw the best and the worst of the people of the towns gathered on the water fronts to watch your steamboat come round the bends and veer in toward the landings. They had been summoned by the music of the whistle, and they knew her name before they saw her, for no two whistles on the river were alike. You went ashore perhaps and mingled with the friendly people, talked with them, and learned the local gossip and the latest news.

You moved on then, upriver or downriver, passing close to other craft and exchanging greetings and the time of day. They were steamboats—those other craft —larger or smaller than your own, side-wheelers and stern-wheelers, high-pressure and low-pressure boats. They were rafts and barges, loaded almost to the sinking point with whisky, flour, and pork. They were houseboats and showboats. They were skiffs and ferries. Occasionally, if it was spring, they were the famous, Wabash

UPRIVER OR DOWNRIVER, PASSING CLOSE TO
OTHER CRAFT.

River "glass boats"—crude flatboats steered by a stern
oar and surmounted by a cabin stocked with glass and
chinaware that would replenish the cupboards and deco-
rate the parlors of farm and village housewives all the
way down to New Orleans.

On the river in those days, you saw the whole of
midwestern society and scenery glide past you to the
music of your steamboat's whistle and her paddle wheels,
and you enjoyed the additional thrill of entrusting your
life for a time to men who knew the mysteries of the
rivers as a small boy knows the contents of his own
trousers pockets.

Of one of those men—the captain of a passenger
and freight packet on the New Harmony, Evansville,
and Mt. Carmel run, folks used to sing a certain song:

"He wasn't no saint with a gilt-edge crown—
His language'd shatter a church steeple down—
He'd a thirst in his throat that nothin' could drown
An' a fist like a blacksmith forge!"

Some said he had only to hurl an epithet at an obstructing towhead or snag and it would explode and
vanish in a thousand pieces. Others said you could hear
him swearing up or down river twenty minutes before
his whistle became audible. But no one, except his pilot,
dared to challenge his authority or his wisdom on the
rivers. By the divine right of brains, blasphemy, and
brawn, he was a king.

Some of those former despots are still left along the
shores of the Wabash—old fellows now, most of them,
retired to front porches and rocking chairs, their palaces
of yesterday sunk or dismantled, but their natural titles
to sovereignty still unimpaired. Their heads are filled

with many memories. They can tell strange tales. But they do not tell them readily. They fear they may not be believed. And confidence they must have, for confidence was once their daily bread. After all, it is only twenty-five years since the *Island Queen,* one of the last of the Wabash packets, went down in fifteen feet of water while taking a load of hay, horses, and mules to the Stum farm on Fox Island, and what is twenty-five years to them? The wreck of the *Island Queen* happened only yesterday! Their memories are fresh. They deserve to be believed.

Once started, their yarns are endless. They specialize in the bizarre, the violent, and the ironic. They favor the story of the boat that sank with seventeen head of cattle penned on her maindeck and bobbed to the surface a week later when the carcasses became so bloated that they floated her. They relish the fate of the miserly captain who paused in a race to take aboard a man who was signaling him from the shore, only to discover that the man was not signaling him at all but only batting a swarm of mosquitoes away from his face. They grow solemn over the changes the river makes in its course every spring, telling how, in that season, the Illinois farmer you passed on an upriver trip often appeared on the opposite bank, on the return trip, a newly baptized Hoosier, wringing out his clothes and setting his drenched house in order for a year of farming in Indiana. They speak of explosions and gun fights and stove hulls as another man might speak of chigger bites. If you did not already know that almost anything can happen on the Wabash, you might find it hard to believe them.

46

The *Juno*

T HE *Juno* was a side-wheeler that plied the Wabash in the sixties. John R. Hugo built and captained her, and his brother, Jenk Hugo, piloted her. They picked up cargoes of grain and cattle and occasionally carried a passenger or two. The *Juno* was not a floating palace, by any means. She had only one engine and a wooden cogwheel and you could hear her coming and recognize her without a whistle. Folks along the Wabash made up a song about her once that goes like this:

"She was warped in the hull and broad o' beam
An' her engine whistled with the waste o' steam—
An' a two-mile jog agin Wabash stream
Was her average runnin' gait."

But the *Juno* served her purpose, and the Hugo brothers were proud of her.

On the night of February 18, 1865, the *Juno* was headed for New Orleans with a load of pork and flour. She had no passengers; but, in addition to Captain John and Pilot Jenk, the two engineers, and a co-pilot named Beal, Mrs. Jenk Hugo, Mrs. Beal and the Beal baby were aboard. The river was high and so were the spirits of the Hugo brothers; for they had a good cargo and every riverman liked the prospect of a trip to New Orleans. But when they approached Neal's Bend, a mile or so above New Harmony, their rejoicing came to an abrupt end. They were engaged in a heated and unprecedented quarrel.

It was all because of the middle shoal at Neal's Bend, which left two channels in the river. The west channel, on the Illinois side, was clear and wide. The east channel, on the Indiana side, was filled with snags. But the east channel was considerably shorter. Captain John, thinking of his cargo, was all for playing safe and taking the west channel. But Pilot Jenk, confident of his skill, held out for the east channel. For a half hour, they argued, while the *Juno,* paddling downstream, drew rapidly nearer the shoal. Captain John had wisdom and the authority of ownership on his side. But Pilot Jenk had determination—and something else that was even stronger. He had the rank of pilot, and, on any boat under way, the pilot is king.

For that reason, when she arrived at the middle shoal at Neal's Bend, the *Juno* swung eastward into the snag-infested Indiana channel.

There was nothing spectacular in the *Juno's* sinking. She simply struck a snag, heaved up on one end, sighed heavily as the water rushed through the gash in her belly, and then settled gently into a cradle of more snags, which held her cabins up out of the water. Captain John swore and Pilot Jenk tried to exonerate himself; but that was all the confusion the wreck created aboard. The women, knowing the river as well as their husbands, had no fear for their safety; and the engineers soon saw that the engine could be salvaged. So eventually Captain John quieted down and began to blow the distress whistle and a farmer appeared in the dawn and rowed all hands ashore.

The engine and the cargo were salvaged, but there was no saving the *Juno* herself. The Hugos had to leave her to the river and to fate.

Fate appeared on the scene very shortly in the persons of half the townspeople of New Harmony. They came in rafts and skiffs and swarmed about the *Juno*, like flies around sugar. They played their role well, stripping off all the structure that could be pried loose and carrying it back with them to the town. There, for years afterward, their houses and sheds and outside stairways were patched with parts of the steamer's storm deck, and a half dozen privies were graced with ornamental deck railing.

Fate having finished, the river took up its task; and it was the river that won the *Juno* her place in Wabash history. First, the middle shoal began to make down upon the steamboat, covering her decks and eventually her cabins with silt and sand. This process lasted for a quarter of a century. The river bottom slowly rose and engulfed the steamboat, like a growing anthill. Driftwood piled up. Little islands sidled over and attached themselves. Trees began to sprout until a thick growth of them— willow and cottonwood—covered the whole surface. At last, a large island had been formed where the *Juno* sank.

"Juno Island" the people of New Harmony called it; and, for the next thirty years, the shelving bar that ran out from it was a favorite bathing point for young people born long after the wreck of the old steamboat.

But the river was not through. In the 1920's, it sent a cutoff through another island upstream and began to eat away the sand and silt it had piled over the *Juno* years before. The willows and the cottonwoods lost their hold in the shifting soil, tumbled into the water, one by one, and floated off downstream. The little islands that had scurried over to join their fate with Juno broke away and dissolved or set up housekeeping elsewhere. Eddies dug into the earth that was left. Sand swirled upward and was spewed out into the current. Finally, rising like a ghost from the river bed, the *Juno* reappeared.

For several years she stood in the middle of the river, gaunt, stripped, bleached, and sand-streaked. Then the river once more took pity on her and, in one surging flood, swept the old carcass and its whole foundation away.

Today, there is only a smooth, clear expanse of water where Juno Island used to be; but somehow it seems to tell, with mute eloquence, the whole story of the steamboats on the Wabash. They came. They conquered. They prospered. They grew extravagant and reckless. They vanished. And now there is only the silent water, flowing placid and undisturbed.

PART EIGHT

Politics and Poetry

47

-- And Then Some!

THE per capita interest in politics in the Wabash valley is greater than in any other part of the country. Meet any Hoosier out of swaddling clothes and you meet a potential political argument. On buses and trains, in streets and in offices, at weddings and funerals, in the fields and on their front porches, the Hoosiers are at all times ready to pause for a discussion of the issues and candidates of the day; for a Hoosier would almost rather "talk politics" than eat fried chicken!

And they like their politics with all the finishings in Indiana. They love long speeches. They expect exaggeration and gesticulation. They demand cleverness and courage and handshaking. They appreciate these embellishments as other men appreciate Gothic steeples and fine murals, not because they are useful, but because they are art. In the name of political art, they will put up with a lot—these Hoosiers. They will even stand for a long spell of corruption and skulduggery now and then, if they are cleverly practiced and make a good show. But, in the end, they usually swing back to their own sound and healthy convictions. Forensics and even knavery may entertain them; they cannot lead them long astray.

Oliver H. Smith, as a candidate for Congress many

years ago, once addressed a crowd in Ripley County for two hours. When he had finished, an old man who had been leaning against a tree through it all and listening intently, roared out:

"Mr. Smith, that was the best speech I ever heared. I agree with everything you said. But I'd like to ask you one question."

"Most certainly," replied the orator.

"Air you a-goin' to vote fur General Jackson?"

"No, sir; I shall vote for Henry Clay."

"Well, Mr. Smith, that was a durn fine speech— but you won't git my vote!"

In 1856, Cassius M. Clay was scheduled to make an abolition speech in Huntington. The folks in Huntington set very little store by abolitionists and they prophesied that Mr. Clay would never reach the end of his address.

When the day arrived, Cassius M. Clay climbed up on the platform and laid three objects on the table before him.

One was the Constitution of the United States.

"I may have occasion to refer to it," he explained.

Another was the Bible.

"I reckon no political speech is much good without a few quotations from Scripture."

The third was a horse pistol.

"This-here is a paperweight—but I'll use it on any Demmycratic scamp that dares to interrupt me!"

The crowd cheered. They listened respectfully to every word he had to say. At the end, they applauded him loudly. Then they marched off to the polls and voted against him, just as they had originally intended to do.

Cassius M. Clay's was the spirit the Hoosier liked

and still likes in politics. Plenty of barbecue, good liquor, long-winded oratory, courage, wit, and hearty handshakes still draw the crowds on the banks of the Wabash and may sometimes even capture a few votes. Certainly the absence of any one of these attractions spells defeat.

In one of the large cities of the state, they still tell how, in 1916, Charles Evans Hughes lost thousands of votes by refusing to speak in their largest auditorium because it was too ramshackle. In 1910, Theodore Roosevelt, passing through Richmond, Indiana, failed to leave his train and address a large crowd gathered to meet him, with the result that he contributed to the defeat of his friend and fellow Progressive, Albert J. Beveridge. Six years later, John Worth Kern refused to disappoint the people of Brookville, where he had always delivered the closing speeches of his campaigns, and, by so doing, he defeated himself, because he disappointed many more people who were expecting him in the city of Indianapolis.

To win an election in Indiana, you have to be everywhere at all times—and then some!

A certain Hoosier politician tells how once his car broke down beside the wall of one of the state's hospitals for the insane. While he was repairing it, an inmate peered over the wall and engaged him in conversation.

"What's your business, friend?" the inmate asked.

"I'm a candidate for Congress."

"You ain't crazy, are you?"

"No."

"Ever been crazy?"

"No."

"You ought to try it. It beats politics!"

Just before the Civil War, the newborn Republican

party received much of its first strength and encourage-
ment in Indiana; and, two decades earlier, the Democratic rooster is said to have been hatched in Indiana.

The political chanticleer is, indeed, a Wabash bird,
for it was in Terre Haute on the river's banks that he
first began to crow, during the Van Buren-Harrison
campaign of 1840. The Whigs were saying that Little
Van was a used-up man, and certainly he was not making
much headway against the flood of hard cider with which
the friends of Old Tippecanoe had inundated the Wabash
valley. The principal organ of Hoosier Democrats at that
time was the *Wabash Enquirer* published at Terre Haute
by a man named Chapman, but Mr. Chapman seemed to
lack confidence in Little Van's success. Finally, one of
the party leaders got after him and gave him a lesson in
political campaigning. "You must never express any
doubts, Chapman. You must always appear sure and confident. You must crow, Chapman, crow!" Thereafter, in
the columns of the *Wabash Enquirer*, Chapman crowed.

But unfortunately for the Democrats, Mr. Chap-
man's instructions leaked out, and soon every Whig paper
in the state was taunting its rival in big black letters:
"CROW, CHAPMAN, CROW!" The discomfiture of
Chapman and the Democrats was completed when a
waggish poem appeared in the *Spirit of Seventy-Six*, a
Whig sheet published in Indianapolis. It was entitled
"Song of Jim Crow":

> "Let all de British Tory
>   Who feel so very low,
> Keep stiff de upper lip
>   And give a loud Crow.
> Brag about and bet about
>   And grin just so,

And every time you meet a Whig
Give a loud Crow.

"Massa Van he frightened,
Everybody know.
Still he scold at Amos
Cause he doesn't Crow.
Brag about and bet about,
And grin just so;
And never lose de spirits,
But give a loud Crow."

Indiana has sometimes been called the home of America's vice-presidents, both Republican and Democrat. Four Hoosiers—Schuyler Colfax, Thomas A. Hendricks, Charles W. Fairbanks, and Thomas R. Marshall— have been elected to the office; and three others (Let their well-earned anonymity remain inviolate!) have been unsuccessful candidates. Of the speakers of the lower house in Washington, three have been Hoosier congressmen.

Irvin S. Cobb explains "Indiana's magnificent yield of vice-presidents" in the following manner:

"Indiana gives us our vice-presidents and our vice-presidential candidates because she is the average American state. And by the same token, the average Indianian makes suitable vice-presidential material because he is absolutely just that— average. If he were sub-average he couldn't get the nomination and if he were super-average he wouldn't take it."

It is true that the vice-presidency of the United States is a doubtful honor. Thomas Marshall himself once remarked, when he was a candidate for the office: "The vice-presidency of the United States is not an occupation: it's a disease!" And yet, the very fact that a candidate could make such a remark about the office to which he was aspiring would indicate that the candidate, if not the office, was above average. Lank, drawling, witty, and lovable Tom Marshall, with his twinkling eyes and Mark Twain mustache, was certainly one of the least "average" vice-presidents that Washington has ever known.

It must be remembered that Irvin S. Cobb is a humorist and a Kentuckian. Humorists are given to exaggeration, and Kentuckians, like all good neighbors, are likely to underestimate the talents of the folks next door. Mr. Cobb probably overlooked the fact that Abraham Lincoln, while he was born in Kentucky and elected to the presidency from Illinois, attained his manhood and formed his character in Indiana. And two other presidents (not vice-presidents!) have borne the stamp of the Hoosier. William Henry Harrison's political reputation was established on the banks of the Wabash at Vincennes and Tippecanoe, and upon it he built his successful campaign. His grandson, Benjamin Harrison, though born in Ohio, was a senator from Indiana at the time he was elected president.

The Wabash country has produced other distinguished political figures. John Hay, Lincoln's secretary and later ambassador to Great Britain and secretary of state under two presidents, was born in Salem, Indiana. Robert Dale Owen, legislative parent of the Smithsonian Institution and an early crusader for women's rights and public schools, lived on the banks of the Wabash. Daniel W. Voorhees—"The Tall Sycamore of the Wabash"— for years was one of the most brilliant orators in the United States Senate. In Indiana lived the shrewdest master mechanic who ever constructed a political machine west of Tammany—Thomas Taggart. And Indiana today is still producing men whose names are prominent in national affairs—McNutt, Van Nuys, Minton, and Ludlow.

48

Two for Posterity

Average—?

Two twentieth century Hoosiers alone will refute any argument that Indiana's role in politics has been only average. Their names are Albert J. Beveridge and Eugene V. Debs.

A slim, blue-eyed youth, with a mop of yellow hair and a determined jaw, Albert J. Beveridge moved into Indianapolis in the eighties straight from DePauw University, where he had won every prize that was offered for oratory. He was no ordinary young man, and he knew it. Although he was poorer than Job's turkey, he had no intention of wasting his talents on the long, hard struggle expected of young lawyers in their early careers. He went directly to Benjamin Harrison, then the biggest name in the capital, and asked to be allowed to read law in the former president's office. That bearded and dignified little man rejected him coldly. But Beveridge was undaunted. He applied to his second choice, the firm of McDonald and Butler, and was accepted.

Once started, Albert J. Beveridge began to build for the future. He joined the Meridian Street Methodist Church and was soon ushering the "best" people of the city to their pews. He accepted every speaking engagement that was offered to him. He learned all the cosmopolite's tricks of speech and dress. When he set up his own law office, he paid strict attention to details, furnishing it more elaborately than his nonexistent bank balance and clients warranted. By the year 1899, he was ready to ask Indiana for a seat in the United States Senate —but only because he knew that Indiana was ready to give it to him.

Senator Beveridge was an imperialist in those early days, a believer in the principle that might makes right. His heroes were Napoleon and Richelieu—and Albert J. Beveridge. He went to the Philippines and returned with his preconceived faith in our manifest destiny on those islands strengthened by what he had seen. He believed not only that the United States should keep the Philippines, but also that we should take anything else we could get. The Anglo-Saxon race was destined by God to rule and improve the world, and Albert Beveridge was God's prophet. Brilliantly he preached the doctrine of nationalism and imperialism wherever he went, and his maiden speech in the Senate drew the greatest crowd that had packed its galleries since the maiden speech of Daniel W. Voorhees years before.

Then, at the height of his career among the aristocrats, Beveridge's faith in their God-given wisdom inexplicably collapsed. In his forties, he was visited by the light which most conservatives of his kind usually abandon with the visions of their teens. It was the light of political liberalism. He had always believed that the wealth of the land, as well as its people, should be controlled by the state; but now, for the first time, he saw that the state was the people. He became a trust

buster—a friend of the people. He traveled the length
and breadth of the land preaching the new religion of
Theodore Roosevelt. All his brilliant talents he cast in
unreservedly with the lot of the Progressive party. And,
with the Progressive party, he inevitably fell.

Albert J. Beveridge dreamed all his life of the presidency, and no man ever trained himself more conscien-
tiously for that high office. It seemed to his friends that
he never slept. His insatiable mind was always working,
ferreting out the information that a true statesman must
have, culling it from books, from conversations, from
firsthand experience, from philosophic meditation. But
two obstacles stood between Beveridge and the honor
he dreamed of. One was the people, whom he discovered
too late. The other was himself, whom he never learned
to forget.

The other twentieth century Hoosier whose name
reflects political honor upon his state loved the people
too well and himself too little for success in politics. For
four years, he was the city clerk of Terre Haute, and,
from 1885 to 1887, he was a representative in the Hoosier
state legislature. He was nominated for the presidency
six times. But he never dreamed, like Beveridge, of being
elected to that office. His sole concern was for the cause
to which he was devoted and the men and women for
whom he worked. His close friend, James Whitcomb
Riley, once wrote of him:

> "And there's Gene Debs—a man 'at stands
> And jest holds out in his two hands
> As warm a heart as ever beat
> Betwixt here and the Jedgment Seat."

Eugene V. Debs was born in Terre Haute in 1855. His parents were poor and there were nine other children in the family, which was bound together by a filial affection that impressed everyone who knew them. The Debses owned a small grocery store and they needed Gene's help in it, but the boy's compassion for others who lived in poverty was already so strongly marked that his mother and father dared not let him clerk in their store. He might have given everything away! So, at fifteen, he went to work in the Vandalia carshops in Terre Haute and, within a year, he was firing a locomotive. He had many other jobs after that, but his heart remained always in railroading.

In politics, Debs began as a Democrat, and he might have gone far in the ranks of the Democratic party. His sincerity was obvious even to his enemies. His simple eloquence was as irresistible as Lincoln's. When he was a Hoosier legislator, his nominating speech for Daniel W. Voorhees to the United States Senate won him state-wide recognition, and he might have secured a privileged place for himself in the shade of the Tall Sycamore. But his experience on the railroad had set him dreaming, and already he was beginning to fear that his dreams could never be realized within the ranks of one of the old-line parties.

"What can we do for labor?"

He heard the question on the lips of Democrats and Republicans alike, and he was growing contemptuous.

" 'What can we do for labor,' " he cried. "It is the old, old query. . . . It is the language of the slave-catcher, the slave-pen, the slave-block, and the slave-plantation. We hear it yet . . . but our ears are regaled by another and more manly query . . . which is, 'What can labor do for itself?' The answer is not difficult. Labor can organize, it can unify, it can consolidate its forces. This done, it can demand and command."

When the first all-inclusive union of railway men was organized and Debs was offered its presidency, he gave up his Democratic prospects and accepted. But characteristically he accepted only on the condition that the salary should be $3,000 a year, instead of $5,000. After that, his life was devoted to the cause of labor.

The first real test of Debs's courage came in 1894. The workers in the Pullman shops in Illinois struck and other railroad men tried to aid them by refusing to work on trains that hauled Pullman cars. The United States mail became involved, and President Cleveland stepped in. Throughout the strike, Debs urged the workers to abstain from violence of any kind, but he insisted upon the right of all workers to unite in assisting the Pullman strikers. It was not the workers who were obstructing the mails, he argued, but the railroads themselves, by their persistence in hauling the cars that were the subject of the controversy. For his insistence, Debs was eventually tried without a jury and sent to jail for six months. It was during that term that he was converted to socialism.

For the next thirty years, he was the leader of the Socialists, six times their candidate for the presidency. His opponents soon learned that their own rallies were doomed to failure if they were staged in cities where he was speaking; he could draw Democrats and Republicans away from their own gatherings by the thousands—and in spite of the admission fee which his party always charged at its meetings. But he was not only the greatest orator in his party. He was its greatest organizer. He was one of the few men in political history who have known the secret of holding theoretical and practical idealists together. During those thirty years, Eugene Debs was the party; for, without him, it would have collapsed or disintegrated many times.

Like many other Americans, Debs opposed our entrance into the World War; but, unlike most of them, he refused to keep his opinions to himself. Even after war was declared, he continued to speak in behalf of peace, until the government eventually arrested him for violation of the Espionage Act and sentenced him to ten years of imprisonment.

It has been said that the Espionage Act was the most stringent war law ever enforced in modern history and that, if such a law had been in force in this and other countries during other wars, Edmund Burke, Lloyd George, William Gladstone, and James Russell Lowell would have gone to prison for their expressions of opinion. Certainly Debs himself never acknowledged the justice of his punishment. He refused to ask for pardon, even after the war was over. "It is the government that should ask me for pardon," he insisted. And there must have been many Americans who agreed with him; for when he ran for the presidency in 1920 as Convict Number 2273, he polled nearly a million votes. A year later, he was released by President Harding. But he was never officially pardoned.

He was never *un*officially pardoned, either, by many who continued long after the war to persecute him and curse his name. In 1922, a Hoosier governor, Warren T. McCray, addressing a gathering of the American Legion at Indianapolis, expressed regret that an archtraitor of America had his home in Indiana; and, when a motion was made to have members of the state Legion convention march past the Debs home in Terre Haute shouting "Traitor!" Governor McCray approved.

"For this extremely patriotic speech," Debs replied, "Governor McCray was lauded as a great American patriot. . . . It so happened that while Governor McCray was enacting the role of Patriot-in-Chief of the United States and winning the vociferous plaudits . . . he was at the same time fleecing, plucking, and skinning suckers in a dozen states."

For this "fleecing, plucking, and skinning," the patriotic governor was later sentenced to a ten-year term in the same prison from which his "archtraitor" had been released.

Eugene Debs possessed rare combinations of qualities, both as a man and as a politician. He combined gentleness and courage; but, stranger still, he combined a talent for organization with an uncompromising devotion to his principles. Truth was the guiding star of his life. He spoke the truth as bluntly to his friends as to his enemies. Flattery was not in him. A year before his death, at the age of seventy when most men have grown sentimental over the friends who still rally round them, Debs stood on a platform in Steeg Park in Terre Haute, tall, lean, bald, bent forward from the waist, his long arms giving powerful emphasis to his speech; and the undecorated words he flung at the laboring men gathered to hear him were these:

"The politician tells you how intelligent you are to keep you ignorant. I am going to tell you how ignorant you are to make you intelligent. Do you suppose that if you acted intelligently, you would be the ones who build palaces and live in hovels?"

Average—?
Well, hardly!

49

Sheep in Wolves' Klothing

Even when Indiana sins, there is nothing "average" in the holiday she takes from political morality. Let the skeptic consider the shameful interlude of the early 1920's.

On Sunday afternoons in those years, especially in summer, the towns along the Wabash were silent and empty in the hot sunshine. On the lawn of the Catholic parish house, a black-robed priest might be seen sprinkling his flower beds or smoking his afternoon cigar; on Main Street, two or three swarthy, hook-nosed merchants might be engaged in argument and gesticulation in front of their shops; the isolated Italian or Polish family not yet Hoosierized down by the railroad tracks would of necessity be spilled over a grassless yard, driven out of the house by the centrifugal force of numbers and exuberance; and, down by the river, although the windows and doors of the shanties would be closed, as if against the plague, there would be blue smoke curling from tin chimneys, the smell of frying catfish, and the low, sweet music of Negro voices. But in all other places the silent emptiness would prevail.

It was more than the habitual Sunday stupor that oppressed the Wabash towns in the early 1920's. The deserted streets, the drawn window shades, the Sunday papers lying unopened in porch swings were indicative of something more ominous than universal slumber induced by dull sermons and too much fried chicken. The white, Protestant, native-American citizens of the towns were not asleep. With a few exceptions, they were gone —departed for the day and gathered in the hills behind the river on a mission that vitally concerned everyone they had left behind.

The Bible-thumping preacher was there in those hillside gatherings—lank, rubber-lipped, narrow-eyed, burning with hate while he beamed good-fellowship. A few years before, he would have forsaken his calling if there had been anything else to which his limited talents could have been applied. The tiny spark of revelation had long since flickered out in him, and he knew it was only a matter of months until his thumbed and oft-repeated sermons would no longer suffice to hold his pulpit. His wife wore the discarded dresses of his deacons' womenfolk. His children were underfed. The church itself was falling into disrepair. Then, one Sunday, a procession of masked men, bearing a cross in flames, marched, unannounced, down the aisle of his church and laid an offering of one hundred dollars in the collection plate. That was only the beginning. Thereafter the empty pews filled up and the church began to grow. Now the preacher was sleek and happy. His church was remodeled. A vast auditorium, ostensibly devoted to a men's Bible class, had been added. He lived in a new parsonage. His wife wore the latest styles. His children were in eastern colleges. But, better than all this, he had come into his own spiritually as well as mentally. At last, he was launched upon a crusade against the menace to his faith that his little, bogey-haunted mind had always feared. He—once a lowly parson—was to save the world from the hideous machinations of the Pope of Rome!

The businessman was there on the hillside—round, bald, rosy-cheeked, innocuous. He had once been prosperous, but something had gone wrong with business. He had joined the Odd Fellows and the Elks as well as the Rotary, but it had done no good. Sometimes he attributed the slump to the after-effects of the administration of "that fellow Woodrow Wilson." Sometimes he suspected that it was the result of a bolshevik plot. But, most of the time, he was sure that all his misfortunes could be traced to that little Jew who had moved in across the street and set up in competition. When, one day, a group of his friends gathered in his office and explained how he could recapture prosperity by joining a new fraternal order limited only to men like himself, he gladly signed on the dotted line and paid his ten dollars. Now things were booming again, and his small, pulpy soul throbbed with enthusiasm for the benefits of one-hundred-per-cent-Americanism.

The politician was there—silent, cautious, ponderous, hiding his face behind a cloud of cigar smoke. His first concern in all things was votes. Where they came from, how they were obtained, or what they stood for was of no importance. The tally sheets at the polls made no record of such things. All his life he had dealt in votes, discarding a handful here in order to win a larger handful there, surreptitiously espousing one cause here in the hope that he would not be exposed when he espoused the opposite cause there. Sometimes he had been successful. At other times he had failed. He had learned to expect the bad with the good. Then, one day, a committee had waited upon him and explained how he might assure himself of permanent success. By joining a fraternal order that was a solid and indestructible voting unit, he could count on one constant block of votes and, at the same time, because of the secrecy of the order, continue to appeal for votes from its enemies. He had joined, and so far the system had worked. He was beginning to believe that he had entered the politician's millennium.

The poor white was there—a thin, hollow-chested wisp of a man, with close-set eyes, pale lips, and an ancestry that meandered deviously back to the hills of the South. He had never had any fun, and the thought of others having it fired him with helpless indignation. His kind had been despised in the old South, but he kept alive in his speech the tradition of southern pride and aristocracy. Before the Civil War, his folks had been lower in the social scale than slaves, but he loved to boast of what he would do if a "nigger" ever so much as glanced at his mother or sister. He "got religion" periodically, renounced worldly pleasures, and signed the pledge; but he continued to speak knowingly of thoroughbred horses, mint juleps, and fox hunting, while he drove a battered Ford, secretly drank white mule, and kept a rusty pistol in his top bureau drawer. In his heart of hearts, he knew that he was a social anomaly, a hypocrite, and a coward, and the secret knowledge seared his thin soul. Then, one day, an acquaintance stopped him on the street and told him how he could realize all that he pretended to be, how he could hold a mysterious, incomprehensible title that was more high-sounding than that of a southern colonel, how he could actually put the "nigger" in his place and enjoy the prestige of an ac-

knowledged leader of the land, how he could spy upon
and put an end to the fun that licentious and irreligious
folks were having and thereby have some fun for himself, how he could at last redeem his lifelong boast that he
was as good as anyone else. So he paid his ten dollars and
was entering the promised land.

But in larger numbers than the bigots and money
seekers and politicians and downtrodden in the hillside
gathering were the average Hoosiers—tall, short, lean,
fat, prosperous, not so prosperous, male and female—
Hoosiers whose tradition has always been to join any
group that offered a badge or a uniform: Knights of
Pythias, Knights of Columbus, Masons, Odd Fellows,
Redmen, Owls, Eagles, Eastern Star, Daughters of Isa-
bella, Moose, Elks, Rotary, American Legion, Kiwanis,
Ben Hur. They had no specific grudge against the Catholics and the Jews. Their neighbors and best friends were
Catholics and Jews. They did not despise the Negro or
the "foreigner." They rather loved the darkies who
mowed their lawns and mopped their kitchen floors; and
as for "foreigners"—well, they had seen only a few in
all their lives, and they seemed harmless enough. But the
opportunity to wear a new robe, learn a new set of
rituals and passwords and handgrips, and band together
in a new hierarchy was too much for them. They came
in flocks, like innocent sheep; and for five years they
were led, like sheep, to the polls by their fanatic or self-
seeking shepherds and eventually driven to political
slaughter.

In those early days, however, it was fun for them—
the innocent as well as the guilty—gathered mysteriously
on a remote hillside in their new white robes, shivering
with excitement as they waited for their leader.

"He is coming," the rumor would begin. "The Old Man is coming!"

They did not know who he was—this "Old Man" —they only knew that his ways were as unpredictable and all-powerful as the ways of God; and, for the moment, they found him much more awe-inspiring than the "Potentates," "Chancellors," "Worshipful Masters," and "Exalted Rulers" to whom they had formerly given their allegiance. The "Old Man" was also the "Grand Dragon" of the state; but they preferred the simpler title. It made them feel closer to him, without in any way impairing his authority and omnipotence.

"The Old Man will be here soon! He will come!"

The whispered promise filled them with pride as well as expectancy. They were his favorites, his Tenth Legion. No matter how important his other duties, he would not fail them.

"He is coming all the way from Washington. The president called him to the White House for advice, because the pope has been plotting again to invade America. But the Old Man will get here in time!"

The pope! Fists clenched. Under the white hoods, eyes flashed patriotic anger. Another popish plot! But the Crossbacks would never take the country as long as there was still good, red, one-hundred-per-cent-American blood to flow on sacred soil and the Old Man to lead the charge!

"The Old Man!"

Overhead, the whine of a motor silenced them. They looked up. In the blue sky, a tiny, black speck circled, like a buzzard, and grew larger. As it spiraled downward, they recognized at last the beautiful, cream-colored airplane. Then they were able to read the letters

—K.K.K.—printed in flaming red on the bottom of the fuselage. A shout went up. A woman fainted. Others began to dance and sing. The white robes undulated down the hillside in a foamy wave toward a level field.

"The Old Man!"

Like an angel, like God himself, he had come down out of heaven to keep his tryst with them; and now he was there in the field, climbing out of his beautiful plane, magnificent and awful in full regalia of scarlet, white, and gold.

For an hour, he spoke to them. Many could not even hear his voice: the assembly was so large. But it was enough just to see him there, resplendent in his robes, leaning earnestly forward, gesticulating, pointing occasionally toward the gold cross that topped the spire of a Catholic church on a distant hillside. That last was worth the whole day of waiting. They roared and lifted their arms in wrath and quaked with the spirit of godliness that once had stirred their ancestors at camp meetings in these same hills. They did not have to be reminded that an arsenal of the pope's was buried beneath that church, that the German or Irish parishioners secretly practiced in military drill. They knew!

"The Old Man!"

Then, as quickly as he came, he was gone. His plane circled upward and disappeared in the sky, returning to the hangar a few miles away whence it had come on its dramatic and well-timed flight. Behind him, he left the white-robed men and women in a frenzy of self-righteousness that was to end in the flame of a cross on the hillside—a fiery cross designed to strike terror and contrition into the hearts of all un-Americans who might see it throughout the summer night.

"The Old Man!"

In those days, he was not an old man. He was young, blond, handsome, well-built, magnetic, a Texan still in his early thirties. His name was D. C. Stephenson, and he came to southern Indiana in the beginning of the decade and established himself in the coal business. In 1922, he attempted to win a Democratic nomination for Congress, but was so badly defeated that he allied himself thereafter with the Republican party. He was a man of little education, but he knew how to organize men and hold them together by appealing to their passions. Almost before anyone was aware of his presence in the state, he had become a power, having secretly garnered churchmen and laborers and businessmen and politicians by the thousands into the fold of Klannishness. At the height of his power, with four hundred thousand voters behind him, he moved into Indianapolis as the ruler of the Republican party and, through it, the state. From a sumptuous and well-guarded office in the capital he directed the policy of the *Fiery Cross,* the Klan's journal, gave orders to the governor and the legislature, accumulated a fortune, and laid his plans for moving on to Washington.

To appeal to churchmen, he attacked the bootleggers and kept the pagan pomp of Romanism ever before their eyes. To hold the more powerful bootleggers, he limited his attacks to their smaller competitors. To stir up the citizens of northern mill towns, like Gary and Hammond, he emphasized the foreign menace. To assure the loyalty of the poor whites, he urged the need of keeping the Negro in his place. To attract businessmen, he stressed the value of fraternal organization and Klannishness. For those thousands whose acme of happiness was the vicarious pleasure of spying, he revived the defunct Anti-Horse Thief Laws of the pioneers, which enabled almost anyone to become a constable and pry into the affairs of his neighbors. For the odds and ends that were left without a scapegoat, he reserved the ever-available Jew.

When, at last, the Ku-Klux Klan itself began to fear his power and H. W. Evans, the national leader, called him over into Ohio and asked for his resignation, he gave it indifferently. By that time, he no longer needed the Klan. In Indiana, he was able to boast, "I am the law!"

For four or five years, D. C. Stephenson *was* the law in Indiana, until the sheep, grown rapacious in their wolves' clothing, began to turn upon each other. A reign of terror commenced. Where once only the non-Klansman lived in darkness and dread, suspicious of all his friends and neighbors, now the Klansman himself began to guard his speech, not knowing what spy or alien informer he might be talking to, even within his own order. The capitol was in chaos. Corruption, backbiting, vice, and betrayal were the order of the day. A former governor had already traded his good name for the anonymity of a penitentiary number. Other officials were well qualified to join him. But so many were involved that no one knew where the break would come or who would first "get" whom.

The solution was natural and inevitable. They had got into the mess by listening to the Old Man. He was the one to get them out of it. In the fall of 1926, they turned on him and gave him a number and the privilege of lifetime retirement in the state prison at Michigan City. But in his indictment they ignored his activities in the Ku-Klux Klan and the statehouse. His sentence was based on a charge of "malicious mayhem" and the "murder" of a girl.

That winter, the Hoosiers settled back in their rocking chairs and breathed easily for the first time in years. It would be a long time before the old prestige of the state in national politics could be restored; but, at last, the way seemed clear. Those who had had no part in the Klan's activities revived their waning faith in justice and determined to do what they could for the rehabilitation of Hoosier honor. Those who had joined the Klan innocently, impelled only by the Hoosier's passion for joining, sheepishly destroyed their regalia and resolved to think twice next time.

But the rest, driven to cover, carefully folded their robes away in dark closets against the day when organized intolerance would again come into its own. Whether or not that day ever does come again to the banks of the Wabash depends largely upon their undeterminable numbers; for their kind, in any region, never change.

50

A Bumper Crop of Writers

IND a young Hoosier who does not want to be the President of the United States and the chances are that you have found one who wants to be a writer. If the vice-presidency is a disease on the banks of the Wabash, the writing of books is an epidemic. Nowhere else in the nation is the *cacoëthes scribendi* so prevalent. Before the World War of 1914-1918, a local statistician stopped adding up the numbers on passing freight trains long enough to ascertain that Hoosier pens had produced fifteen thousand volumes. Since the war, no one has been able to keep up the tally.

A list of only the better known works of Hoosier writers reads like a syllabus of popular American literature for the last half century:

> *The Hoosier Schoolmaster*
> *Ben Hur*
> Ridpath's *Histories*
> *When Knighthood Was in Flower*
> *Dorothy Vernon of Haddon Hall*
> *Alice of Old Vincennes*
> The *Little Colonel* books
> *Freckles*
> *Little Orphant Annie*

Graustark
The House of a Thousand Candles
Fables in Slang
Seventeen
An American Tragedy
Middletown

The names of only a handful of the many Hoosiers who are writing today form a cross section of contemporary American literary talent: Theodore Dreiser, Howard Brubaker, Charles A. Beard, Margaret Weymouth Jackson, George Jean Nathan, J. C. Furnas, Elmer Davis, George Ade, and Booth Tarkington.

John Finley was the first Hoosier to be inoculated with the writing bug. He started the literary epidemic in the Wabash country when, in 1830, the Indianapolis *Journal* published a poem of his entitled "The Hoosier Nest." It described the Hoosier pioneer cabin.

> "One side was lined with divers garments,
>   The other spread with skins of varmints;
>   Dried pumpkins overhead were strung,
>   Where venison hams in plenty hung;
>   Two rifles placed above the door;
>   Three dogs lay stretched upon the floor,—
>   In short, the domicile was rife
>   With specimens of Hoosier life."

Once started, there was no stopping the Hoosier pen. Lawyers, preachers, and politicians, because they traveled about more than other people and had an opportunity for comparisons, began to write their impressions of the country. The best of them was Oliver H. Smith, whose *Early Indiana Trials and Sketches* is full of wise and witty observations and racy anecdotes. Since his time, the output of local histories and memoirs in the Wabash country has almost exceeded the corn crop.

First in time among the Hoosier writers to achieve a national reputation was Edward Eggleston. Although he wrote *The Hoosier Schoolmaster* long after the rough pioneer days were past, this masterpiece, published in 1870, was one of America's first conscious attempts at realism in literature. The Hoosiers were angered by the book when it first appeared, and there are still many who refuse to believe that the author ever saw Indiana. But he was a native Hoosier. He was born and brought up in Indiana and, even after he went away and became a pastor in Brooklyn, he returned to the state for many visits. His childhood was spent quietly in cultured homes in Vevay and Madison, but his Bud Means was the result of first hand observation on numerous excursions into the backwoods of the forties. In Madison today, the author's relatives still point out the spot on Ryker's Ridge, high above the town, where the Hoosier school-house is said to have stood.

Since Eggleston's day, novelists have sprouted all over the Wabash country. Many of them have been plowed under, but a great number have produced crops that reached vast markets. General Lew Wallace—the most unliterary of them all—probably had the greatest financial success. That stern, brisk, military, little man wrote *Ben Hur* before he had seen the Holy Land and, from it and *The Fair God* and *The Prince of India*, made a fortune which he did not need. He went to Turkey as the American ambassador and shocked the world by shaking hands with the sultan, thereby winning that amazed potentate's lifelong admiration and friendship. Returning to Crawfordsville, he designed and built a study which foreshadowed the architecture of early twentieth century municipal fire stations and devoted the rest of his life to the enjoyment of his reputation. A few years before his death, he put an end to the Golden Age of Indianapolis—which, for a decade, had been a "city of homes"—by constructing its first apartment house, which he called the Blacherne, after the palace of the Emperor of Constantinople in *The Prince of India*. It is now the annex of the Spink Arms on busy, metropolitan Meridian Street.

Like the general, Maurice Thompson, a fellow townsman, preferred the faraway and long ago to the immediate Hoosier scene; and Charles Major, down in Shelbyville, indulged in the same imaginative literary wanderings—although he produced one local-color yarn for children, *The Bears of Blue River*, which is a classic in Indiana and deserves to be one everywhere. But it was not until Meredith Nicholson and Booth Tarkington came along that any real effort was made to transpose the Hoosier scene into fiction.

Meredith Nicholson calls himself a "provincial American"; and, early in his career, he demonstrated his affection for his native province in *A Hoosier Chronicle*, although he has since become better known for other works which are unrelated to the Hoosier scene.

Booth Tarkington has been quoted as saying, "I had no real success until I struck Indiana subjects." It was with *The Gentleman from Indiana* in 1899, when he was thirty, that he began to attract attention; and it is from his novels deriving from the Indiana background—*Penrod, Seventeen, The Magnificent Ambersons, Alice Adams*—that he has won his greatest successes. Although Mr. Tarkington has traveled far from Indiana in some of his more recent literary ventures and although he now spends much of his time outside the Hoosier state, he still bears the indelible mark of the Hoosier and, as a man and as a writer, is an example of the best in the Indiana tradition—unaffected, understanding, courageous, and, in all things, thoroughly sound. He holds to-day—and fully merits—the undisputed title of Dean of Hoosier writers.

Booth Tarkington and Meredith Nicholson were members of the famous colony that flourished in Indianapolis just before the Blacherne era and attracted more talented and brilliant men than any other such colony outside New York. Lew Wallace was there, of course, stopping over between Crawfordsville and Constantinople, and Charles Major came up often from Shelbyville. Former President Benjamin Harrison was still living then, gracing the broad streets of the city with his portly and dignified figure, in the company of a half dozen former ambassadors. Senator Fairbanks, of the Mephistophelian beard, was much in evidence; and Albert J. Beveridge and John Worth Kern, with his high, stiff collar, little bow tie, and inevitable cigar, were well along in their careers. Dreamy-eyed David Graham Phillips and genteel Maurice Thompson were there, too, and learned men like William H. English and Jacob P. Dunn. George Ade has described a visiting lecturer of those days making the mistake of inviting all literary men and women to join him on the platform. The entire audience swarmed up to his side!

But none of those many men of Indianapolis in the nineties inspired young Tarkington and Nicholson more than the spry and dapper little figure of James Whitcomb Riley. That Indianapolis colony was synonymous with the name of Riley. In fact, the name of Indiana itself suggests the name of Riley to most people; for he knew the state as no other man has known it before or since, and with his knowledge he won a popularity that has been exceeded by that of only one other American poet—Longfellow.

Riley was born in Greenfield, Indiana, in 1849 and attended a school on the National Road, which distracted him from his studies but gave him his first glimpse of the variety and vagaries of human nature. He tried to study law, as his father desired; but after his mother's death, he quarreled with his father and left home to become a traveling sign painter with the Wizard Oil Company.

Those were glorious days for the sandy-haired, loose-jointed boy with the large, lustrous eyes, riding beside "Doctor" McCrillus on the medicine wagon over the Hoosier countryside, stopping in settlements and villages to play the guitar, recite, or paint, as his part of the shows, and, afterward, scribbling half the night at the verses which years later were to make him famous. He acquired in those days his "iron mask"—his rather sharp and unpoetic expression—to conceal his sensitiveness to all the impressions that crowded in upon him. He acquired, too, his skill as a recitationist and his inexhaustible stock of Hoosier characters and his accurate knowledge of their speech.

But it took him a long time to find out what he was destined to do. Once he was driven completely off his course by the brilliance of Ole Bull's playing in an Indianapolis concert. For a year, Riley carried the violinist's picture in his "reticule," and all his spare time was devoted to practice on his own violin. Then, one day, he smashed his thumb in a door, and his musical ambitions suddenly ended. His first book of verse was published when he was thirty, and thereafter, like Abe Lincoln, he was gradually propelled to success by the efforts of men who loved him rather than by ambitions of his own. He lived to have his portrait painted by Sargent and to become the dean of Hoosier letters, and, when he died in 1916, his poems were an essential part of the furnishings of every Hoosier home. But he never lost the shyness and simplicity that made him sensitive to all the humble joys and griefs of Hoosier life.

Other poets have shone on the Hoosier horizon. Joaquin Miller was born in Indiana. So was William Vaughn Moody. But Riley was the Hoosier Poet. He knew the woods and fields of Indiana. He knew its farms and its farmers, its crops, its language, its children, and its creeks and rivers. He knew the appetizin' flavor of the air "when the frost is on the punkin and the fodder's in the shock." He loved the scent of clover and the pagan delights of boyhood in "wortermelon time." He liked the sunshine spread on country roads "as thick as butter on country bread"; but when God "sorted out" the weather and sent rain, rain was his choice. Like most Hoosiers, he preferred the summer; but he could be happy when there was "winter without" because in Indiana there was always "warmth within" and his head was full of stories—the kind of stories the Raggedy Man used to tell " 'bout Giunts, an' Griffuns, an' Elves, an' the Squidgicum-Squees 'at swallers therselves"! But, best of all, he loved the "noon-time an' June-time, down around the river," that time—

" 'Long about knee-deep in June,
 'Bout the time strawberries melts
On the vine—"

Riley is the Hoosier Poet, because he saw the Hoosier world through the eyes of a child, as all Hoosiers persist in seeing it throughout their lives. No matter where they go or what they do in later life, their Hoosier childhood remains a part of them and gives them their characteristic good nature and quiet, if often pungent, humor. It is as if they felt compelled to repay nature for the blessings it showered upon them when they were children.

Humor is one of the principal characteristics of Riley's writings. But it crops up in every Hoosier's literary efforts, just as it colors his politics and his daily life. Inevitably, therefore, some Hoosier writers have devoted their talents exclusively to humor. At the head of this group stands George Ade, whose *Fables in Slang* are at once indigenous to the Hoosier mind and universal in their ironic challenge. But another man speaks more characteristically for the Wabash country at the same time that he penetrates just as deeply into the foibles of human nature. His name is Kin Hubbard, the creator of Abe Martin of Brown County.

Brown County, in the heart of Indiana, is now the habitat of Indiana's artists; but the originals of Kin Hubbard's creations may still be observed in the log cabins of the back country and round about the town of Beanblossom. Sitting on a slack, barbed-wire fence, his slouch hat pulled down over his wide and disarming eyes, his shoulders hunched, like a crow's, in his tight, black coat, and his hands jammed deep into the pockets of his baggy pants, Abe Martin has managed to observe

the whole history of man's dreams and delusions and de-
linquencies in the doings of his fellow Hoosiers in
Brown County.

When several English sparrows light on the roof of
the blacksmith shop and Abe remarks that they "give the
locality quite a metropolitan appearance," he opens a
horizon beyond the limits of Beanblossom and lets you see
the ridiculous grimace of all America in its growing
pains. When he announces that "Miss Tawney Apple's
niece wuz prematurely drowned yesterday while walkin'
in a canoe," you realize that much of life is a fool-
hardy procession and you remember the times when you
yourself went "walkin' in a canoe." The lost innocence
and idle glory of the day when the male was supreme
in society are recaptured in his laconic report that "while
goin' after fishin' worms in a field where his wife wuz
plowin', Tipton Bud found a Indian dart." Abe Martin
needs but a few words. "Tilford Moots's mother-in-law
is visitin' him anyhow," he says; and you know all.

A town like Beanblossom exists nowhere except in
Indiana, but the Tawney Apples, Fawn Lippincuts, Tipton Buds, and Cale Fluharts are everywhere in this world.
It is unfortunate that the Abe Martins are not so
numerous.

These are not all the writers of the Wabash country.
There are many more—like George Barr McCutcheon
and Gene Stratton-Porter—whose names are familiar to
everyone, and still others—like Mary Hartwell Cather-
wood and May Louise Shipp—whose names are not so
familiar. There are historians and scholars, too, of first
rank, men like Beveridge and Dunn and English. And
there are also the entertainers, whose professions make
them first cousins of the littérateurs and very definitely

products of the Hoosier spirit: Charles Butterworth, of Hollywood and radio fame; Joe Cook, of Evansville and Broadway; Cole Porter, master of sophisticated wit and intricate rhythm; and the creator of that modern dance classic, "Stardust"—Mr. Hoagy Carmichael.

With one notable exception, all the writers of Indiana have one quality in common—a certain mellow optimism—and the reason is obvious. Almost all of them were born and brought up in comfortable homes. Riley was often poor as a young man, but his boyhood home was the home of a moderately successful country lawyer. Tarkington's family—an "old" family, as Indiana families go—were able to educate him at Princeton. Eggleston came of aristocratic Virginia stock. Lew Wallace's father was an army officer and, at one time, governor of the state. Maurice Thompson's was a wealthy farmer and, before that, a plantation owner in the South.

Until recently, such has been the background of most Hoosiers. Dire poverty and the congestion of city life, which breed the pessimistic, the critical, and the rebellious mind, have been almost unknown in Indiana. A Hoosier family, even without much money, could be comfortable and happy and well-fed in that bounteous land; and every Hoosier child, even those of the cities, has had the mellowing influence of rural scenes and rural society to shape his character. Hoosier writers have been mostly optimistic and gentle, because they have been fortunate; and, while their social consciences may have been dulled by their good fortune, it is to their credit that such physical and spiritual ease as they have known have bred in them good humor and an appreciation of life, rather than egotism and intolerance.

The one notable exception to the common spirit of

Hoosier writers is Theodore Dreiser. Oddly enough, the author of *An American Tragedy* was born in the home town of the state's one genuine rebel in politics—Eugene Debs. Still more interesting is the likelihood that Dreiser's name will survive the names of most Hoosiers in the history of American literature.

Dreiser's childhood and youth were not "comfortable." In Terre Haute, where he was born, his large family of brothers and sisters never knew actual want, but they came very close to it. In Terre Haute—and later in Sullivan, Vincennes, and Evansville—they were often wondering where their next meal would come from; and, on one occasion, Theodore was sent home from his parochial school because he had no shoes.

But from Theodore Dreiser's autobiography one gathers that it was the Catholic church, the parochial school, and the religious fanaticism of his father against which he rebelled more than the harshness of poverty or the limitations of Hoosier society. The elder Dreiser, as his son describes him, was a tyrant, a darkly passionate man constantly oppressed by the consciousness of sin. A German immigrant, he seemed unable to adjust himself to the free and democratic life of America, and Theodore Dreiser seems unable to forgive him for his ineptitude and his bigotry.

Theodore Dreiser left Indiana before he began to write. Yet, whenever he recalls his native Hoosier background or revisits it, he grows as nostalgic and sentimental as all the others. In his autobiography and some of his travel books, there are pages of pure lyricism that James Whitcomb Riley might have written. He recaptures his boy's enthusiasm for roaming in the fields and woods about Sullivan. He has a strong Hoosier affection for creeks and rivers. His delight is exclamatory when, for the first time, he comes under the spell of the river-town of Evansville in the eighties.

And it was Theodore Dreiser who wrote the words for the famous nostalgic song composed by his brother, Paul Dresser:

"O the moonlight's fair tonight along the Wabash,
 From the fields there comes the breath of new-mown hay;
 Thro' the sycamores the candlelights are gleaming,
 On the banks of the Wabash far away."

51

This Is the Wabash

This is the story of the Wabash, and yet it is not the Wabash itself. The Wabash is something more than topography, history, and statistics. It is, rather, the things a Hoosier remembers when he hears that magic name.

The Wabash is the smell of clover in June, of hay and sweetgrass. It is a dome of blue and golden sky, piled high with white clouds, and sun-soaked days filled with the hum of insects. It is the harvest moon and stars, like a chandelier of jewels, in purple nights. It is the folks on their front porches waiting to go down and look at the river. It is the soft drawl of friendly voices, the creak of rockers, the scuffle of small boys, and the laughter of pretty Hoosier girls.

The Wabash is the taste of crisp fried chicken and hot biscuits, of watermelons and cantaloupes, sweet roasting ears and homemade bread spread thick with yellow butter. It is fields of golden wheat and rich green corn, the song of redbirds, catbirds, and turtledoves, and the lazy dip of oars in a sluggish bayou. It is milkweed and Jimson weed and ironweed, white with dust; the haze of autumn over a far, low-flung horizon; the flavor of ripe persimmons; a big, black mule rolling on its back in a barn lot; a bursting corncrib; and the contented cluck of brown hens in the sun.

315

''O, THE MOONLIGHT'S FA

"TONIGHT ALONG THE WABASH."

The Wabash is men who greet you with a friendly "howdy" and tell you readily about themselves and their folks and whether they vote Republican or Demmy-cratic. It is women who wear aprons and sunbonnets and work miracles in their kitchens. It is barefoot boys on country roads, with nigger-killers dangling from the pockets of their dusty overalls and strings of "yeller catfish" slung over their shoulders. It is the song of darkies and the long, slow, rich, and mellow laughter of folks, both black and white, who have time to laugh at solemn, homespun humor.

The Wabash is spacious towns and cities, dozing in the sun. It is comfortable homes with wide porches, broad lawns, and dark shade trees. It is long, straight, concrete highways, with road signs suggesting a reduced speed of sixty miles per hour at the infrequent curves. It is clusters of flour mills and canning factories. It is tall buildings with plenty of room about them. It is fine schoolhouses and community centers. It is the drone of a lawn mower on a summer afternoon; the well-thumbed pages of a book from the public library; the scrape of roller skates over asphalt; the murmur of many voices in a schoolroom; the proud faces of parents at a high school commencement; the pride of men and women in native sons and daughters.

The Wabash is the old-time religion that some-times lifts and sometimes destroys men's hearts. It is lodge meetings and Rotary clubs and literary circles. It is political rallies and barbecues and moonlight excur-sions. It is watermelon feasts, hay rides, love-making, fist fights, and laughter.

The Wabash is Indiana; and to every Hoosier, wherever he lives, Indiana means "home."

PART NINE

Bibliography and Acknowledgments

Headwaters

Of the many books I have read and consulted in my study of the Wabash story, the one that surveys the history of the early years with the most scholarly approach and the greatest literary charm is *Indiana: A Redemption from Slavery* by Jacob Piatt Dunn. For a general impression beyond the years of the Civil War, however, one must turn to Logan Esarey's *History of Indiana*, which is thorough and satisfying, in the manner of a good textbook. *The Centennial History and Handbook of Indiana*, by George S. Cottman, is another excellent survey of the Indiana story and has the additional merit of individual chapters on each county in the state.

For the history of early French explorers and adventurers, I relied principally upon the writings of the Frenchmen themselves, but I found *La Salle and the Discovery of the Great West*, by Francis Parkman, and *The French Adventurer*, by Maurice Constantin-Weyer, of special value in re-creating the atmosphere of those early times. Of the accounts of the great campaign at Vincennes, no one's is more exciting than that of George Rogers Clark himself; but Temple Bodley and James Alton James have applied the tools of modern research to the story and produced very valuable biographies.

There are many early travel books that describe the Hoosier scene in the first few decades of the nineteenth century. The three that have left the most lasting impression with me are: *Early Indiana Trials and Sketches*, by O. H. Smith; *The Wabash: Or Adventures of an English Gentleman's Family in the Interior of America*, by J. Richard Beste; and *A Tour Through Indiana in 1840*, by John Parsons, which is a diary recently discovered and edited by Kate Milner Rabb. Other firsthand accounts can be found scattered through the many volumes of *Early Western Travels, 1748-1846,* a collection edited by Reuben Gold Thwaites, and, of course, the Indiana Historical Publications.

In his own time, countless eulogies of the first governor of Indiana Territory appeared, masquerading as biographies; but they are of value only to the student of the excesses of political propaganda. In 1926, the Indiana Historical Collections were increased by a biography written by Dorothy B. Goebel. It is a thorough history, but is as unimaginative as most Ph.D. theses. *Old Tippecanoe* by F. Cleaves, published after this book about the Wabash was completed, is the first well-balanced and literary biography of William Henry Harrison to date. The Tecumseh story, on the other hand, has been treated by many authors in many forms.

It is a fairly simple matter to ascertain the facts relating to the Rappite settlement on the Wabash, although the Rappites kept no written records. Concerning the Owenites, however, who were forever taking their pens in hand, there is the greatest confusion. George B. Lockwood, in *The New Harmony Movement,* has published the only attempt to organize the complete New Harmony story, and he has pioneered valiantly; but confusion and contradiction are rife in his book. In recent years, several scholars have gone to New Harmony to avail themselves of the vast store of material in the town's library and to write the definitive history, but so far all of them seem to have given up in despair. When that book is written—and written well—it will be one of the most delightful and fascinating volumes to emerge from the sources of American history.

Albert J. Beveridge's two volumes still remain the best study of the life of Abraham Lincoln up to 1858, although Emanuel Hertz's edition of the papers of William H. Herndon has thrown new light on the character of the Civil War president and Mrs. Bess V. Ehrmann's little volume, entitled *The Missing Chapter in the Life of Abraham Lincoln,* offers an assortment of new material related to Lincoln's Indiana years. William Wesley Woollen's *Biographical and Historical Sketches of Early Indiana* contains interesting anecdotes about some of the other political figures of Indiana, and Claude G. Bowers, who is a political figure of importance himself, has written several good biographies of more recent Hoosier statesmen. On the subject of Indiana writers, there is very little besides Meredith Nicholson's small book called *The Hoosiers,* which was written at the turn of the century.

These, along with my diggings in many old newspaper files, are the more notable of the literary sources I used in writing the Indiana story. But a great part of the story was not the result of work among books and newspapers. Instead, it came from my own life among the people of the Wabash valley and from the people themselves. An acknowledgment is due, first of all, to them, all the friends and acquaintances who have given me generously their time and assistance.

Specifically, I wish to thank the following for the services they have rendered me: Professor James B. Hedges, of Brown University; Mr. Richard McGinnis; Dr. Charles F. Leich; Mr. Howard A. Wilson, of the University of Wisconsin; Mrs. Kathleen Robb McRoberts; Mr. Richard Hanson; Mr. William B. Carlton; Mr. Levi Grigsby; Mr. John R. Frazier, of the Rhode Island School of Design; Professor I. J. Kapstein, of Brown University; Mrs. Harry G. Leslie; Mr. Charles B. Enlow; Mr. Frank H. Hatfield; Mr. M. E. Garber; Mrs. Elsie Lustig Clough; Miss Louise M. Husband, librarian of the Workingmen's Institute in New Harmony; Mrs. Sarah L. Denton and the staff of the Willard Library in Evansville; Miss Evelyn Chase and the staff of the Rhode Island School of Design Library; and the staffs of the Central Library in Evansville, the Terre Haute Public Library, the Providence (Rhode Island) Atheneum, the Providence Public Library, the Harvard University Library, the Concord (Massachusetts) Public Library, and the Indiana State Historical Library.

I would thank my wife, Ellen Cameron Wilson, for her reading of the manuscript, her helpful criticism, and her patience with me while I was writing it. And my list of acknowledgments would certainly be incomplete without the name of the late Constance Lindsay Skinner, who, in the year preceding her death, advised and encouraged me constantly.

More than anyone else, I would thank my father, William E. Wilson, for his unfailing interest and helpfulness. He is, in a sense, the coauthor of this book, by virtue of the stimulus his enthusiasm has provided. His own and my mother's fine Hoosier characters have been at all times the models I have kept before me when I wished to consider the best that the Wabash country has produced.

Bibliography

Books

AIKMAN, DUNCAN, *The Hometown Mind*. New York: Minton, Balch and Company, 1926.

ANBUREY, THOMAS, *Travels Through Interior Parts of America* (2 vols.). London: William Lane, 1789.

BALL, T. H., *Northwestern Indiana from 1800 to 1900*. Chicago: Donohue and Henneberry, 1900.

BARCE, ELMORE, *The Land of the Miamis*. Fowler, Ind.: Benton Review Shop, 1922.

BENTON, E. J., *The Wabash Trade Route in the Development of the Old Northwest*. Baltimore: Johns Hopkins University Studies, 1903.

BERNHARD, DUKE OF SAXE-WEIMAR EISENACH, *Travels Through North America During the Years 1825 and 1826*. Published in Philadelphia, 1828.

BESTE, J. RICHARD, *The Wabash: Or Adventures of an Engglish Gentleman's Family in the Interior of America* (2 vols.). London: Hurst and Blackett, 1855.

BEVERIDGE, ALBERT J., *Abraham Lincoln, 1809-1858* (2 vols.). Boston: Houghton Mifflin Company, 1928.

BIRKBECK, MORRIS, *Notes on a Journey in America from the Coast of Virginia to the Territory of Illinois*. London: James Ridgway, 1818.

BLAKE, KATHARINE EVANS, *Heart's Haven*. Indianapolis: Bobbs-Merrill Company, 1905.

BODLEY, TEMPLE, *George Rogers Clark*. Boston: Houghton Mifflin Company, 1926.

BOND, BEVERLY W., *The Civilization of the Old Northwest*. New York: The Macmillan Company, 1934.

325

BOWERS, CLAUDE G., *Beveridge and the Progressive Era.* New York: The Literary Guild, 1932.

———— *The Life of John Worth Kern.* Indianapolis: The Hollenbeck Press, 1918.

BOYD, THOMAS, *Mad Anthony Wayne.* New York: Charles Scribner's Sons, 1929.

BURNET, MARY O., *Art and Artists of Indiana.* New York· The Century Company, 1921.

BURNS, LEE, *Early Architects and Builders of Indiana.* Indianapolis: Indiana Historical Collections, 1935.

CATLIN, GEORGE, *Indians of North America* (2 vols.). London: H. G. Bohn, 1845.

CAUTHORN, HENRY S., *History of the City of Vincennes.* Terre Haute: Moore and Langen, 1902.

CHAMBERLAIN, E., *The Indiana Gazeteer.* Indianapolis: Chapman and Spann, 1850.

CLARK, GEORGE ROGERS, *Account of the Capture of Vincennes.* Boston: Old South Leaflet, No. 43.

CLEAVES, F., *Old Tippecanoe.* New York: Charles Scribner's Sons, 1939.

COBB, IRVIN S., *Indiana.* New York: George H. Doran Company, 1924.

COCKRUM, WILLIAM H., *Pioneer History of Indiana.* Oakland City, Ind.: Press of the Oakland City Journal, 1907.

CONSTANTIN-WEYER, MAURICE, *The French Adventurer: The Life and Exploits of LaSalle.* New York: Macaulay Company, 1931.

COTTMAN, GEORGE S., *Centennial History and Handbook of Indiana.* Indianapolis: Max R. Hyman, 1915.

COX, SANDFORD C., *Recollections of the Early Settlement of the Wabash Valley.* Lafayette: Courier Steam Book and Job Printing House, 1860.

DEBS, EUGENE V., *Voices of Revolt* (Vol. IX). New York: International Publishers, 1928.

DICKEY, MARCUS, *The Youth of James Whitcomb Riley.* Indianapolis: Bobbs-Merrill Company, 1919.

DICKEY, MARCUS, *The Maturity of James Whitcomb Riley*. Indianapolis: Bobbs-Merrill Company, 1922.

DILLON, JOHN B., *A History of Indiana*. Indianapolis: Bingham and Doughty, 1859.

DREISER, THEODORE, *A History of Myself—Dawn*. New York: Liveright, 1931.

———— *A Hoosier Holiday*. New York: Lane, 1916.

DUNN, JACOB P., *Indiana: A Redemption from Slavery*. Boston: Houghton Mifflin Company, 1888.

———— *True Indian Stories*. Indianapolis: Sentinel Printing Company, 1908.

EARLE, ALICE MORSE, *Two Centuries of Costume in America* (2 vols.). New York: The Macmillan Company, 1903.

EGGLESTON, E., and SEELYE, LILLIE E., *Tecumseh and the Shawnee Prophet*. New York: Dodd, Mead and Company, 1878.

EGGLESTON, GEORGE CARY, *The First of the Hoosiers*. Philadelphia: Drexel Biddle, 1903.

EHRMANN, BESS V., *The Missing Chapter in the Life of Abraham Lincoln*. Chicago: Walter M. Hill, 1938.

ELLSWORTH, HENRY WILLIAM, *Valley of the Upper Wabash, Indiana, with Hints on its Agricultural Advantages*. New York: Pratt, Robinson and Company, 1838.

ENGLISH, WILLIAM HAYDEN, *Conquest of the Country Northwest of the River Ohio, 1778-1783, and Life of General George Rogers Clark*. Indianapolis: Bowen, 1896.

ESAREY, LOGAN, *A History of Indiana* (2 vols.). Indianapolis: B. F. Bowen and Company, 1918.

———— *History of Indiana*. New York: Harcourt, Brace and Company, 1922.

EVANS, MADISON, *Biographical Sketches of the Pioneer Preachers of Indiana*. Philadelphia: J. Challen and Sons, 1864.

EWBANK, LOUIS B., *Morgan's Raid in Indiana*. Indianapolis: Indiana Historical Society Publications, 1923.

FOULKE, WILLIAM DUDLEY, *Life of Oliver P. Morton*. Indianapolis: Bobbs-Merrill Company, 1899.

GOEBEL, DOROTHY B., *William Henry Harrison*. Indianapolis: Indiana Historical Collections, 1926.

GOODRICH, DEWITT C., and TUTTLE, CHARLES R., *An Illustrated History of the State of Indiana*. Indianapolis: Richard S. Peale and Company, 1875.

HAYS, ARTHUR HOMER, *Notawkah, Friend of the Miamis*. Caldwell, Idaho: Caxton Printers, Ltd., 1932.

HERTZ, EMANUEL (Editor), *The Hidden Lincoln, from the Letters and Papers of William H. Herndon*. New York: Viking Press, 1938.

HINSDALE, B. A., *The Old Northwest*. New York: Townsend MacCoun, 1888.

HODGE, FREDERICK WEBB, *Handbook of American Indians North of Mexico* (2 vols.). Washington: Government Printing Office, 1907-1910.

HOLDEN, ANGUS, *Elegant Modes in the Nineteenth Century*. New York: Greenberg, 1936.

ILLICK, JOSEPH S., and DEAM, CHARLES C., *Common Trees of Indiana*. Washington, D. C.: American Tree Association, 1927.

JAMES, JAMES ALTON, *The Life of George Rogers Clark*. Chicago: Chicago University Press, 1928.

―― (Editor), *George Rogers Clark Papers (1771-1781)*. Springfield, Ill.: Illinois State Historical Library, 1912. 73rd Congress, 1st Session, 1934.

JOHNSEN, JULIA E. (Compiler), *Ku Klux Klan*. New York: The H. W. Wilson Company, 1923.

KALLEN, HORACE M., *Culture and Democracy in the United States*. New York: Boni and Liveright, 1924.

LAUGHTON, CLARA E., *Reminiscences of James Whitcomb Riley*. New York: Fleming H. Revell Company, 1916.

LEMCKE, J. A., *Reminiscences of an Indianian*. Indianapolis: The Hollenbeck Press, 1905.

LEVERING, JULIA HENDERSON, *Historic Indiana*. New York: G. P. Putnam's Sons, 1909.

LILLY, ELI, *Prehistoric Antiquities of Indiana*. Indianapolis: Indianapolis Historical Society, 1937.

LOCKRIDGE, ROSS F., *La Salle*. Yonkers-on-Hudson: World Book Company, 1931.

LOCKWOOD, GEORGE B., *The New Harmony Movement*. New York: D. Appleton and Company, 1905.

LYND, R. S. and H. M., *Middletown*. New York: Harcourt, Brace and Company, 1929.

——— *Middletown in Transition*. New York: Harcourt, Brace and Company, 1937.

MARGRY, PIERRE (Editor), *Découvertes et Etablissements des Français dans L'Amérique Septentrionale*. Published in Paris, 1879.

MECKLIN, JOHN MOFFATT, *The Ku Klux Klan*. New York: Harcourt, Brace and Company, 1924.

MOORE, EDWARD E., *A Century of Indiana*. New York: American Book Company, 1910.

MORISON, SAMUEL E., and COMMAGER, H. S., *The Growth of the American Republic* (2 vols). London: Oxford University Press, 1937.

NICHOLSON, MEREDITH, *The Hoosiers*. New York: The Macmillan Company, 1900.

OGG, FREDERICK AUSTIN, *The Old Northwest*. New Haven: Yale University Press, 1921.

OSKINSON, JOHN M., *Tecumseh and His Times*. New York: G. P. Putnam's Sons, 1938.

OWEN, ROBERT DALE, *Threading My Way*. New York: G. W. Carleton and Company, 1874.

PAINTER, FLOY RUTH, *That Man Debs and His Life Work*. Bloomington, Ind.: Indiana University, 1929.

PALMER, FREDERICK, *Clark of the Ohio*. New York: Dodd, Mead and Company, 1929.

PARKMAN, FRANCIS, *LaSalle and the Discovery of the Great West*. Boston: Little, Brown and Company, 1910.

PAXSON, F. L., *History of the American Frontier* (*1763-1893*). Boston: Houghton Mifflin Company, 1924.

PEARS, THOMAS, *New Harmony*. Indianapolis: Indiana Historical Collections, 1933.

PEARSON, T. GILBERT (Editor), *Birds of America*. Garden City: Garden City Publishing Company, 1936.

PIRTLE, ALFRED, *The Battle of Tippecanoe*. Louisville: John P. Morton and Company, 1900.

QUAIFE, MILO M., *The Capture of Old Vincennes*. Indianapolis: Bobbs-Merrill Company, 1927.

RABB, KATE MILNER (Editor), *A Tour Through Indiana in 1840: Diary of John Parsons*. New York: Robert M. McBride and Company, 1920.

SANDBURG, CARL, *Abraham Lincoln, the Prairie Years* (2 vols.). New York: Harcourt, Brace and Company, 1926.

SCHNITTKIND, HENRY, *The Story of Eugene Debs*. Boston: National Educational Committee, Independent Workmen's Circle, 1929.

SHETRONE, HENRY CLYDE, *The Moundbuilders*. New York: D. Appleton and Company, 1930.

SKINNER, CONSTANCE LINDSAY, *Pioneers of the Old Southwest*. New Haven: Yale University Press, 1921.

SMITH, O. H., *Early Indiana Trials and Sketches*. Cincinnati: Moore, Wilstach, Keys and Company, 1858.

SMITH, REV. WILLIAM C., *Indiana Miscellany*. Cincinnati: Poe and Hitchcock, 1867.

SMITH, WILLIAM HENRY, *The History of the State of Indiana*. Indianapolis: B. L. Blair Company, 1897.

SNEDECKER, CAROLINE DALE, *The Town of the Fearless*. Garden City: Doubleday, Doran and Company, 1931.

STUART, BEN F., *History of the Wabash and Valley*. Delphi, Indiana: Longwell-Cummings Company, 1924.

SWEET, WILLIAM WARREN, *Circuit-Rider Days in Indiana*. Indianapolis: W. K. Stewart Company, 1916.

SWIGGETT, HOWARD, *The Rebel Raider*. Indianapolis: Bobbs-Merrill Company, 1934.

THWAITES, REUBEN GOLD, *Early Western Travels, 1748-1846* (32 vols.). Cleveland: A. H. Clark Company, 1905.

TICKNOR, CAROLINE, *Glimpses of Authors.* Boston: Houghton Mifflin Company, 1922.

TRISSAL, FRANCIS M., *Public Men of Indiana.* Hammond, Ind.: W. B. Conkey, 1922.

TRUESDELL, MARY VAN HOGEL, *Tippecanoe: A Legend of the Border.* Published in 1840.

UNITED STATES CONGRESS, *Wabash River, Ohio, Indiana, and Illinois.* Washington: U.S. House Document No. 100, 73rd Congress, 1st Session, 1934.

UNITED STATES ENGINEERS, *Flood Control Plan, Wabash and Tributaries.* Louisville: U. S. Engineers' Office, 1938.

WALLACE, LEW, *Lew Wallace: An Autobiography.* New York: Harper and Brothers, 1906.

WARWICK, EDWARD, and PITZ, HENRY C., *Early American Costume.* New York: The Century Company, 1929.

WINGER, OTHO, *The Lost Sister Among the Miamis.* Elgin, Ill.: The Elgin Press, 1936.

WOOLLEN, WILLIAM WESLEY, *Biographical and Historical Sketches of Early Indiana.* Indianapolis: Hammond and Company, 1883.

Newspapers and Periodicals

CORDELL, R. A., "Limestone, Corn, and Literature; the Indiana Scene and Its Interpreters," *Saturday Review of Literature,* December 17, 1938.

Corydon *Democrat.*

Delphi *Citizen,* 1931.

Evansville *Courier,* 1925, 1938.

Evansville *Daily Journal,* 1863.

Evansville *Journal,* 1868.

Evansville *Press,* 1925, 1936-1939.

FROST, STANLEY, "The Masked Politics of the Klan," *World's Work*, February, 1928.

Hancock Democrat, Greenfield, Ind., 1926.

Indiana Gazette, Vincennes, Ind., 1804.

Indianapolis *Journal*, 1840.

Indianapolis *News*, 1925.

Indianapolis *Star*, 1925.

Madison *Courier*.

MERRITT, DIXON, "Klan and Anti-Klan in Indiana," *Outlook*, Dec. 8, 1926.

New Harmony *Advertizer*.

New Harmony *Disseminator*, 1831.

New Harmony *Gazette*, 1825.

New Harmony *Times*.

Outdoor Indiana.

Spirit of Seventy-Six, Indianapolis, 1840.

TAYLOR, ALVA, "What the Klan Did in Indiana," *New Republic*, November 16, 1927.

Terre Haute *Star*, 1925.

Terre Haute *Tribune*, 1925.

Wabash Enquirer, Terre Haute, 1840.

Western Sun and General Advertiser, Vincennes, 1830.

Western Sun, Vincennes, 1807.

Index

"Grand Prairie," 10, 22, 100
Great Lakes, 7, 8, 18, 27, 252
Green River, 230
Grigsby, Natty, 212, 235
Grigsby family, 199, 207, 208, 222
Grounendyke's Mills, 266
"Grouseland," 88
Gulf of Mexico, 8, 9

Hall, Squire, 234
Hamilton, Lieutenant Colonel Henry,
    45-52, 54, 55, 59, 67, 68, 236
Hanks, Dennis, 206, 210, 212-214, 222,
    234
Harding, Warren G., 291
Harmony (Harmonie), 11, 116-127
Harrison, Benjamin, 87
Harrison, Benjamin, President, 284,
    286, 307
Harrison, William Henry, 10, 82-91,
    162-170, 173, 176, 252, 259,
    282
  President, 96
  Tippecanoe, 92-96
Hay, Major Jehu, 45, 49, 67, 68
Hay, John, 284
Hayne, Robert Young, 239
Helm, Captain Leonard, 44, 48-52, 66,
    67
Hendricks, Thomas A., 257, 283
Hendricks, William, 173
Henry, Patrick, 55
Highland Laddie, steamboat, 229, 266
Highlander, steamboat, 177, 239
Hobson, General, 263, 264
Hoosier Chronicle, A., 306
"Hoosier Nest, The," 304
Hoosier Schoolmaster, The, 303, 305
Hoosiers, 1-11, 13-16
  characteristics, 184-187
  cooking, 14, 186
  Civil War, 255-264
  origin of name, 187, 188
  schools, 243-246
Hubbard, Kin, 310, 311
Hughes, Charles Evans, 281
Hugo, Jenk, 272

Hugo, John R., 272-274
Huntington, Indiana, 280

Illinois, 10, 69, 162-164
  "Country," 24, 54
  County of, 69
  Lincoln in, 236-240
Imperialism, 287
Independence, steamboat, 229
Indian summer, 73-77
Indiana, 10, 69, 162, 163
  Civil War, 255-261
  constitution, 1816, 172-175, 181-185
  politics, 279-285
  slavery conflict (see Slavery)
  food, 186
  free state, 175
Indiana Gazette, 166, 238
Indiana Territory, 87, 162-163
Indiana University, 244
Indianapolis, 20, 177, 182, 243, 263,
    267, 281, 282, 291, 292, 307-314
  literary colony, 307-314
Indianapolis Journal, 304
Indians, 7-112
  corruption, 87-90
  evictions, 97-101
  first legal victory, 97
  French and, 24-27
  in Indiana, 73-96
  with British, 44-52, 54, 68
  (see also individual tribes)
Irish, 46, 187
Iroquois tribe, 19
Island Queen, packet, 271
Italians, 187

Jackson, Margaret Weymouth, 304
Jefferson, Thomas, 53, 88
Jennings, Jonathan, 168, 170-175, 178
Jesuits, 22, 40
Jews, 295, 297, 301
Johnson, Captain Adam, 257
Johnson, John, 174
Johnston, John, 234
Johnston, Sarah Bush (see Lincoln,
    Sarah Bush)
Joliet, Louis, 20-23